Fauré Studies

Fauré Studies showcases new research from leading scholars in the United States, United Kingdom, and France into this influential French composer of the fin de siècle. The book features interpretations of individual works and musical analyses, as well as studies of compositional pedagogy, social history, and aesthetics. Accessible to a wide range of readers, this volume also provides a valuable overview of Fauré research from the composer's lifetime to the present. As part of *Cambridge Composer Studies*, *Fauré Studies* advances new research into this major composer, which includes recently launched critical editions of his music.

CARLO CABALLERO is Associate Professor of Music at the University of Colorado, Boulder. He is the author of *Fauré and French Musical Aesthetics* and has published essays in *Victorian Studies*, *19th-Century Music*, the *Journal of the American Musicological Society*, and many edited collections. His current projects include studies of social continuities in French music from the eighteenth to the twentieth centuries, the historiography of nineteenth-century ballet, and a second monograph on Fauré.

STEPHEN RUMPH is Associate Professor of Music History at the University of Washington. He is the author of *The Fauré Song Cycles* (forthcoming). Other publications include *Beethoven after Napoleon* (2004) and *Mozart and Enlightenment Semiotics* (2011) and articles in the *Journal of the American Musicological Society*, *Journal of the Royal Music Association*, *19th-Century Music*, and other journals. In 2015 he co-organized the international conference "Effable and Ineffable: Gabriel Fauré and the Limits of Criticism." He sings professionally as a lyric tenor.

CAMBRIDGE COMPOSER STUDIES

Fauré Studies

Edited by

CARLO CABALLERO
University of Colorado, Boulder

STEPHEN RUMPH
University of Washington

Shaftesbury Road, Cambridge CB2 8EA, United Kingdom

One Liberty Plaza, 20th Floor, New York, NY 10006, USA

477 Williamstown Road, Port Melbourne, VIC 3207, Australia

314–321, 3rd Floor, Plot 3, Splendor Forum, Jasola District Centre, New Delhi – 110025, India

103 Penang Road, #05–06/07, Visioncrest Commercial, Singapore 238467

Cambridge University Press is part of Cambridge University Press & Assessment, a department of the University of Cambridge.

We share the University's mission to contribute to society through the pursuit of education, learning and research at the highest international levels of excellence.

www.cambridge.org
Information on this title: www.cambridge.org/9781108453233

DOI: 10.1017/9781108692267

First published 2021
First paperback edition 2023

A catalogue record for this publication is available from the British Library

Library of Congress Cataloging-in-Publication data
Names: Caballero, Carlo editor. | Rumph, Stephen C. editor.
Title: Fauré studies / edited by Carlo Caballero, Stephen Rumph.
Description: [1.] | New York : Cambridge University Press, 2021. | Series: Cambridge composer studies | Includes bibliographical references and index.
Identifiers: LCCN 2019049501 (print) | LCCN 2019049502 (ebook) | ISBN 9781108429191 (hardback) | ISBN 9781108453233 (paperback) | ISBN 9781108692267 (epub)
Subjects: LCSH: Fauré, Gabriel, 1845-1924–Criticism and interpretation.
Classification: LCC ML410.F27 F37 2021 (print) | LCC ML410.F27 (ebook) | DDC 780.92–dc23
LC record available at https://lccn.loc.gov/2019049501
LC ebook record available at https://lccn.loc.gov/2019049502

ISBN   978-1-108-42919-1   Hardback
ISBN   978-1-108-45323-3   Paperback

For Jean-Michel Nectoux

Contents

Figures

Tables

Music Examples

Contributors

BYRON ADAMS University of California, Riverside

CARLO CABALLERO University of Colorado, Boulder

ROBERT O. GJERDINGEN Northwestern University

SANDER GOLDBERG University of Oregon and University of California,
Los Angeles

ROY HOWAT Royal Academy of Music and Royal Conservatoire
of Scotland

SYLVIA KAHAN State University of New York, Staten Island

HERVÉ LACOMBE Université Rennes 2

JEAN-MICHEL NECTOUX Independent scholar (formerly at Bibliothèque
nationale de France)

STEVEN RINGS University of Chicago

STEPHEN RUMPH University of Washington

MATHIEU SCHNEIDER Université de Strasbourg

LESLEE SMUCKER Independent scholar and artist

Acknowledgments

Fauré Studies grew out of an international conference held in 2015 at the University of Washington, "Effable and Ineffable: Gabriel Fauré and the Limits of Criticism." We extend our warmest thanks to all the speakers, performers, and audience members at that memorable event. This book, however, is no mere proceedings. While the chapters by Lacombe, Gjerdingen, Adams, Goldberg, Schneider, Howat, and Rings originated in papers presented in 2015, they have been greatly expanded and reworked. Those by Kahan, Caballero and Smucker, and Rumph represent entirely new work.

Fauré Studies primarily targets music scholars, but it also addresses topics and works of interest to performers, students, and general readers. The three opening chapters (Kahan, Lacombe, Gjerdingen) have broad aims, treating issues of patronage, critical discourse, and pedagogy. Adams' chapter on the Requiem, Fauré's best known work, lies at the center of the book. The two chapters that follow focus on the opera *Pénélope*, one of Fauré's least known works, yet one of his most complex and rewarding. After forty years of silence, two nearly simultaneous productions of *Pénélope* in 2015 – one staged expressly for the Seattle conference – allow us to suggest that these essays might mark a timely return of this opera to the repertoire. Four other chapters (Rumph, Caballero and Smucker, Howat, and Rings) likewise focus on works or groups of related works. The final chapters broaden out again as Caballero and Smucker address French orientalism, situating musical styles in the context of aesthetic and political trends, and Rings develops his analysis of the Thirteenth Nocturne from insights drawn from Vladimir Jankélévitch's philosophy. In short, after a cultural conspectus at the outset, the book plunges into an inviting forest of musical works, then re-emerges on headlands whose horizons recover some of the breadth of the early chapters.

We are grateful for the generous financial support of the University of Washington School of Music and Simpson Center for the Humanities, which made possible the 2015 conference. We also thank Dan Wallace Miller and Vespertine Opera, Julia Tai and Philharmonia Northwest, Dean Williamson, and the singers and technical staff who mounted the inspiring production of *Pénélope*. Thanks are also due to the students of Carlo Caballero's doctoral seminar ("Gabriel Fauré and His World") in spring 2016, where several of the Seattle papers, kindly provided by their authors, provided a basis for enjoyable and often searching discussions. Finally, Kate Brett, Eilidh Burrett, and the rest of the team at Cambridge University Press have lent much-needed support, patience, and encouragement at all stages of the project.

All Fauré scholarship owes its impetus to the groundbreaking research of Jean-Michel Nectoux. Although he was unable to attend the 2015 conference, Nectoux graciously contributed a foreword that recounts his research journey and offers his unique perspective on Fauré scholarship from the composer's lifetime to the present. We gratefully dedicate this volume to him.

~ | Looking Back on a Journey

JEAN-MICHEL NECTOUX[*]

Let us begin by considering how Gabriel Fauré (1845–1924) made a way for himself in France between about 1855 and 1909. As for the posthumous international development of research into his music, that will be the focus of the latter part of this text.

Fauré's long life gives one pause. One might describe it as a slow but constant and courageous ascent. Really, nothing destined this boy from Ariège, deep in the south of France, to become one of the glorious figures of the French Republic – the Republic that would one day confer on this modest man the extraordinary honor of a national funeral, like that of Victor Hugo.

We remark that since he was intended from childhood to become a church musician, he did not follow the educational path taken by the majority of French musicians and attend the Paris Conservatory, an institution founded by the National Convention in 1795. He was only nine years old when he was enrolled instead in the excellent École de musique classique et religieuse that had just been founded by Louis Niedermeyer, and he would study there from 1854 to 1865. At the École, a capital encounter took place: he met Camille Saint-Saëns, his teacher and soon his friend, who took over piano instruction after Niedermeyer's death in 1861. Fauré's beginnings as an organist were rather modest. He languished in the loft of the Church of Saint-Sauveur in Rennes (1865–69); on returning to Paris, he became organist at Notre-Dame de Clignancourt (1870) and then at the swank parish of Saint-Honoré-d'Eylau (1871). After the war he played the choir organ at Saint-Sulpice, a post he passed along to his friend André Messager when he had to replace Saint-Saëns at La Madeleine during the older composer's tours. His professional life stabilized in 1877 when he became choirmaster of the same church, a post that put him in the public eye. Saint-Saëns was then principal organist at La Madeleine, an even more prominent position, which he yielded to his former student in 1896. Fauré was more than fifty years old when he

[*] I wish to thank Carlo Caballero and Stephen Rumph for their invitation to contribute to the present volume.

received his first mark of official recognition, also in 1896: his appointment as professor of composition at the Paris Conservatory, where he succeeded a celebrated figure in French music, Jules Massenet.

As for his candidacies for election to the Academy of Fine Arts (the Institut), Fauré experienced two wounding disappointments. In 1894, he received four votes while his triumphant rival Théodore Dubois (1837–1924) got nineteen. He was no luckier in 1896: Charles Lenepveu (1840–1910) received nineteen votes against four for Fauré. The composer of *La bonne chanson* would reach the venerable age of sixty-four before being elected to the Academy of Fine Arts in 1909.

Examination of Fauré's professional life in the years around 1900 makes one wonder how and when he found time to compose. Appointed Inspector of Musical Instruction in 1892, he had to crisscross France to evaluate the activities of conservatories in the major cities, a role that required endless trips and the redaction of detailed reports on his return to Paris. After 1896, he continued this work on top of his obligations at La Madeleine and the Paris Conservatory; his work as a musical critic for *Le Figaro* after 1903 added yet another layer. In 1905, at the age of sixty, he finally could abandon his exhausting labors as inspector, organist, and professor of composition to assume the directorship of the Conservatory, an appointment that greatly astonished Parisian musical circles, since the composer had never been a student there.

As for the dissemination of his works, Fauré had to endure an extremely slow uptake by publishers with scant conviction in his merits. Hartmann published four of his songs in 1871,[1] and these were transferred five years later to Antoine Choudens, who issued his first songs individually, drop by drop, and finally published twenty together in 1879. The young Fauré's relations with Choudens were always difficult. As early as 1870, the composer wrote his friend Julien Koszul, "I shall send you the 'Gavotte' one of these days ... I'll also tuck in a copy of my *romance* 'S'il est un charmant gazon,' which is about to come out. Choudens, apparently quite a comedian, gave it the title 'Rêve d'amour'! I would never have thought of that."[2] In 1879, the young composer broke off relations with the surly publisher when the latter adamantly refused to bring out the radiant Piano Quartet, Op. 15. In a letter to his confidante Marie Clerc, the composer diagnosed Choudens with "quartetto-phobia" and added, "Very well! This

---

[1] "Lydia," "Hymne," "Mai," and "Seule."

[2] Gabriel Fauré, *Correspondance, suivie de Lettres à Madame H.*, ed. Jean-Michel Nectoux (Paris: Fayard, 2015), 29.

little snub has undoubtedly been more significant for me than I would ever have thought. It's really the end of the line. If I knew M. Geoffroy Saint-Hilaire, I would ask him why the anatomical collection in the Jardin des Plantes does not have any publishers' skeletons!"[3] Op. 15 would be issued by Julien Hamelle who, for better or worse, became Fauré's regular publisher from 1880 to 1905 and greatly vexed the composer.[4] Fauré would later find in Henri Heugel (1906) and Auguste and Jacques Durand (1913) publishers of quite another level of commitment.

* * *

While Fauré's music often met with favorable reviews in the press of his time, only much later did it inspire extensive critical study, scant examples of which appeared during his lifetime. In 1888, Hugues Imbert published a chapter in his book *Profils de musiciens* whose title page, unfortunately, identified the composer as "J. Fauré," typical of the Parisian press who frequent confused the famous baritone Jean-Baptiste Faure (1830–1914) with the young composer.[5] Faure was famous for playing the title roles in *Don Giovanni* and *Guillaume Tell* at the Paris Opéra, but he also occasionally composed vocal music. He lives on in memory thanks to the astonishing collection of paintings, including Manet's *Déjeuner sur l'herbe*, which he bequeathed to posterity.

In 1909, the monthly magazine *Musica* honored Fauré with a special issue, and in 1914 Louis Vuillemin wrote a short book, *Gabriel Fauré et son œuvre*, brought out by the composer's own publisher Durand.[6] During World War I, Georges Jean-Aubry devoted a few pages to Fauré in his collection *La musique française d'aujourd'hui*, to which Fauré contributed a preface.[7] Émile Vuillermoz reprinted his articles on *Mirages* and the Second Piano Quintet in a collection entitled *Musiques d'aujourd'hui*, and Fauré honored his former pupil with a short preface to this

---

[3] Ibid., 84.

[4] See Nectoux, "Un début dans la vie d'artiste: Gabriel Fauré et ses premiers éditeurs," in *Noter, annoter, éditer la musique: Mélanges offerts à Catherine Massip*, ed. Cécile Reynaud and Herbert Schneider (Geneva: Droz, 2012), 565–577.

[5] Hughes Imbert, *Profils de musiciens* (Paris: Fischbacher et Sagot, 1888), 57–78. The composer's personal copy (private collection) bears this inscription: "To M. Gabriel Fauré | Kind and affectionate recollections | H. Imbert."

[6] *Musica* 77 (February 1909); Louis Vuillemin, *Gabriel Fauré et son œuvre* (Paris: A. Durand et fils, 1914).

[7] Georges Jean-Aubry, *La musique française d'aujourd'hui* (Paris: Perrin, 1916); the chapter on Fauré is on pp. 72–81.

volume.[8] Joseph de Marliave had consecrated two remarkable articles to Fauré's music just before the war, which were republished in the posthumous volume *Études musicales* in 1917.[9] In October 1922, under the editorship of Henry Prunières, *La revue musicale* honored Fauré with a special issue. It opened with a short memoir by the composer himself, recalling his student days, and continued with essays by Émile Vuillermoz, Maurice Ravel, Roland-Manuel, Charles Kœchlin, Florent Schmitt, Roger-Ducasse, Alfred Cortot, Nadia Boulanger, and René Chalupt. Most of the authors were former composition students of Fauré's, and some of the essays remain significant because of their direct insights into the composer's world.[10] Fauré died in November 1924, and Alfred Bruneau, observing a hallowed tradition, delivered a long eulogy at the Académie des Beaux-Arts when he inherited the late composer's chair, a speech that was later published as a pamphlet.[11] As for Fauré's work as a musical critic for the daily paper *Le Figaro*, a selection of his articles, sensibly regrouped by the composers under review, was published in 1930 under the title *Opinions musicales*.[12]

This bibliographical overview may seem rather slender. Yet one must stress that from the moment of his death Fauré's work attracted a veritable cult. The first substantial books about him appeared, written by his former students: a study by Charles Kœchlin which continues to be of great interest, and a belated one by Émile Vuillermoz.[13] But we must draw even more attention to the writings of Philippe Fauré-Fremiet (1889–1954), the composer's younger son. He published a biography of his father in 1929,

[8] Émile Vuillermoz, *Musiques d'aujourd'hui* (Paris: G. Crès, 1923), 1–20. We should also add the very short essay at the start of André Cœuroy's *La musique française moderne* (Paris: Delagrave, 1924).

[9] Joseph de Marliave, *Études musicales* (Paris: Félix Alcan, 1917). The opening section of the book, headed "Un musicien français: Gabriel Fauré," includes two essays: "Sa musique de piano" [1909], 1–34; and "Pénélope" [1913], 35–60. De Marliave (1873–1914) died in battle on August 24, 1914. He is best known for his book on Beethoven's string quartets, published in 1925 with a preface by Fauré. Ravel dedicated the splendid Toccata from *Le tombeau de Couperin* to the memory of de Marliave.

[10] Gabriel Fauré, special issue of *La Revue Musicale* 4, No. 11 (October 1, 1922).

[11] Alfred Bruneau, *La vie et les œuvres de Gabriel Fauré* (Paris: Charpentier et Fasquelle, 1925).

[12] Gabriel Fauré, *Opinions musicales*, ed. P.-B Gheusi (Paris: Rieder, 1930). Nicolas Southon is currently working on a complete edition of Fauré's critical writings.

[13] Charles Kœchlin, *Gabriel Fauré* (Paris: Alcan, 1927; second edition, Paris: Plon, 1949). Émile Vuillermoz, *Gabriel Fauré* (Paris: Flammarion, 1960), completed only a few months before his death; the English translation by Kenneth Schapin (Philadelphia: Chilton, 1969) contains valuable additions: a chronology, catalogue of works, an index, and an important discography by Steven Smolian. For the record, let us also mention, despite its extremely irritating approach, the book by Georges Servières, *Gabriel Fauré* (Paris: Laurens, 1930).

and then published a new version in 1957 that includes the additional essays "Réflexions sur la confiance fauréenne" and "Notes sur l'interpréta- tion," as well as an important catalogue of works arranged by opus number and a discography covering the years 1926–1957.[14] We also have Philippe Fauré-Fremiet to thank for an edition of the composer's letters to his wife Marie, published under the title *Lettres intimes*.[15] Unfortunately, these letters were published without critical notes or an index, but the 300-odd pages offer the reader glimpses into the workshop of a composer who was always secretive. Indeed, a few weeks before his death, he wrote to his wife, "When I am back in Paris, each day I shall set about giving you, so that you may burn them, all my sketches, all my rough drafts, all those things of which I wish nothing to subsist after I am gone. This worry haunted me while I was ill. You will help me to appease it."[16] This invaluable corpus of letters still awaits a truly critical edition, which it obviously merits.[17]

In 1945, the composer's centenary prompted various publications. We may mention Claude Rostand's *L'œuvre de Fauré* and the more personal work of Fauré's near-homonym and friend, Gabriel Faure (no accent mark!), which includes interesting excerpts from letters he received from the composer.[18] Above these looms the important volume brought out by Éditions de la Revue musicale, *Le centenaire de Gabriel Fauré (1845–1945)*, which includes "La genèse de Pénélope" by Philippe Fauré-Fremiet, "Le centenaire de Gabriel Fauré" by René Dumesnil, and a study by Georges Jean-Aubry on an operatic project, "Gabriel Fauré, Paul Verlaine et Albert Samain, ou Les Tribulations de 'Bouddha': Lettres inédites."

Certain aspects of Fauré's work prompted specialized studies, for example, Marguerite Long's little book *Au piano avec Gabriel Fauré*, which brings together personal memories and the advice of an interpreter who fostered a sort of cult of the composer – a cult of which she firmly believed herself the sole priestess.[19] In the 1960s and 1970s, we must admit, Fauré's music suffered from a certain disaffection. The generation of fervent

---

[14] Philippe Fauré-Fremiet, *Gabriel Fauré* (Paris: Rieder, 1929), an edition illustrated with nearly 100 high-quality (rotogravure) images (second edition, Paris: Albin-Michel, 1957).

[15] Fauré, *Lettres intimes*, ed. Philippe Fauré-Fremiet (Paris: Grasset, 1951).

[16] Ibid., 295 (October 14, 1924). Translation from Carlo Caballero, *Fauré and French Musical Aesthetics* (Cambridge: Cambridge University Press, 2001), 241.

[17] The original documents are held by the Bibliothèque nationale de France, Département de la Musique.

[18] Claude Rostand, *L'œuvre de Fauré* (Paris: J. B. Janin, 1945), of little interest; Faure, *Gabriel Fauré* (Paris: Artaud, 1945).

[19] Marguerite Long, *Au piano avec Gabriel Fauré* (Paris: Julliard, 1963). Long was the widow of Joseph de Marliave, cited above in note 9.

Fauréans born in the 1880s dwindled and musical France was focused on the discovery of newer works stretching from Bartók to Messiaen, from Stockhausen to Boulez . . .

* * *

Although Debussy, Fauré, and Ravel are often invoked as a triumvirate, we must recognize that, of the three, Fauré remains by far the least understood, the least famous, and the least often performed. This state of affairs provokes and, indeed, merits speculation. The composer's creative activity developed in an era when Parisian musical life was dominated by the lyric stage, and we may remark, when we consider Fauré's work as a whole, that he embraced, first and foremost, the intimate media of song, piano music, chamber music, and religious music. His rare symphonic essays did not meet with success or even with the composer's own approval, and he destroyed most of his scores, often keeping only a few themes for much later redeployment.[20]

While his work certainly has spectacular moments – we may recall the unjustly forgotten *Prométhée* (1900) and the beautiful design of *Pénélope* (1913) – Fauré is a musician of understatement; he lacks the orchestral mastery of his student Ravel and the inventive freedom of Debussy. Whoever would follow the lines of his music must listen attentively and tune into the harmonic language, so rich in surprises, which may startle listeners on first hearing. Fauré is a musician of the unexpected. To the very end, and with ever greater boldness, he explored harmonic landscapes uniquely his own. But his muse remained reserved, shadowy, only attaining splendor in his final years. Nonetheless, who would deny that the traits so peculiar to his aesthetic are also its assets? The musician operated in a highly personal universe that ultimately satisfied him. Witness the astonishing letter he wrote to his former teacher Saint-Saëns in October 1893: "My dear Camille, if, by chance, you wake up one morning in a state of disgust and nausea over Meurice and Vacquerie's *Antigone* . . . pass it along to me! Incidental music is the only kind [of theatrical composition] that more or less suits my small means!"[21]

* * *

[20] Symphony in F, Op. 20 (1866–73), from which he recycled two movements; Concerto for Violin, Op. 14 (1878–9), two movements composed and performed and only one (the Allegro) extant; Symphony in D Minor, Op. 40 (1884), performed and destroyed.

[21] Fauré, *Correspondance*, 213. Fauré was referring to incidental music for a revival of Sophocles' *Antigone*, translated by Paul Meurice and Auguste Vacquerie. The premiere took place at the Comédie-Française on November 21, 1893 with music by Saint-Saëns.

Why Fauré? I found myself being asked this question again and again by people surprised by this choice I had taken as a young man. To tell the truth, I would have liked to commit myself to Ravel's music, which I spent my leisure hours listening to in recordings by Vlado Perlemuter and Samson François. In 1975, the centenary of Ravel's birth, I curated a Ravel Exposition in the great gallery of the Bibliothèque nationale de France, interviewing those few surviving witnesses who knew the composer, such as Madeleine Grey, the mezzo-soprano who recorded the *Chansons madécasses* under Ravel's direction. But I judged, not without some good sense, that the last word on the composer had been written by his devoted follower Roland-Manuel (1891–1966) and by the man who would become my teacher, Vladimir Jankélévitch (1903–85).

Fauré's music slowly but surely captured me. In fact, it had attracted me for many years, and with hindsight I feel that a series of happy accidents led to my impassioned, fascinating research into this most secret of musicians. In my early adolescent years, I was beguiled by certain songs, like "Automne," "Au bord de l'eau," and "Les berceaux," which I discovered thanks to Colette Ledran, my music teacher at the Lycée de Montgeron.[22] Each week she gathered around her piano some older students who came to sing the works that with flawless musical instinct she recommended to us. And so we sang together passionately (and in French) *An die ferne Geliebte* by Beethoven or Cherubino's "Voi che sapete" from Mozart's *Le nozze di Figaro*. But I particularly remember the ravishing voice of Jocelyne Vessières singing "Dove sono," the Countess's second aria from the same opera, or Mélisande's song from Debussy's opera:[23]

Mes longs cheveux descendent jusqu'au seuil de la tour,
Mes cheveux vous attendent tout le long de la tour,
Et tout le long du jour, et tout le long du jour.

Saint Daniel et Saint Michel
Saint Michel et Saint Raphaël
Je suis née un dimanche,
Un dimanche à midi.

---

[22] My first biography, *Fauré* (Paris: Seuil, 1972), is dedicated to her. She is also one of the three dedicatees of my recent *Gabriel Fauré: Catalogue des œuvres*, in *Œuvres complètes de Gabriel Fauré*, Vol. 7, No. 1 (Kassel: Bärenreiter, 2018).

[23] She was the daughter of André Vessières, a remarkable Arkel in *Pelléas* at the Opéra-Comique. He can be heard, under the baton of Ernest Ansermet, in a 1960 recording, later reissued on compact disc.

Mæterlinck in fact wrote five versions of Mélisande's song. John William Mackail, who translated *Pelléas et Mélisande* for the London production in 1898, chose a different one, which Fauré set to music (in English):

The King's three blind daughters
Sit locked in a hold.
In the darkness their lamps
Make a glimmer of gold.

Up the stairs of the turret
The sisters are gone.
Seven days they wait there,
And the lamps they burn on.

What hope? says the first,
And leans o'er the flame.
I hear our lamps burning,
O yet! if he came!

O hope! says the second,
Was that the lamps' flare,
Or a sound of low footsteps?
The Prince on the stair!

But the holiest sister,
She turns her about:
O no hope now for ever,
Our lamps are gone out.

But I should evoke an even more distant period of my life, my childhood – in a family where music was always present, loved, and practiced. My maternal grandfather, René Brille, possessed a superb bass-baritone voice, having received his musical training from the brothers of the Collège Saint Joseph in Dijon, where he was called upon to sing Gregorian chant in the boys' choir of the Cathedral of Saint-Bénigne. After he became an engineer, stationed just east of Paris in Gagny, he partici-pated actively in the choir of the parish of Saint-Germain, of which he was also president. I still have vivid memories of the times he invited me to climb the organ loft as a boy to add my voice to the church choir during Christmas Masses. Seized with passion and astonishment, I beheld the organist Mademoiselle Ravassard lavish the full energy of her hands and feet on the consoles and pedalboard. The choir and organ music were then directed by the composer Roger Calmel (1920–98), a student of Messiaen and Milhaud and long-time professor at the Maîtrise de Radio France. Under his direction, I heard on many occasions and with a thrill that has survived the passage of many years Fauré's first youthful masterwork, the *Cantique de Jean Racine.*

* * *

During the long and difficult months of the revolution of May 1968, after the prospect of university examinations evaporated, I began to study Fauré's chamber music, perhaps his most characteristic field of creativity. I soon realized that most of the books devoted to him offered few details concerning either the chronology or the analysis of these masterpieces. Driven by the energy and audacity of youth, I decided to go back to the autograph sources, manuscripts, and letters. Eager to deepen my research by consulting the composer's own archives, I got in touch with his daughter-in-law, Mme. Philippe Fauré-Fremiet (née Blanche Felon, 1895–1983), who received this young scholar in an unforgettable manner. She welcomed me into nothing less than the last home of the composer, at 32 rue des Vignes in Paris, where he moved in April 1911. Fauré's presence still seemed palpable. Nothing appeared to have changed for half a century in the vast apartment situated on the fifth floor of a classic bourgeois building of the sixteenth arrondissement. A long hallway opened onto a dining room to the left; then came the composer's study, facing the street. It was an intimate room draped in red cloth, with black woodwork picked out in gold. Above the white marble hearth rose a mirror fashioned in Louis XVI style; on the wall were many watercolors, drawings, and paintings by the composer's father-in-law, the sculptor Emmanuel Fremiet (1824–1910). A medium-sized Erard grand piano occupied a large part of the room,[24] and there was still a divan upholstered in grey velvet which stood against black-and-gold wooden doors that would have opened onto the dining room. A bay window with a view of greenery graced this studio where the composer worked and slept. In the entry hall one could see to the right the immense atelier, two stories high, belonging to the composer's wife Marie, née Fremiet.[25]

[24] This piano from 1914 was bequeathed along with John Singer Sargent's oil portrait of the composer to the Musée de la musique, Cité de la Musique–Philharmonie de Paris (inv. E. 995.6.157), as was a plaster bust of the musician by Emmanuel Fremiet (inv. E. 995.6.157), which is visible in a well-known photograph of the composer in front of his piano in his studio.
[25] She had a talent for drawing but also tried her hand at sculpture. According to Blanche Fauré-Fremiet, when she died (1926) only formless attempts were found in her studio.

Over the course of May and June 1968, in a Paris lacking all means of communication, I used up the last liters of petrol in my little car to cross the capital, almost deserted, to come to work in the Fauré archives. I would eventually spend innumerable fascinating hours there consulting original documents that Blanche Fauré-Fremiet brought me with unflagging trust and patience. Her attention, willingness to help, encouragement, and friendship were a constant source of support. In the large atelier at rue des Vignes, two black wooden file-cases were placed at my disposal, containing an impressive collection of manuscripts, letters, and photographs of the musician. A few years later, in 1979, I took great joy in welcoming them into the collections of the Département de la musique of the Bibliothèque nationale, where, as a young curator, I cataloged them.

Ever modest, Blanche Fauré-Fremiet maintained from the outset that she could in no way guide my research, especially in the absence of her late husband. She suggested that I approach Vladimir Jankélévitch, the celebrated philosopher and long-established professor at the Sorbonne, who was friendly with the Fauré family. He had already devoted three indispensable works to the composer in 1938, 1951, and 1974.[26] I enjoyed the privilege of many long conversations with the philosopher in his beautiful apartment at 1 Quai aux Fleurs, situated near the tip of the Île de la Cité. During our meetings, sitting near his study and piano, I had an unforgettable view of the spire of Notre-Dame. Under his direction I wrote a dissertation entitled "Fauré et le théâtre" (1980).

I count among my most moving memories of those years the two interviews I held in January and February 1971 with the composer's older son, Emmanuel Fauré-Fremiet (1883–1971), a renowned researcher in comparative embryology and professor at the Collège de France. This old man – witty, the essence of charm – relayed the memory of how on summer nights in Bougival he heard *La bonne chanson* sung by Emma Bardac accompanied by his own father ... During my studies at the Institut de musicologie, I encountered another great teacher in Yves Gérard, a researcher at the Centre national de la recherche scientifique (CNRS), known for his catalogue of the works of Boccherini and also responsible for the Saint-Saëns archives housed in the Château de Dieppe. Under his direction I published an edition of the correspondence between Fauré and Saint-Saëns, the composer's teacher and friend.

---

[26] Vladimir Jankélévitch, *Gabriel Fauré et ses mélodies* (Paris: Plon, 1938); *Gabriel Fauré: Ses mélodies et son esthétique* (Paris: Plon, 1951); and *Gabriel Fauré et l'inexprimable* (Paris: Plon, 1974).

In a wave of youthful enthusiasm, I expressed my surprise to François-Régis Bastide at the absence of Fauré from the illustrated paperback collection "Solfèges," of which he was series editor at Éditions du Seuil. Replying by post, and to my great surprise, he informed me that he had already commissioned the book but preferred to reassign it to me. Such is the origin of the little illustrated volume that appeared in 1972.[27] Since that time, I have published a number of different books about the composer,[28] ending with a thematic catalogue of his works, the fruit of half a century of research.[29]

* * *

It gives me great satisfaction to recount and applaud the very important growth of scholarship around Gabriel Fauré. Norman Suckling's book remains a pioneering work,[30] which presaged the wide international trend toward research on Fauré that developed first in France, the United Kingdom, and the United States, and later in Spain, Japan, and elsewhere. I am also pleased to cite here the works of Robert Orledge, Marie-Claire Beltrando-Patier, Robin Tait, Jonathan Barrie Jones, Marie-Maud Thomas, Jessica Duchen, Carlo Caballero, and Graham Johnson.[31] In 1995, the sesquicentenary of Fauré's birth inspired the first scholarly colloquia on his music: one was held in Lennoxville, Québec, and the contributions were edited and translated by Tom Gordon; the other took place in Munich,

---

[27] Augmented editions appeared in 1986 and 1995 also from Seuil.

[28] Nectoux, *Gabriel Fauré, 1900–1977*, Phonographies, 1 (Paris: Bibliothèque nationale, Département de la phonothèque nationale et de l'audiovisuel, 1979): a discography including radio recordings. My most recent work has been published by Librairie Arthème Fayard: *Gabriel Fauré, Les voix du clair-obscur*, 2nd revised edition (Paris: Fayard, 2008) and the *Correspondance* (2015) cited above, which includes a large selection of letters, hitherto unpublished, from the composer to his mistress Marguerite Hassselmans, whose important role in his life is known to all students of the composer.

[29] Nectoux, *Gabriel Fauré: Catalogue des œuvres* (Kassel: Bärenreiter Verlag, 2018).

[30] Norman Suckling, *Fauré* (London: J. M. Dent; New York: E. P. Dutton, 1946).

[31] Robert Orledge, *Gabriel Fauré* (London: Eulenburg, 1979); Orledge, second edition, 1983; Marie-Claire Beltrando-Patier, "Les mélodies de G. Fauré" (State thesis, Université de Strasbourg II, 1978); Robin Tait, *The Musical Language of Gabriel Fauré* (New York: Garland, 1989); *Gabriel Fauré: A Life in Letters*, trans. and ed. J. Barrie Jones (London: Batsford, 1989); Marie-Maud Thomas, *La musique de chambre de Gabriel Fauré: Une étude de style* (Port-au-Prince: [n.p.], 1994); Jessica Duchen, *Gabriel Fauré* (London: Phaidon, 2000); Carlo Caballero, *Fauré and French Musical Aesthetics* (Cambridge: Cambridge University Press, 2001); Graham Johnson, *Gabriel Fauré: The Songs and Their Poets*, with translations of the song texts by Richard Stokes (London: Guildhall School of Music & Drama; Farnham, Surrey: Ashgate Publishing, 2009).

with the proceedings published in German by Peter Jost.[32] We should also highlight the important bibliographic guide by Edward R. Phillips; Mutien-Omer Houziaux's study on the Requiem, Op. 48; the short book (in Spanish) on Fauré's piano music by Beatriz Montes; and the recent short book in French by Jacques Bonnaure.[33] This leaves out the many articles about Fauré's music in musicological journals, mostly in French and English.

* * *

The wide-ranging array of research cited above now sustains the *Œuvres complètes de Gabriel Fauré*, a monumental edition being published under the auspices of Bärenreiter-Verlag in Kassel, Germany. This vast enterprise, in the care of our remarkable editor Annette Thein, will number thirty volumes and, without doubt, will assure the broad international dissemination of this admirable music into the future. Bärenreiter deserves the highest recognition, including my personal gratitude, for undertaking this labor. I have entrusted to my friend Nicolas Southon the important responsibility of serving as editor-in-chief of the *Œuvres complètes*, for which I thank him. I continue in the capacity of general editor.

Translation by Carlo Caballero

---

[32] *Regarding Fauré*, ed. and trans. Tom Gordon (Amsterdam: Gordon and Breach, 1999); *Gabriel Fauré: Werk und Rezeption*, ed. Peter Jost (Kassel: Bärenreiter, 1996).

[33] Edward R. Phillips, *Gabriel Fauré: A Guide to Research* (New York and London: Garland, 2000); Phillips, *Gabriel Fauré: A Research and Information Guide*, second edition (New York and London: Routledge, 2011); Moutien-Omer Houziaux, *À la recherche "des" Requiem de Fauré* (Liège: Société liégoise de musicologie; Paris: Klincksieck, 2000); Beatriz C. Montes, *Gabriel Fauré al piano* (Madrid: Nauclero, 2012); Jacques Bonnaure, *Gabriel Fauré* (Arles: Actes Sud/Classica, 2017).

1 | Patrons and Society

Gabriel Fauré's "Other" Career in the Paris and London Music Salons

SYLVIA KAHAN

On April 10, 1903, on the occasion of his promotion to the rank of Officier of the Légion d'honneur, *Le Figaro* described Gabriel Fauré in this way:

No [such] reward could cause more rejoicing in the hearts of musicians, for no one is more purely musical than Fauré, no one is imbued with more poetry – so much so that his delightful *Lieder* have earned him the appellation of the French Schumann.

Modest, almost shy, and yet with a fine mind, Fauré is above all a tender and sweet dreamer.[1]

It was these qualities of poetic sweetness and modesty – in addition to the genius of his music – that endeared the composer to almost everyone who knew him. And yet, despite the many accolades that came Fauré's way over the course of his career, the renown of the composer and his works during his lifetime was achieved slowly and with difficulty. The modesty and shyness alluded to by the *Figaro*'s journalist stemmed, in part, from Fauré's insecurities about his talent and his ability to succeed as a composer, professionally and financially. He was never able to make a living from composition, and he was overburdened by his hardworking daily life as a church musician, suburban piano teacher, and freelance musician. In 1892, he also took on the position of inspector of conservatory education in the branches of the national music and choir schools, a post that involved relentless administrative work and interminable train travel. It was only in middle age (beginning in the mid-1890s) that Fauré was able to achieve an estimable degree of recognition and respect as a composer.

Fauré's hard-won success was due, in no small part, to the performances of his works in the artistic, aristocratic, and upper-bourgeois music salons in Paris and London, and to his championship by the hosts and hostesses of these salons, who offered professional opportunities and material support at crucial moments in the composer's career. This study will

---

[1] "Instantané: Gabriel Fauré," *Le Figaro*, April 10, 1903, 1. Unless otherwise noted, all translations from the French are my own.

provide a brief overview of the social milieus and patronage that played such an important role in the ascent of Fauré's reputation in the wider musical world.

The music salon was at the height of its popularity as Fauré began to make his way in Paris musical circles. Salons dedicated to literature, philosophy, and the art of conversation had been established during the Enlightenment, but, beginning in the 1830s, musical performance became the express purpose of certain gatherings. Music salons were hosted not only by musicians such as Rossini and Offenbach, but also by members of the aristocracy such as Napoleon's niece, Princesse Mathilde, and Liszt's lover, Comtesse Marie d'Agoult. The period following the Franco-Prussian War of 1870–1 saw a proliferation of music salons in artistic-musical, literary, aristocratic, and upper-bourgeois circles. While the wider public's musical consumption was mostly satisfied by opera and ballet (or, for those with more taste for the popular, at *café-concerts*), those "connoisseurs" who yearned for more intimate music-making found havens in the pleasing domestic surroundings of the salon's hosts and hostesses, many of whom performed alongside the greatest performing artists of the era. In this socially fluid post-war period, musicians were welcomed into the salons of the upper classes, who received on a chosen "day." Composers of art song and chamber music who were unsuccessful in having their works performed in the official concert societies – the Société des Concerts du Conservatoire, the Concerts populaires (later, the Concerts Pasdeloup), the Concerts Colonne, and, some years later, the Concerts Lamoureux – were able to hear their works performed in refined surroundings before an audience of passionate, sophisticated, and socially influential music-lovers. The Société nationale de musique (founded in 1871), whose goal was the advancement of French contemporary music, was composed primarily of composers and musicians playing for other composers and musicians.[2] Thus, the salon emerged as one of the only venues where new music could be promulgated among relatively diverse and fluid groups of sophisticated music-lovers.[3]

---

[2] A member of the Société nationale de musique since its creation in 1871, Fauré first served as secretary of the organization and subsequently, in 1886, as its treasurer. Three of his chamber works, eighteen of his songs, and four symphonic works were given their first performances under the auspices of the SNM between 1872 and 1885. See Michel Duchesneau, *L'Avant-Garde musicale à Paris de 1871 à 1939* (Sprimont: Mardaga, 1997), 19–21.

[3] For a discussion of Paris salon culture, see Chapters 2 and 3 of my *Music's Modern Muse: A Life of Winnaretta Singer-Polignac* (Rochester, NY: University of Rochester Press, 2009).

Early Promoters: Pauline Viardot and the Clerc Family

Shortly after Fauré moved to Paris in 1871 to begin a career as a young organist, he was introduced by his teacher and mentor Camille Saint-Saëns to the salon of the internationally renowned singer and composer Pauline Viardot. Fauré quickly ingratiated himself into the brilliant Viardot circle, where he met an extraordinary group of artistic personalities that included Charles Gounod, Gustave Flaubert, Ernest Renan, Ivan Turgenev, and George Sand. Pauline Viardot took a liking to Fauré, and soon began to serve as his musical advisor and social intermediary, recommending him to her friends and associates as a potential pianist-accompanist in their salons and a teacher of piano.[4] His modesty and shyness notwithstanding, Fauré loved to circulate in society; his dramatic good looks and natural charm were attractive to men and women alike. He formed a romantic attachment (broken off in 1877) with Pauline Viardot's younger daughter, Marianne; he also became friends with Madame Viardot's violinist son Paul Viardot, who was the dedicatee of Fauré's Violin Sonata in A Major, Op. 13 (composed 1875–6). This score, a deservedly celebrated staple of the violin repertoire, might not have been made accessible to the public so expeditiously were it not for the intercession of two new friends whom Fauré met around the same time: Camille and Marie Clerc. The Clercs – he a well-to-do engineer and she a talented amateur musician – hosted their own salon of artists and musicians in the fashionable Rue de Monceau; in the summers, the music-making and artistic camaraderie were transplanted north to the Clercs' summer home in Saint-Adresse, in Normandy, where Fauré was a constant guest and musical participant. In the Clercs, Fauré found not only a close and welcoming family circle but also encouragement for his creativity, sorely needed by a young composer who doubted the value of his works. Marie Clerc became a surrogate mother for Fauré. She encouraged him to push past his natural indolence and lack of ambition, in the words of Jean-Michel Nectoux, "leading him out of an adolescence that continued well beyond his thirtieth year."[5] Under her supervision, Fauré applied himself to his work. His diligence bore fruit; the Violin Sonata in A Major was written almost entirely under the Clercs' roof during the summer of 1875 (he would begin work on his Piano Quartet in C Minor, Op. 15, the following summer).

[4] Jean-Michel Nectoux, *Gabriel Fauré: Les voix du clair-obscur* (Paris: Fayard, 2008), 61.
[5] See Jean-Michel Nectoux, (ed.), *Gabriel Fauré: His Life through His Letters*, trans. J. A. Underwood (London and New York: Marion Boyars, 1984), 31.

It was Camille Clerc, however, who brought about Fauré's first great professional coup. A skilled businessman, Clerc convinced the German music-publishing house of Breitkopf & Härtel to publish the Sonata in A Major. It was inconceivable that such a long and daunting work by an unknown composer could be accepted by such a renowned publisher, but Clerc negotiated the deal by convincing the publishers that Fauré was a young artist with "a great future" – and by convincing Fauré to forgo payment in exchange for the prestige of being taken on by such a prestigious house.[6] Camille Clerc intervened again on behalf of Fauré in 1877, when Camille Saint-Saëns gave up his post as organist at the Church of the Madeleine. Théodore Dubois subsequently assumed the position, leaving open the post of *maître de chapelle* (choirmaster). Clerc promptly asked a friend to speak on Fauré's behalf to the curate of the Madeleine (with Saint-Saëns working behind the scenes as well to promote his former student, and Fauré also securing a recommendation from Gounod). In late April, Fauré was awarded the prestigious post.[7]

Fauré's Career in the Salons

In the decades that followed – from the period of his appointment as *maître de chapelle* at the Madeleine (1877) until his ascendancy to the directorship of the Paris Conservatoire (1905) – Fauré became a regular fixture in the salons of the aristocracy and the upper bourgeoisie. For all intents and purposes, music-making in the salons became an additional profession – often an unwelcome supplementary chore at the end of a long hard day. Yet, the salons could also provide a respite from the daily grind. His 1883 marriage to Marie Fremiet, a woman to whom he was temperamentally unsuited, quickly proved to be emotionally unsatisfying; on top of that, his wife was a homebody, while Fauré was a social animal. As a consequence, Fauré chose to spend more evenings out than at home. There is no question that it was exhausting to keep up the affable sociability and *politesse* required, especially in the more exclusive salons of the *gratin* (upper-crust society), but the composer was adept at assuming

---

[6] Letters pertaining to the publication of the Violin Sonata, Op. 13 are published in Gabriel Fauré, *Correspondance, suivie de Lettres à Madame H.*, ed. Jean-Michel Nectoux (Paris: Fayard, 2015), 34–45.

[7] Letters detailing Fauré's application for and subsequent attainment of the post of *maître de chapelle* at the Madeleine are published in Fauré, *Correspondance*, 47–55.

the mask of charm and deference required. Despite the complexities of the social strata that needed to be navigated, the salons always held out the possibility of new professional contacts – and money – to be made. The critic Louis Aguettant would describe the "Fauré of the salons, moving languidly through the swirl of high-society denizens, a satisfied smile on his face, like some ancient Olympian deity who has had his fill of incense."[8] Debussy was less tactful: "Fauré is the musical mouthpiece [*porte-musique*] of a group of snobs and imbeciles."[9]

But the artistically knowledgeable and appreciative *mélomanes* (music-lovers) in attendance in the salons who offered encouragement of and admiration for Fauré's talents made the nonstop participation in salon life worth the effort. Jean-Michel Nectoux writes:

Certainly Fauré frequented the Paris salons, as did all his colleagues . . . It must be stressed, however, that, unlike the young Proust, Fauré did not value the social round for its own sake. There was nothing of the snob about him; everyone who knew him emphasizes the simplicity of his life and manners. He made regular appearances only in those salons where people were genuinely interested in his music.[10]

Indeed, a substantial number of salon hosts and hostesses were passionately interested in his music. Many first performances of Fauré's music took place in the salons, and a substantial number of Fauré's works bear dedications to the long list of enlightened *mélomanes* who welcomed his compositions and his artistry into their music rooms.[11] Consciously or unconsciously, Fauré may have crafted some of his music to suit the domestic spaces in which it was most likely to be performed: by virtue of their modest proportions and the small forces needed for their execution, his songs, piano music, and chamber music naturally lent themselves to performances in private homes. Graham Johnson has suggested that, in the 1880s at least, Fauré's compositional style (as least in so far as the song repertoire was concerned) was influenced, in part, by "the standards and demands of the salon": often, the melodic lines of his songs were not too difficult to be undertaken by amateurs (a good number of whom had vocal

---

[8] Louis Aguettant quoted in Nectoux, *Les voix du clair-obscur*, 297.

[9] Claude Debussy to George Hartmann, August 9, 1898, in Claude Debussy, *Correspondance 1872–1918*, ed. François Lesure and Denis Herlin (Paris: Gallimard, 2005), 415.

[10] Nectoux, *His Life through His Letters*, 195.

[11] Details of the dedications of Fauré's songs to his salon hosts and hostesses are provided in Graham Johnson, *Gabriel Fauré: The Songs and Their Poets*, with translations of the song texts by Richard Stokes (London: The Guildhall School of Music & Drama and Farnham, Surrey: Ashgate, 2009).

SYLVIA KAHAN

training), and the accompaniments were suffused with the harmonic subtleties and "understated eroticism" that permeated his music.[12] Indeed, given the erotic nature of much of the music of the Belle Époque, musical performance could often serve as a form of artistic "seduction."[13] And Fauré, with his dark good looks and air of charming inscrutability, was capable of arousing intense ardor in his listeners through his keyboard artistry. According to one eyewitness, "When Fauré sat down [at the piano], letting his plump hands wander along the keyboard, improvising a prelude to some song that [my godmother] was going to sing, all conversation ceased, and we listened, charmed."[14] Not surprisingly, the composer was frequently called upon to play the piano – as a soloist, a duo-piano or four-hands partner, or as an accompanist to the host or hostess who wanted nothing better than to perform Fauré's songs with the composer at the piano. The singer Émilie Girette, an accomplished amateur, wrote in her diary that "to be accompanied by 'him' is to know happiness, artistic happiness, the purest of happiness – the only kind, perhaps, that comes close to being in love."[15]

Often, entire *soirées* were devoted to "all-Fauré" programs.[16] These programs included not only short works but also more extended compositions: a traversal of Fauré's opera *Prométhée* (1900), accompanied by two pianos, took place in February 1902 in the salon of the Jean Girette family. One month later, in the same salon, a performance of the complete Requiem, conducted by eminent pianist Alfred Cortot, was performed before a "chic audience," as Émilie Girette recorded in her diary, with the host and hostess serving as soloists and with the composer seated among the guests. Girette noted that Fauré was "delighted" by her performance of the "Pie Jesu" – and there is no reason to think otherwise.[17] In a letter written that year to the Comtesse Greffulhe, Fauré alluded to his eternal quest to find the perfect interpreters of his vocal music. "I don't

[12] Ibid., 164.
[13] In my Introduction to *Music's Modern Muse*, 20, I argue that attendance at private musical gatherings served as a sublimation of, or substitution for, sexual activity.
[14] Geneviève Sienkiewicz, "Ce ... et ceux que j'ai aimés" (unpublished manuscript), cited in Myriam Chimènes, *Mécènes et musiciens: Du salon au concert à Paris sous la IIIe République* (Paris: Fayard, 2004), 69.
[15] Émilie Girette, diary entry of June 19, 1903, cited in ibid., 44–45.
[16] All-Fauré programs were performed, for example, in the salons of Madeleine Lemaire (June 17, 1902), Albert Blondel (January 1907), and the Comtesse de Maupeou (January 15, 1908).
[17] Émilie Girette, diary entry of March 25, 1902, cited in Chimènes, *Mécènes et musiciens*, 142, 144.

know any among the professional [singers]," he wrote. "It's the amateurs who know how to translate me and who understand me best."[18]

Marguerite Baugnies, Madame de Saint-Marceaux

One of the salons where Fauré could relax and be himself was that of Marguerite (Meg) Baugnies née Jourdain (1850–1930), who, following the death of her first husband, painter Eugène Baugnies, married sculptor René de Saint-Marceaux in 1892. The dedicatee of Fauré's First Nocturne (1875) and the *mélodie* "Après un rêve" (1877), Marguerite Baugnies created a hybrid salon, where class lines were blurred and where composers, renowned musicians, and talented amateurs shared the pleasures of high-level performance – or sophisticated improvisation – in unpretentious surroundings and attire. A woman of keen musical instincts, wide-ranging tastes, high standards, and unabashed (sometimes severely critical) opinions that she did not hesitate to share, Meg used her wide network of acquaintances to promote the music and careers of the composers who frequented her salon, turning her private space into a veritable laboratory for the performance of new works: among the countless compositions that were heard for the first time in the Baugnies/Saint-Marceaux salon, Debussy's *Pelléas et Mélisande* is perhaps the most famous.

Fauré would often arrive late to Meg's *vendredis* (Fridays), more formally dressed than the other attendees, having "just left the home of one of his duchesses in evening attire" – but within minutes of arrival, he would be making four-hand music with fellow composer and École Niedermeyer schoolmate André Messager: "Often side by side on one of the piano benches, Fauré and Messager improvised four-hand music, competing in sudden modulations and unexpected changes of key. They both liked that game."[19] Fauré was among the privileged small circle of favored composers, and Meg's diary is filled with details about performances of his works in her music room. Two Fauré cycles – *La bonne chanson* (1894) and *La chanson d'Ève* (1910) – were performed frequently in the Saint-Marceaux salon, often with the composer at the piano;[20] on

---

[18] Fauré to the Comtesse Greffulhe, "Samedi" [November 1902], published in Fauré, *Correspondance*, 292–294.

[19] Marguerite de Saint-Marceaux, quoted in Colette, "Un salon de musique en 1900," in *Journal à rebours* (Paris: Fayard, 1941), 53.

[20] In her diary (published as *Marguerite de Saint-Marceaux, Journal 1894–1927*, ed. Myriam Chimènes [Paris: Fayard, 2007]), Madame de Saint-Marceaux notes numerous performances of

SYLVIA KAHAN

many occasions, Meg, a serious and well-trained amateur pianist and
singer, was the featured soloist.[21]

Meg's desire to help Fauré extended beyond the salon. In 1881, she
and Eugène Baugnies hosted Fauré in Bayreuth, where they attended
performances of *Lohengrin* and *Tristan und Isolde*.[22] In 1888, during a
financially difficult time in Fauré's life, Meg organized a lottery (kept
secret from the beneficiaries), the proceeds of which paid for another
trip to Bayreuth for Fauré and Messager.[23] When Fauré became a composition professor at the Conservatoire (1896), Meg featured works of his
students – including Charles Kœchlin, Florent Schmitt, and, especially,
Maurice Ravel – in her salon offerings. She supported Fauré and pro-
moted his compositions even after the deafness that first manifested itself
in 1898 worsened over the next two decades, causing the musician to
stumble frequently during performance.[24] "Poor genius friend," she
wrote in 1916. "With patience and resignation he accepts his malady;
his heart is as big as his talent."[25]

Fauré's songs cycles in her music salon. *La bonne chanson* was performed on June 15, 1894
(p. 87), May 9, 1895 (98), February 2, 1896 (128), May 21, 1901 (244), May 16, 1906 (435),
January 30, 1914 (excerpts, 790), May 25, 1923 (1197), and June 5, 1923 (1199). Excerpts from
the not yet completed cycle *La chanson d'Ève* were performed on February 22, 1907 (473) and
December 25, 1908 (528); the complete cycle was performed on March 27 and 29, 1911 (641),
October 1, 1911 (666), March 3, 1916 (890), and February 4, 1927 (1248).
[21] In her introduction to the *Journal*, 40–41, Chimènes describes the diligence with which Saint-
Marceaux worked to perfect her piano-playing and her vocal abilities, even late into middle age.
When she sang contemporary repertoire, she worked with the composers themselves. Fauré
personally coached her before her salon performances of his music, especially *La bonne
chanson*, which she performed often in her salon.
[22] See Fauré's letter to Marie Clerc of September 23 [1881], in Fauré, *Correspondance*, 104–105.
[23] See Nectoux, *His Life through His Letters*, 71, and Fauré's undated letter to Marguerite Baugnies
[July 27, 1888], in Fauré, *Correspondance*, 146–147.
[24] This is important new historical data, placing the composer's incipient deafness three years
earlier than the date proposed by Jean-Michel Nectoux. Nectoux claimed 1902 to be the year of
the onset of Fauré's deafness (see Nectoux, *Les voix du clair-obscur*, 381). He leaned on the
evidence of Fauré's letter to his wife from August 6, 1903, in which the composer revealed that
his loss of hearing "remains terribly frightening and saddening!" as well as another letter from
two days later, in which Fauré complained that "for a year now, the plummeting [of my ability
to hear], from that point of view, has been terrible"; Gabriel Fauré, *Lettres intimes*, ed. Philippe
Fauré-Fremiet (Paris: La Colombe, 1951), 72–73. But in a diary entry dated December 2, 1898,
Marguerite de Saint-Marceaux notes, "[Fauré] is going deaf, poor friend": Saint-Marceaux,
Journal, 187.
[25] Saint-Marceaux, diary entry of April 12, 1916, *Journal*, 893.

Comte Robert de Montesquiou and Comtesse Élisabeth Greffulhe

Fauré was introduced to the aesthete Comte Robert de Montesquiou (1855–1921) at a performance of the Société nationale de musique either in 1886 or early 1887. The highly refined, impeccably dressed count, a self-proclaimed arbiter of taste, was no doubt attracted as much by Fauré's striking good looks as by his beautiful music. On April 26, 1887 the Comte hosted a soirée of his songs; the invitations were printed on pink Japan paper.[26] He became Fauré's "literary advisor," introducing him to poets as yet not set by the composer – the most important of whom was Paul Verlaine, whose poetry inspired Fauré to write some of his greatest vocal music.

Montesquiou subsequently became Fauré's means of entry into the poshest salons of the Paris aristocracy, including those of Princesse de Cystria, the Comtesse d'Haussonville, the Comte and Comtesse de Saussine (in whose salon the first performance of Fauré's great song cycle, *La bonne chanson* took place),[27] the Comtesse de Chevigné, the Comtesse de Gauville, and the Princesse Potocka.[28] But the most important person to whom Montesquiou introduced Fauré was his cousin, the Comtesse Greffulhe (1860–1952). Known as the "beauty queen of Paris," Élisabeth Greffulhe was the daughter of the Belgian prince and diplomat Joseph de Caraman-Chimay and his musically gifted wife, née Marie de Montesquiou-Fezensac (Robert de Montesquiou's aunt). The Caraman-Chimays were without fortune, but raised their children in a household that valued culture and music. At age eighteen, Élisabeth married Vicomte (later Comte) Henry Greffulhe, heir to a vast banking fortune and a future politician. In the exclusive salon that she established soon after her marriage, Élisabeth Greffulhe welcomed the cream of the worlds of art, music, literature, science, and politics.

The Comtesse knew of Fauré, having heard him conduct the choir at the Madeleine, her parish church. In 1887, she invited him to perform in her

[26] Anne de Cossé Brissac, *La Comtesse Greffulhe* (Paris: Perrin, 1991), 74; "À travers Paris," *Le Figaro*, April 28, 1887, 1.

[27] "Mondanités: Réceptions," *Le Gaulois*, April 27, 1894. The title of Fauré's song cycle does not appear in the notice, only the report that "M. Maurice Bagès sang the newest *mélodies* of Gabriel Fauré" before the "most purely 'upper-crust' (*gratin*) audience." Nectoux mentions in *Les voix du clair-obscur*, 56 that another one of the first performances of the cycle took place at the home of painter Madeleine Lemaire.

[28] See Nectoux, *Les voix du clair-obscur*, 296–297 for a full list of the hosts and hostesses from the aristocracy, the upper bourgeoisie, and the artistic milieus in which Fauré performed.

spring musical gatherings. That June 1887, Fauré conducted a performance
of Wagner's *Siegfried Idyll* in the Greffulhe salon, scheduling an additional,
unbudgeted rehearsal the day of the concert; "In that way," he wrote, by
way of an excuse, "we can *get close to* perfection."[29] Élisabeth Greffulhe's
passion for Fauré's music was heartfelt, and for nearly two decades she
served as a faithful patron, providing moral and material support, always in
short supply for the composer. In August, the Comtesse invited Fauré,
stressed by overwork and suffering from chronic migraines, to spend four
days at her palatial vacation home in Dieppe; his companions during the
brief respite included Montesquiou; painters Jacques-Émile Blanche,
Walter Sickert, and Paul Helleu; and Prince Edmond de Polignac, an
eccentric, talented composer from the aristocracy. Upon his return to
Paris, he composed a graceful orchestral *Pavane*, expressly intended for
the Greffulhe salon. He subsequently asked Montesquiou to write some
accompanying text that would render the work "suitable to be danced and
sung"; the Comte acceded to Fauré's request, adding, as Fauré described to
his patroness, "sly coquetries by the female dancers and great sighs by
the male dancers that will singularly enhance the music."[30] The *Pavane* –
today one of Fauré's most popular works – was dedicated to Élisabeth
Greffulhe, who made it the centerpiece of a *fête* that she gave in the Bois de
Boulogne on July 21, 1891, on which occasion the work – in fulfillment of
Fauré's original conception – was performed by a mime and a troupe of
dancers, accompanied by an invisible chorus and orchestra.[31] On April 26,
1887, the Comtesse hosted what might have been the first "all-Fauré"
program in a salon setting.[32]

The Comtesse also had a hand in disseminating another beloved work
by Fauré. On January 16, 1888, the first performance of the composer's
Requiem took place at the Madeleine. Originally written for the funeral of a
wealthy parishioner, the work was so enthusiastically received that Fauré
took it upon himself to arrange additional performances; for the second of

---

[29] "... de cette façon nous pourrons côtoyer la perfection!" Letter to the Comtesse Greffulhe of
June 9, 1887, in Fauré, *Correspondance*, 125.
[30] Fauré to the Comtesse Greffulhe, [September 29, 1887], in Fauré, *Correspondance*, 132.
[31] Printed program of the Greffulhe soirée of July 21, 1891, Fonds Montesquiou, BnF-Mss, NAfr
15038, folder 117. In addition to the Fauré *Pavane*, the concert included works by J. S. Bach,
Wagner, Edmond de Polignac, Xavier Perreau, and a recitation of poems by Robert de
Montesquiou. A note in Montesquiou's hand at the bottom of the printed program indicates
that the same program was repeated at a soirée hosted by Montesquiou in his Paris apartment.
[32] "Échos: À Travers Paris," *Le Figaco*, April 28, 1887.

these, on May 4, 1888, the Comtesse Greffulhe and the Prince de Polignac discreetly underwrote the expenses.[33]

Not content to limit her artistic activities to the domestic sphere, the Comtesse, who had superior organizational skills and an unmatched network of connections, yearned to branch out beyond the confines of domestic music-making. In 1890, she launched the Société des grandes auditions musicales de France, whose dual goals were "1) to give major performances of complete musical works by older or contemporary [composers], and 2) to constitute a center for French composers, in order to assure in our country the primacy of French works, [an honor] too often reserved for foreigners." In the early stages of the Société's planning, the Comtesse Greffulhe proposed a merger between her new organization and the Société nationale de musique, with herself as president: she needed the support of professional musicians, and, in return, she could offer a substantially larger financial base than the SNM was able to garner through subscriptions. Fauré served as intermediary between the two organizations. Ultimately, after heated discussions among the members of the SNM's executive committee, the merger was rejected. Fauré explained in a delicate letter to the Comtesse that "the SNM was founded in 1871 with the goal of highlighting French modern music *to the exclusion* of all other music." The merger of the two societies, Fauré continued, would risk exacerbating the tensions that already existed in the organization between those who categorically wanted to exclude foreign music and those (including the SNM's president Vincent d'Indy) who were open to more inclusivity and diversity in its concert programming. "You can see the resultant battles, the coalitions ... the successive resignations of the older members and their replacement by the younger members ... [As] for me, who really owes a lot to our poor Société, I don't want to be its executioner!!"[34] The merger never took place, but the SNM's executive committee became a "consulting" body for the programming of the "Grandes auditions," which presented diverse large-scale works, from Handel oratorios to Wagner and Strauss operas. Fauré's music was included in the concert offerings.[35] The Comtesse Greffulhe remained Fauré's staunch supporter, writing letters on his behalf to the members of the Institut when the composer became a

---

[33] Edmond de Polignac to the Comtesse Greffulhe, undated "bleu" (telegram) [April 1888], Fonds Greffulhe, AP 101 (II), folder 106, Archives nationales, Paris.

[34] Fauré to the Comtesse Greffulhe, [February 3, 1890], in *Correspondance*, 163.

[35] "À travers Paris," *Le Figaro*, May 29, 1894.

candidate for election.[36] Mindful of Fauré's impecunious state, Élisabeth Greffulhe sent gifts through the years to Fauré's wife and children, who regarded her as a sort of "fairy godmother."[37]

Winnaretta Singer, Princesse Edmond de Polignac

Throughout his years as a salon musician, Fauré was obliged to navigate any number of complex social relationships with individuals and within networks. But no relationship, perhaps, was so complicated as his friendship with Winnaretta Singer, the future Princesse Edmond de Polignac (1865–1943), known during her lifetime as *la grande mécène* – the Great Patron. Daughter of American sewing-machine magnate Isaac Singer and his Parisian-born wife Isabella Boyer, Winnaretta became a millionaire upon her father's death in 1875.[38] She demonstrated talent in both art and music, and received lessons in painting, piano, and organ.

In 1879, the widow Singer married again, to Dutch-born violinist and tenor Victor Reubsaet, who claimed to come from noble ancestors. Helping himself to his wife's enormous fortune, he bought himself a ducal title, becoming the so-called Duc de Camposelice. He went on to purchase an extraordinary collection of stringed instruments, including a double quartet of precious Stradivariuses. It was thus that the young Winnaretta was able to hear the great works of the chamber music repertoire performed in the family salon. Isabella and Victor often entertained their guests with performances of the operatic and song repertoire; Winnaretta was often called upon to accompany them on the piano or organ. Extremely shy, she drew inspiration and psychological comfort from the great music that took place in her home.

Winnaretta's and Fauré's paths first crossed in the early 1880s, when they became neighbors during their respective summer vacations in Normandy. As mentioned earlier, the Clercs, who hosted Fauré, organized numerous gatherings for the colony of artists and musicians in residence during the summer months. It was during one of these that Winnaretta

---

[36] Letters pertaining to Fauré's 1893–4 candidacy for the Institut are published in Fauré, *Correspondance*, 214–217; letters pertaining to his 1909 candidacy – which he won, after nine rounds of voting – appear in ibid., 354–357.

[37] Nectoux, *Les voix du clair-obscur*, 182.

[38] Most of the information on Winnaretta Singer, Princesse Edmond de Polignac, in the current study can be found in my *Music's Modern Muse*; see also her own "Memoirs of the Late Princesse Edmond de Polignac," *Horizon* 12, No. 68 (August 1945), 110–140.

first heard Fauré perform his own works. "From the first," she would later write in her memoirs, "I was enthusiastic about them, for they seemed to me ... worthy to rank with those of Chopin or Schumann."[39] Although they were twenty years apart in age, an easy rapport sprang up between them. Fauré recognized Winnaretta's keen sensitivity to art and beauty, and Winnaretta was enthralled by Fauré's ardor and simplicity and his impassioned compositions: he was her first musical mentor.

The growing rift between Winnaretta and her mother and stepfather led her to leave the family home as soon as she reached the age of twenty-one (1887). She promptly had her fortune transferred to her own name and soon thereafter purchased a large property with two houses in the Passy district of Paris (16th arrondissement). Recognizing that she could not circulate in polite society as a single, unchaperoned woman, she chose a husband; in doing so, she joined the ranks of industrialists' daughters who married into the aristocracy – they were called "dollar princesses." Prince Louis de Scey-Montbéliard, whom she wed in July 1887, came from a respected aristocratic family and was happy to ally his title with his intended's sewing-machine fortune. The marriage was not a happy one: Winnaretta had, by this point, acknowledged her attraction to women, and her husband, understandably, had not bargained for a sexless union. During the four years that they kept up the socially imposed pretense of marriage, Winnaretta solidified her standing in the Paris music world. She frequented the salons, including that of Meg Baugnies, who became a role model.

She engineered an introduction to Élisabeth Greffulhe – who normally did not consent to receive women that she considered below her in social standing – and subsequently contributed 10,000 francs to the Comtesse's Société des grandes auditions, which gave her "lifetime membership."[40] In 1889 (at exactly the moment when she legally separated from her husband), she sponsored a concert of new works by the SNM, further strengthening her growing reputation as an important music patron.[41]

She also established her own salon, and before long, the Scey-Montbéliard music room became known as a haven for the musical avant-garde. She struck up a friendship with Emmanuel Chabrier, whose music was thought to be too advanced for most tastes. In 1888, to help convince the Paris Opéra to mount his newest opera, *Gwendoline*, the

---

[39] Polignac, "Memoirs," 118.
[40] Fonds Greffulhe, Archives nationales, AP 101 (II), folders 129 and 149.
[41] Fauré to the Princesse de Scey-Montbéliard, [c. April 9, 1889], Fondation Singer-Polignac, Paris, reproduced in Fauré, *Correspondance*, 149–150.

Princesse offered to host a salon performance of the work, featuring singers from the Opéra, with Chabrier accompanying on piano, Fauré on the harmonium, and d'Indy and Messager on percussion.[42] The opera was not the only work on the program: Fauré conducted his song "Clair de lune" (on a poem of Verlaine), orchestrated for the occasion. As Graham Johnson observes, that soirée "marked the deepening of a remarkable relationship between the Princesse and himself – something that might almost be termed an artistic partnership, a friendship that survived vicissitudes and deserves the epithet 'lifelong.'"[43] That summer, Winnaretta participated, with Meg Baugnies, in the "secret lottery" that brought Fauré and Messager to Bayreuth; together, she and Fauré attended a performance of *Die Meistersinger* that left both awestruck.[44]

After her separation from her husband, Winnaretta remodeled the two adjoining houses on her property. The reconstruction included construction of an *atelier* designed for painting and music-making, equipped with two Steinway grands and a custom-built Cavaillé-Coll organ. Winnaretta intended the new space to become the heart of the house, a center for the most up-to-date manifestations of art and music, brilliant enough to attract the cultured elite of Paris society. As a tribute to the deepening of her friendship with Fauré, she commissioned him to write a short musical work with a mutually agreed-upon libretto or poetic text; for this, he would be paid the princely sum of 25,000 francs (as a basis of comparison, he was earning an annual salary of 3,000 francs as choirmaster at the Madeleine). Fauré enthusiastically accepted the offer. Winnaretta thought to engage Verlaine as the librettist for a treatment of a *commedia dell'arte* theme. Verlaine agreed to compose a poem for the project, but disappeared shortly thereafter: he was in the hospital, in a state of severe physical depletion. Alcoholic and syphilitic, his life had become, in Fauré's words, "an endless to-and-fro between the pub and the poorhouse."[45] It became increasingly apparent that, even with financial enticements, Verlaine would never be able to concentrate on his work. Talk of making "The Life of Buddha" the subject of the project was bantered about. Poets Maurice Bouchor and Albert Samain were considered to pick up where Verlaine had left off. Samain was ultimately engaged, but his poetic efforts had no appeal for the composer. And without an inspiring text with which to work, Fauré's

---

[42] Polignac, "Memoirs," 122.   [43] Johnson, *The Songs and Their Poets*, 202.
[44] Polignac, "Memoirs," 121.
[45] Letter to the Princesse de Scey-Montbéliard of January 18, 1891, in Fauré, *Correspondance*, 174.

doubts about his ability to complete the project increased. And so he dithered.[46]

To further complicate matters, Fauré's feelings for Winnaretta had clearly deepened beyond those of friendship and respectful deference: he was falling in love with her, and his letters to her (and to others, including Meg Baugnies)[47] reveal an unmistakable undercurrent of romantic ardor. In March 1891, Winnaretta obtained a civil divorce; in April she left Paris to spend several months in Venice, where she rented the Casa Wolkoff. She invited Fauré, as well as two painter friends Ernest Duez and Roger Jourdain (Meg Baugnies' half-brother) and their wives to stay with her. Fauré arrived on May 18, and the five weeks that he spent there were among the happiest of his life, giving him the repose that he so desperately needed. The lively days and sultry nights inspired him to compose a series of *mélodies* on poems by Verlaine. Although Winnaretta had prepared a room for him with a piano, Fauré preferred to compose at the Café Florian on the Piazza San Marco. There, amidst the hubbub of the popular café, he wrote one of his greatest songs, "Mandoline"; this was soon followed by a second, "En sourdine." The two *mélodies* received their first performance in a little fishing boat rented by Winnaretta, whose deck she had equipped with a "little portable yacht piano." And thus, one night, drifting slowly down the lagoons, Amélie Duez sang Fauré's new songs to his enraptured friends. Three more songs, "Green," "À Clymène," and "C'est l'extase," were completed after Fauré's return to Paris; collectively, the five songs came to be known as the *Cinq mélodies "de Venise,"* and, as dedicatee, Winnaretta's name became forever associated with one of Fauré's most beloved song cycles.[48] In November 1891, "Mandoline" was published in the *Figaro musical*, bearing a dedication to "Madame la Princesse de Scey-Montbéliard."[49]

In February 1892, Winnaretta's marriage was officially annulled by the Vatican. Around that time, Prince Edmond de Polignac – the eccentric aristocratic composer-friend of Fauré, Robert de Montesquiou, and the Comtesse Greffulhe – was in dire straits. He had squandered his meager fortune trying, in vain, to advance his career as a composer over many

---

[46] Letter to the Princesse de Scey-Montbéliard, undated [August 22, 1891], ibid., 200. The full story of the Fauré-Verlaine debacle was recounted for the first time in an article by Georges Jean-Aubry, "Gabriel Fauré, Paul Verlaine et Albert Samain, ou Les tribulations de 'Bouddha'," in *Le centenaire de Gabriel Fauré*, special issue of *La revue musicale* (1945).

[47] Fauré to Marguerite Baugnies, "Vendredi" [June 5, 1891], Fauré, *Correspondance*, 183–185.

[48] Polignac, "Memoirs," 120.

[49] Gabriel Fauré, "Mandoline," *Figaro musical* 1, No. 2, November 1891, 8–11.

long, frustrating years. Of frail constitution, homosexual, and considered by his family to be a crackpot, his future looked hopeless. Montesquiou (who was likely Polignac's lover) urged his friend to make a marriage of convenience with Winnaretta, who, because of her divorce, had lost social standing. Montesquiou pointed out to Prince Edmond that Winnaretta was wealthy, that she was as passionate about music as the Prince – and that she was not sexually interested in men. Élisabeth Greffulhe was enlisted as a female intermediary who could make a parallel case to Winnaretta: Edmond de Polignac would enable the divorced Winnaretta to become a princess once more without being subjected to any sexual demands (in addition to being homosexual, Polignac was also thirty years her senior); moreover, their mutual love of art and music would give them enough common ground for a reasonably happy shared life.[50] With trepidation, both of the interested parties agreed to the plan. To the amazement of all, Winnaretta and Edmond formed an unanticipated bond of deep friendship and affection – they discovered that they were "soulmates." They married in December 1893, and for seven years – until the Prince de Polignac's death in 1901 – they created a loving home: their deep bond was consecrated through music (see Figure 1.1). The most powerful symbol of their union was the music salon they created together; the nonstop music-making that took place in their house was the daily expression of their vows. Within weeks of their marriage, the Polignacs began to host musical gatherings in the *atelier*. The first of these were "organ evenings," during which Paris's great organists (Alexandre Guilmant, Charles Widor, Louis Vierne, and Eugène Gigout, among others) came to perform on Winnaretta's Cavaillé-Coll organ. In the months that followed, vocalists and instrumentalists came to offer songs and chamber music. Contemporary French music was performed as frequently as the standard classical and Romantic repertoire. Early music was also given a prominent place in the Polignac salon: the *atelier* was equipped with a harpsichord that Edmond had inherited from his parents, and Paris's foremost early-music performers were engaged to perform rarely heard treasures of the Renaissance and Baroque eras.[51]

As both family friend and de facto "house musician," Fauré was often on hand to play his own works; his compositions figure in dozens of concert programs given in the Polignac salon in the years 1894–1901 alone. These programs were often recorded in meticulous detail by the society press,

---

[50] See my *Music's Modern Muse*, 72.   [51] See ibid., 79–98.

Figure 1.1 Gabriel Fauré, Prince Edmond de Polignac, and Princesse Edmond de Polignac in front of the Hôtel Polignac, Fontainebleau, *c.* 1895.
Private collection

which added more luster to both the Polignac salon and to Fauré's reputation as a composer.[52] An enthusiastic admirer of Edmond de Polignac's compositions, Fauré was always willing to collaborate in performances of the prince's music. A typical program, given on June 16, 1895, included several works by Polignac, the Schumann Piano Quartet, Fauré's *Élégie* for cello and piano, and a group of his songs, including "Mandoline."[53] Present at this particular *soirée* was a young, unknown writer who had been introduced to the Polignacs in the first months of

[52] Ibid., 372–377. The listing of concert programs performed in the Polignac salon is incomplete, but printed programs and newspaper notices of musical matinées and soirées in the Polignacs' home attest to Fauré's constant presence.

[53] *Le Figaro*, February 8, 1895.

their marriage by Robert de Montesquiou (who would subsequently break off relations with the couple because of their lack of "gratitude" for having engineered the marriage). The Polignac salon provided Marcel Proust with an encyclopedic musical education, introducing him to a diverse range of works spanning three centuries. The future writer of *À la recherche du temps perdu* became an ardent admirer of Fauré's music. In September 1903, under the pen name Horatio, Proust wrote a retrospective article for *Le Figaro*, "The Salon of the Princesse Edmond de Polignac: Music of Today, Echoes of Yesteryear"; in it, Proust praised the "supreme elegance" of the Polignac salon, and listed among the musical performances that he remembered most fondly Fauré's Violin Sonata in A Major, Op. 13.[54] Many Proust scholars believe that the Op. 13 sonata may have perhaps provided a model for the "little phrase" that infiltrates the consciousness of Swann in *Swann's Way*.[55]

As he did with Meg de Saint-Marceaux, Fauré introduced a number of his talented composition students into the Polignac salon. It was thus that Maurice Ravel was introduced to the Polignacs in 1899. Knowing what association with the name of the Princesse de Polignac could do for the reputation of an unknown composer, Ravel undertook an unheard-of feat of musical social-climbing: he dedicated his newly-written piano solo, the *Pavane pour une infante défunte*, to the Princesse – without asking her permission. This presumptive action breached every rule of etiquette. But before Winnaretta could dress down the impertinent Ravel, she was confronted with the work's immediate popularity. Ultimately, she could only conclude, "I was much surprised and deeply touched that he should have attached my name to these lovely pages."[56]

Fauré's perpetual presence in the Polignac salon was at once a testament to Winnaretta's affection for her old friend and her veneration of his music – but also an indication of the proprietary hold that she exercised over "her composer." As for Fauré, he apparently came to terms with his unrequited love – and was surely delighted by the mutual happiness of his two dear friends. At the same time, he was conscious of the fact that he had failed to produce the commissioned vocal work. Winnaretta certainly had not forgotten. In June 1894, she wrote Fauré an imperious letter,

[54] Horatio [Marcel Proust], "Le Salon de la Princesse Edmond de Polignac: Musique d'aujourd'hui; échos d'autrefois," *Le Figaro*, September 6, 1903.
[55] See, for example, the discussion of Fauré and Swann's "little phrase" in Jean-Jacques Nattiez's landmark work *Proust as Musician*, trans. Derrick Puffett (Cambridge: Cambridge University Press, 1989).
[56] Polignac, "Memoirs," 127.

reminding him that it had been four years since he had agreed to write a
work that would "belong entirely to [her]." She wanted to know his
intentions. "It is a great source of melancholy … to know that what
I had believed to be a source of repose, a rare occasion to work freely,
has only become a source of misunderstandings and, for me, some
particularly painful discussions."[57] Fauré was shocked, and responded,
"I am a simple human being, and I don't pretend to be worth either more
or less than any other human; however, I'm fairly certain that I am
superior to what you seem to think!"[58] He promised to fulfill the commission with the next large work that he composed. And, in fact, he kept his
promise, albeit many years later. In 1898, Fauré was engaged by the Belgian
symbolist playwright Maurice Maeterlinck to write the incidental music
for the first London production of his 1882 symbolist play *Pelléas et
Mélisande*, starring the renowned actress Mrs. Patrick Campbell in the
role of the doomed heroine. When the Polignacs arrived in London for
the first performance, on June 21, 1898, Winnaretta was informed by the
composer that he had decided to dedicate the incidental music to her.

When Prince Edmond died in 1901, Fauré conducted the choir and
played the organ at the funeral of his beloved friend. He was astounded to
learn that the prince had bequeathed him 10,000 francs in his will.[59] For
the rest of his life, the composer maintained his affection for his friend and
patron the Princesse. In early 1924 (the year of his death), he wrote her a
brief note: "I see you too rarely and I think so often of the marvelous hours
spent in Paris and Venice, which I owe to *you* – *you*, the unique Winnie in
all the world!"[60] As for Winnaretta, throughout all the years that she held
salon concerts, until 1939, she continually included Fauré's music in her
salon programs, often devoting complete concerts to his work. At the same
time, until the end of her days, she continued to bear a grudge against the
composer for the failure of the Verlaine project. In her memoirs she wrote,

I'm sure that his libretto would have been wonderful, but I am sorry to say that
Fauré refused to write the music … He had a keen sense of humour and was
intensely alive to the absurdity of the pretentious; but although he was sensitive
and sentimental, he was easily carried away by new affections, and was not always

[57] Princesse Edmond de Polignac to Fauré, June 1894, in Fauré, *Correspondance*, 221–222.
[58] Fauré to the Princesse Edmond de Polignac, [June 1894], ibid., 222.
[59] See Fauré's two undated letters [August 12 and September 4, 1901] to the Princesse Edmond de
   Polignac, ibid., 287–288 and 289–290, respectively.
[60] Fauré to the Princesse Edmond de Polignac, January 12, 1924, ibid., 562–563.

a faithful and perfect friend, being too much interested in new ties to trouble much about his old ones.[61]

Fauré's London Patrons

Fauré's music was introduced to British audiences by Camille Saint-Saëns, who performed frequently in Great Britain and routinely programmed Fauré's piano music on his recitals. In 1894, Fauré himself was in London, where he made the acquaintance of Frederick Maddison, a lawyer associated with the British music-publishing house of Metzler and Co., and his composer wife, Adela Maddison.[62] Mr. Maddison secured a contract for Fauré with Metzler. Between 1896 and 1899, the firm published almost two dozen of Fauré's songs and instrumental works, sometimes before they had even appeared in print in Paris. By the time Fauré was engaged by Maeterlinck to write the incidental music for *Pelléas et Mélisande*, his name was well known to British audiences. Graham Johnson calls 1898 Fauré's "British year," for the composer made three trips to Great Britain for concerts within an eight-month period.[63]

Often, Fauré would be hosted in London by Leo Frank Schuster (1852–1927). The son of German bankers, Schuster used his wealth to become an influential patron of art and music. He maintained music salons in his London townhouse at 22 Old Queen Street (Westminster) and in his opulent country mansion at Bray-on-Thames, jokingly nicknamed "The Hut." In these two abodes, he welcomed figures such as John Singer Sargent (who in 1889 had painted a now-famous portrait of the composer), Walter Sickert, and Edward Elgar. Schuster introduced Fauré to London society with an "all-Fauré" program.[64] In 1896 Fauré again traveled to London (in the company of the Princesse de Polignac) to give a concert of his vocal and orchestral works in Schuster's new music room. Among the works performed on that occasion were the four-part song "Madrigal" and the *Pavane*, enthusiastically received by a group of music connoisseurs that included Sargent, Henry James, Lady Randolph Churchill, and her sister

---

[61] Polignac, "Memoirs," 121.

[62] Adela Maddison, a gifted composer, would go on to become one of Fauré's mistresses. The liaison lasted for several years, and Fauré dedicated his Seventh Nocturne to the beautiful Adela. Not surprisingly, Frederick Maddison's relations with the composer soured, and, after 1901, Metzler declined to renew his contract.

[63] Johnson, *The Songs and Their Poets*, 269–270.

[64] "Le Monde et la ville," *Le Figaro*, November 29, 1895.

Lady Leslie.[65] Fauré spent part of the summers of 1906 and 1907 at "The Hut," where the guests also included Sir Adrian Boult. It is likely that it was Schuster who helped Fauré make his way into court circles as well. In March 1908, Fauré spent ten days in London, where he played for the Prince and Princess of Wales and subsequently performed at Buckingham Palace for Queen Alexandra and the Mother Empress of Russia.[66] Fauré thoroughly enjoyed the luxurious treatment that he received as Schuster's guest; according to Nectoux, Schuster was so devoted to Fauré that, in letters to his wife, the composer referred to his host as "my nanny."[67] He wistfully wrote to his mistress Marguerite Hasselmans that the gestures of the valet were "like velvet," adding that "Life like that would be, materially, really very sweet; 'comfort' is truly an English invention."[68]

A Life in Society

In 1896, when Fauré was engaged as professor of composition at the Conservatoire, few knew who he was. *Le Figaro* wrote: "Monsieur Fauré … is not a music-drama composer; he is an organist by profession … Almost entirely unknown by the general public, Monsieur Fauré has the esteem – the very high artistic esteem – of all his confreres and an elite group of dilettantes, who have made of him a cult."[69] On the few occasions when the newspapers mentioned his name, it was in connection with his work as choirmaster or organist at the Madeleine. But, beginning in the late 1880s, Fauré's activities in the salons began to be chronicled in the society columns of the daily newspapers *Le Figaro* and *Le Gaulois*, which reported on the activities in the fashionable music salons. It was, in fact, the aforementioned "dilettantes," the musical hosts and hostesses who appreciated Fauré's music, who kept his name before the public. The composer's participation in a performance of contemporary music at the home of the Princesse de Scey-Montbéliard (the future Princesse de Polignac) was noted by *Le Figaro* in May 1888.[70] *Le Gaulois'* first mention of Fauré's salon activity occurred on February 9, 1891 in connection with a performance of his *mélodies* by renowned operatic

---

[65] See Polignac, "Memoirs," 119.   [66] See Nectoux, *Les voix du clair-obscur*, 288–289.
[67] Ibid., 288.
[68] Fauré to Marguerite Hasselmans, [March 15, 1908], in *Correspondance*, 642–643.
[69] Jules Huret, "Les nouveaux professeurs du Conservatoire," *Le Figaro*, October 16, 1896.
[70] "À travers Paris: Dans le monde," *Le Figaro*, May 16, 1888.

soprano Gabrielle Krauss.[71] Progressively, reports of performances of Fauré's music in the salons began to appear more frequently than reports of his musical activities at the Madeleine. From 1893 onward, notices of "all-Fauré" programs in private venues appeared with increasing regularity; in addition to the aforementioned occasions hosted by the Comtesse Greffulhe and Leo Schuster, the papers took note of salon recitals comprised exclusively of Fauré's work in the salons of the Princesse Alexandre Bibesco, Marguerite de Saint-Marceaux, and the Princesse de Polignac.[72] While a definitive link between these articles and the ascent in Fauré's reputation cannot be established, there is no question that the constant stream of positive publicity emanating from the society press surely helped.

Gabriel Fauré frequented the salons well into his later years, until deafness and the frailties of old age made it impossible for him to circulate in society. Throughout his life he remained ambivalent about salon culture. He complained to Madame Marcel Girette in February 1897 that he was being "flattened" by the "shallow vanity" of the *salonnières* vying for his presence in their music rooms. "My music has been performed TOO MUCH this winter, and my presence is required too often, no doubt to insure that I can't ignore such flattering efforts."[73] But Fauré knew well that the salon was necessary for his career – and there is no denying that the contacts that he made in the private music rooms of the *gratin* helped disseminate his music and promote his advancement in public concert life.

Interviewed by the newspaper *Excelsior* two years before his death, Fauré was asked about his success in the salons. He answered simply: "I was preoccupied with making a living. I had good friends, and when you are unknown by the wider music public, you are happy to be understood by some of those friends."[74]

[71] "Ce qui se passe: Échos de Paris," *Le Gaulois*, February 9, 1891.

[72] See, for example, mentions of "tout-Fauré" programs in the salons of Gaston Berardi in "Mondanités," *Le Gaulois*, February 20, 1894; the Princesse Alexandre Bibesco in *Le Figaro*, April 13, 1896, and *Le Gaulois*, March 9, 1899; the Princesse Edmond de Polignac in "Le Monde et la ville," *Le Figaro*, March 10, 1900 and April 6, 1908; Angèle Duglé in "Le Monde et la ville," *Le Figaro*, May 8, 1896; Marguerite de Saint-Marceaux in *Le Gaulois*, May 9, 1899.

[73] Fauré to Mme. Marcel Girette, February 1897, quoted in Nectoux, *Les voix du clair-obscur*, 230.

[74] Fauré, quoted in Roger Valbelle, "Une gloire de la France: Entretien avec M. Gabriel Fauré," *Excelsior*, June 12, 1922.

Criticism, History, Aesthetics

HERVÉ LACOMBE

Contrary to received wisdom, music has always been connected with language, however tenuously, on at least two levels. First, despite theoretically standing apart from our two principal systems of representation, words and images, music has persistently been linked throughout our history and culture with something beyond itself. Each age has constructed a system of relationships, metaphors, or analogies through which musical scores are conceived and heard – simple examples include a musical "phrase," "high" and "low" pitches, "soft" and "powerful" tones.[1] Second, music has constantly been connected with verbal discourse, whose importance increased throughout the nineteenth century (if only through the proliferation of the press and the growth of writing about music): musical works are not understood and appreciated as unmediated objects, but are filtered through discourses that precede, accompany, and succeed them. Aesthetic theories, critical reception, and historical studies, together with informal conversation, enter into the life of a musical work. It is this second level that will concern us.

Over the course of time, the sedimentation of critical discourse generates a lexicon and ideas that seem to encircle an author and his œuvre. Fauré did not escape this process, even though, paradoxically, the reception and study of his music grew up around the conviction that it was almost impossible to talk about it. Viewed in its time as atypical and offering little purchase to critical commentary, Fauré music's eventually nourished one of the most significant philosophical meditations on music of the twentieth century, that of Vladimir Jankélévitch, which provides the horizon for this essay. Drawing upon the composer's own writings, the critical reception of his works, and Jankélévitch's reflections on both of these, we shall seek to reconstruct a Fauréan conception of music in relation to the idea of the ineffable.

---

[1] See Christian Accaoui, "Les diverses voies de la métaphore et de l'analogie en musique," in *Métaphore et musique*, ed. Inès Taillandier-Guittard (Rennes: Presses universitaires de Rennes, 2015), 13–40.

Jankélévitch and the Music of Fauré

Before Jean-Michel Nectoux's publications, Fauré criticism in France bore the strong imprint of Philippe Fauré-Fremiet in the area of biography, Françoise Gervais in analysis of Fauré's musical language, and Vladimir Jankélévitch in aesthetics.[2] Jankélévitch attracted little attention in anglophone musicology until 2003, when Carolyn Abbate published her translation of *La musique et l'ineffable* (*Music and the Ineffable*). While this work certainly marks a culmination of Jankélévitch's musical aesthetic, it should not overshadow the author's many other writings.[3] As a philosopher, Jankélévitch was known for his work on Bergson, irony, lying, evil, virtue, the moral life, death, and many other themes. An amateur pianist who delighted in reading scores at the keyboard, he published numerous writings on music, in addition to two posthumous works.[4] Fauré enjoys pride of place in this company. (See the Appendix for a full list of Jankélévitch's publications dedicated to the composer.) To the writings devoted to Fauré we may add relevant excerpts from Jankélévitch's other works, such as a book on the nocturne that refers often to Fauré, as well as the many allusions scattered throughout his philosophical works. In short, Fauré creeps in everywhere. Indeed, Jankélévitch began *La musique et l'ineffable* with a quotation from the composer. The philosopher's thought unfolds around the figure of Fauré, taking vocabulary and core issues from the early reception of the composer's works as a point of departure.

Reading Fauré's contemporaries, especially Émile Vuillermoz (1878–1960) and Louis Aguettant (1871–1931), it becomes clear that Jankélévitch took up and continued their critical tradition. Both authors are cited in passing in *Gabriel Fauré et ses mélodies*. But Jankélévitch would later forget to reveal these sources for some of his ideas. Aguettant proposed

---

[2] Françoise Gervais defended a doctoral thesis on June 30, 1954, belatedly published as *Étude comparée des langages harmoniques de Fauré et de Debussy* in *La revue musicale* 272 (special number, 1971).

[3] Carolyn Abbate's related article "Music – Drastic or Gnostic," *Critical Inquiry* 30, No. 3 (2004), 505–553, is more of a conceptual shock (she plucks a single binarism from the vast enterprise of musical inquiry tackled by Jankélévitch) than a true introduction to his thought. As Brian Kane perceptively writes, "such intense fixation on the 'drastic' and the 'gnostic' has perhaps winnowed our concern for breadth of Jankélévitch's thought – as if a writer of so many volumes of music and philosophy could be summarized in one dichotomy" (see "Vladimir Jankélévitch's Philosophy of Music. Introduction," *Journal of the American Musicological Society* 65, No. 1 [Spring 2012], 217). The Colloquy in this issue of the *Journal* provides a useful overview of Jankélévitch's twenty-first-century reception in the United States.

[4] *La musique et les heures*, ed. Françoise Schwab (Paris: Seuil, 1988); *L'Enchantement musical: Écrits, 1929–1983*, ed. Françoise Schwab and Jean-Marie Brohm (Paris: Albin Michel, 2017).

Fauré's music as the archetype of the inexpressible: "All music, of its essence, escapes verbal interpretation, and Fauré's undoubtedly more than others. This dreamer we call Music has a reticent and ungraspable charm: namely grace."[5] The Jankélévitchian vocabulary already appears here, and still more in Aguettant's remarkable article of 1924 entitled simply "On the Death of Gabriel Fauré." The following passage reads almost verbatim like Jankélévitch: "A virtue that none have disputed in Fauré is charm. A subtle vapor hovers over the threshold of his work, a *je ne sais quoi* composed of imponderable things."[6]

Why did the composer exercise such a fascination over the philosopher? His œuvre represented for Jankélévitch the summit of mystery and musicality. More than any other composer's work, it explores, reveals, and expresses what music is, or put differently, the essence of music: it offers the quintessence of music. But even this does not go far enough. Reading Jankélévitch's work in its entirety, we discover that an opposite and complementary viewpoint explains his fascination with Fauré: his music manifests, condenses, and expresses in artistic form a range of issues that haunted the philosopher. Jankélévitch found in the French composer's works, unconsciously at first, what he sought to grasp in the realm of concepts. Furthermore, the philosopher, who was twenty-one years old when Fauré died, was a man whose thought and imagination were permeated by fin-de-siècle culture. In sketching the genealogy of his lexicon, we must measure the degree to which he followed Henri Bergson's conceptual pathways,[7] along with ideas stemming from Romantic reflections on pure or absolute music, and determine to what extent he synthesized through his own intellectual powers ideas contemporary with Fauré, or even written by the composer. Jankélévitch's musical writings are inscribed within, first, a personal and collective history (Louis-Albert Revah has shown, for example, how his privileged canon of musical works is tied to the Second World War and Holocaust);[8] second, the hands-on perspective of a

---

[5] Louis Aguettant, "Les mélodies de Gabriel Fauré" (1903), reprinted in *Les amitiés littéraires: Paul Valéry, Paul Claudel, Gabriel Fauré, Émile Mâle, Louis Mercier, Marcel Ormoy, Robert Browning* (Paris, Turin, and Budapest: Harmattan, 2001), 79. On the question of the unsayable in music, see Timothée Picard, "Musique et indicible dans l'imaginaire européen: Proposition de synthèse," www.vox-poetica.com/sflgc/biblio/picard.html.
[6] Louis Aguettant, "Sur la mort de Gabriel Fauré," *Gazette artistique des Grands Concerts de Lyon* (November 15, 1924), reprinted in Aguettant, *Les amitiés littéraires*, 87.
[7] See Judy Lochhead, "Can We Say What We Hear? Jankélévitch and the Bergsonian Ineffable," in "Colloquy: Vladimir Jankélévitch's Philosophy of Music," 231–235 (see note 3).
[8] Louis-Albert Revah, "Sur la partialité en musique," *Critique* 500–501 (January–February 1989), 57–70.

performer; third, a more general philosophical approach; fourth, the body of musical criticism and writing that came before him; and fifth, the wider constellation of historiographical assumptions that subtend the writing of music history.

The Challenge of an Elusive Œuvre: Fauré in History

From his earliest scores, Fauré posed a challenge to critics who hoped to define his singular art and its effect on listeners. The posthumous debate over his place in the history of music, together with the problem posed by the genres that he favored, which elude normal habits of classification, invites a broader investigation into the grounds by which we evaluate a musical work. "Fauréan art occupies a unique position in the history of music," proclaimed Vuillermoz, a student of the composer and friend of Debussy.[9] Georges Jean-Aubry noted how "in each of his works, everything hangs together through a mysterious coherence."[10] As Ravel insisted, "Fauré's mysterious processes seduce us most and fatigue us least because they are less evident, less noticeable in themselves. Their discretion assures their efficacy."[11] To these questions of value (Fauré's historical position), content (the nature of his music), and language (its mysterious coherence), we must add a fourth concerning the critical commentary on the man and his works. In 1905, Louis Schneider, a critic for *Gil Blas*, remarked that "it is difficult to find concerning M. Gabriel Fauré and, above all, his work anything more than hopelessly brief journalistic notices."[12] Echoing these words, Vuillermoz expressed astonishment in 1913 that Fauré should be the "only great contemporary musician about whom not a single book has been written."[13] Does this mean that his music eludes verbal commentary more than any other, or rather that it suffers an injustice that must be rectified? Fauré offers a particularly valuable subject for this fourfold

---

[9] Émile Vuillermoz, *Musiques d'aujourd'hui* (Paris: Crès, 1923), 2.

[10] Georges Jean-Aubry, *La musique française d'aujourd'hui* (Paris: Perrin, 1916), 79.

[11] Maurice Ravel, "Les mélodies de Gabriel Fauré," *La revue musicale* 3 (October 1922), reprinted in Ravel, *Lettres, écrits, entretiens*, ed. Arbie Orenstein, trans. Dennis Collins (Paris: Flammarion, 1989), 325.

[12] Louis Schneider, "Gabriel Fauré directeur du Conservatoire," *Gil Blas*, June 14, 1905.

[13] Lecture by Émile Vuillermoz read by M. Signoret on April 15, 1913 at the Comédie des Champs-Elysées, typescript, F-Pn: Vma. 5429. A year later, Louis Vuillemin published the first biography of the musician, *Gabriel Fauré et son œuvre* (Paris: A. Durand et Fils, 1914).

inquiry and, therefore, a case study for general historiographical reflection: how do we write music history, and on what ideological basis?

One of the major components in the debate over Fauré's place in music history concerns the relation between value, reputation, musical genres, and institutions. In 1916, Georges Jean-Aubry reported on various contemporary trends – new timbral resources, orchestral innovations, music in the service of the picturesque. He then claimed that Fauré, immune to these tendencies, "remained, above all, enamored of the riches of the piano and the voice, of the inexhaustible inflections of the melodic line."[14] Jean-Aubry thus underscored Fauré's mastery of French song. Yet can the finest *mélodie* rival a symphony? Can a composer who cultivated his talents in less esteemed genres, outside the official venues of the Opéra and major symphonies concert series, receive his due recognition? Charles Kœchlin based a lecture on this question, arguing that "the value of works does not depend in the least on their performing forces or length . . . A single *mélodie* by Fauré is sometimes a masterpiece. His artistry is testimony that he has attained a summit, a *summa* of 'musical civilization.'"[15] Fauré's appointment as director of the Paris Conservatoire, followed by the premiere of *Pénélope* in 1913, brought the composer a belated recognition. Shortly after the revelation of Fauré's opera, Gaston Carraud observed that the composer was still viewed too much as a salon composer, a creator of chamber works, piano pieces, and songs: "People couldn't see anything beyond the highly personal elegance . . . of compositions that were judged small-scale."[16] Jean-Aubry found another explanation in the manner in which music history treats independent personalities. Histories are written, in essence, to describe the tendencies of a period. Yet, as he pointed out, Fauré positioned himself outside these tendencies.[17] The composer was as loath to transgress as to accept blithely the common tongue of his historical heritage. Neither modern nor traditional, but individual, he occupied a place in between.[18] An aspect of the ineffable plays out in the space between what is (tonality) and what is not (normative tonal syntax). As a simple example, we might

---

[14] Jean-Aubry, *La musique française d'aujourd'hui*, 72.

[15] Lecture given for the Concert historique Pasdeloup at the Opéra on March 17, 1921, published as "Gabriel Fauré," *Le Ménestrel* (June 3, 1921), 234.

[16] Gaston Carraud, "Gabriel Fauré," *La Liberté*, May 3, 1913. Carraud explains that the Requiem and *Prométhée* were not often performed.

[17] Jean-Aubry, *La musique française d'aujourd'hui*, 72–80.

[18] Herein lies the "nearly nothing" (*presque rien*, a phrase of Jankélévitch's) that makes all the difference in his music and affects tonality in its overall structure (harmonic progressions), not in its nature (Fauré preserves standard chords, cadential articulations, and the distinction between dissonance and consonance).

consider the first four bars of the Ninth Nocturne, which preserve the main tonality of B minor despite the unfamiliar harmonic progressions and modal "contamination" of the tonal structure. In this way, a *contournement du langage* is achieved, using *contournement* in the double sense of "twisted" (complicated) and "bypassed" (avoided), both having the same goal (the tonic). "At the moment, people prefer Debussy to this powerful, gentle master," wrote Henri Collet (inventor of "Les Six") in 1920. "It is true," he continued, "that the dazzling Debussian revolution was more likely to conquer fashion than the inveterate classicism of Fauré. But the reasons given abroad to justify this preference are so ridiculous that I must rebut them."[19]

Although Debussy's art demands a more delicate analytical approach than Fauré's, it has attracted many more studies. At least one reason for this disparity lies in the place accorded to the two composers in the history of musical modernity. As Carl Dahlhaus has noted, the avant-garde ideal has long dominated the historiographic narrative of twentieth-century music.[20] Fauré's development, however, has more to do with originality (as Carlo Caballero has shown)[21] and continual artistic evolution (corresponding to the nineteenth-century ideal of progress in the sciences and general knowledge) than with the avant-garde.[22] Jankélévitch, with his hostility to the Second Viennese School,[23] abetted Fauré's marginalization, especially since his intellectual orientation directly opposed the structuralist paradigm that came to have a lasting effect on the social sciences in the twentieth century. Jankélévitch overtly criticized structuralism in his review of a 1964 performance of Fauré's Second Piano Quartet: "It seems incredible, in our age of 'structures,' that music could speak so intimately to each heart."[24] His aesthetic directly absorbed the Romantic ideal of an inexpressible essence lying at the core of artistic creation that eludes the grasp of language and reason. Music history is always ideological, insofar as it proceeds from covert or explicit premises, aesthetic categories, hierarchical ranking of composers, and periodizations that are all intellectual constructs imposed onto reality. What does it mean to be classic in

[19] Henri Collet, "La musique chez soi: Le cas Gabriel Fauré," *Comœdia*, December 31, 1920.
[20] See the opening pages of Carl Dahlhaus, *Die Musik des 19. Jahrhunderts* (Wiesbaden: Laaber, 1980, 1988).
[21] Carlo Caballero, *Fauré and French Musical Aesthetics* (Cambridge and New York: Cambridge University Press, 2001).
[22] Like many others, Fauré gradually found himself on the margins of prominent models, whether those initiated by Debussy and his followers, those connected to various Stravinskian styles, or those begun by the Second Viennese School.
[23] See Jankélévitch, *La musique et l'ineffable*, 54–55.
[24] Jankélévitch, *L'Enchantement musical*, 106.

music, asked Kœchlin in a 1921 lecture devoted to Fauré (Henri Collet, as we saw, referred to Fauré's "classicism"). Kœchlin's answer differs utterly from notions of musical classicism derived from Charles Rosen or Leonard Ratner:

It must be clearly understood that Fauré is a pure classic. Regrettably, discussions of musical art tend to reserve that honor for German composers of the eighteenth and nineteenth centuries. They are classics in their compositional methods, their harmonies, their recitatives, their symphonic layouts. There would be much to say about this in a composition textbook. Put simply, it would seem neither reckless nor blasphemous to argue that true classical qualities (notably those of the Greeks) may sometimes be found in other composers. Fauré possesses them.[25]

Kœchlin returned later in the lecture to Fauré's historical position, but now within his native French tradition: "this master strikes us as the most purely musical of artists – profound, sensitive, harmonious, classical, in a word, the greatest of our nation, and the most beloved."[26] Fauré is now *the* great French composer of the early twentieth century.

The dominant canon is Germanic, as Kœchlin reminds us. When Jankélévitch wrote of music, he intended not only to overturn values and concepts but also to stake out a historiographical and moral position. He effected this reversal, first of all, by establishing an alternative "counter-canon" with its own alternative issues.[27] Jankélévitch mostly wrote about French, Spanish, and Russian musicians – Déodat de Séverac; Liszt and Chopin; Rimsky-Korsakov and Musorgsky; Albéniz and Mompou; Satie, Ravel, Debussy, and especially Fauré. As the philosopher Bernard Sève has

---

[25] Kœchlin, "Gabriel Fauré [1]," *Le Ménestrel* (May 27, 1921), 222 (lecture given on March 17, 1921 at the Concerts Pasdeloup). Kœchlin goes on to describe these qualities: "It is the perfect equilibrium between charm and power, between refinement of material and a form that contributes to the truest simplicity, to the purest and most serene splendor, to that impression of the definitive, that the masterpieces of ancient sculpture provide. It is also the concision, the judicious choice of means, the mastery of style and that light undimmed by any dark shadow, the absence of emphasis, and finally, the plentitude and density of phrases that say more than they seem to say, containing beauties that we discover gradually and with ever greater wonder."

[26] Kœchlin, "Gabriel Fauré [2]," *Le Ménestrel* (May 27, 1921), 233 (continuation of the lecture identified in the previous note). Kœchlin, like other French commentators from the early twentieth century, saw in Fauré, and especially *Pénélope* and *Prométhée*, the fulfillment of a classical art, truly Hellenic. For current musicologists, by and large, the composers who ultimately came to be designated as "classics" remain Haydn, Mozart, and Beethoven, whose repertory became canonical in concert programming.

[27] The Germans and the Viennese; questions of form, of the development and evolution of musical language – he has no use for all these. Jankélévitch, who had a particular love of Schumann, would reject him after the Second World War; see Françoise Schwab, Preface to Jankélévitch, *L'Enchantement musical*, 16.

noted, a recurring cluster of family traits emerges across his writing, which fashion the ideal type of the Jankélévitchian composer as a master of reticence, understatement, allusion, and modesty.[28] Already in his first publication on Fauré, Jankélévitch declared war on the German school. By his lights, Beethoven's art was "impure, weighed down with humanity, sociology, and metaphysics, on the same level as everyday life." In opposition to Beethoven, Jankélévitch proposes ... Fauré.[29] An unexpected historical revision!

When Fauré came onto the scene of Parisian musical life during the 1870s, the battle lines were quite different, as were the historiographical stakes. The 1877 premiere of Fauré's First Violin Sonata, Op. 13 at the Société nationale de musique took place just as French music was undergoing a renewal after the military defeat of 1870. Saint-Saëns used this premiere as a pretext to stress the following point: contrary to popular opinion, the most important musical events do not necessarily transpire in the theater. "Over the past few years," he wrote, "we have begun to grasp this truth in France; those who first understood it were accused of betraying the French spirit, dabbling in Germanism, and despising the theater."[30]

The Lexicon of Fauréan Criticism

One of the main challenges for the music historian is to identify a proper vocabulary, cogent ideas, and central issues. This combination (words, ideas, issues) allows us to place a particular work in its proper context and to situate the composer in his own time, so as to reconstruct the contemporary meaning of his works. Jann Pasler has taken this approach in *Composing the Citizen: Music as Public Utility in Third Republic France* (Berkeley: University of California Press, 2009), where she isolates and unpacks the hermeneutic potential of "public utility," a concept borrowed

---

[28] See Bernard Sève, "Nuance et construction: Remarques sur le corpus musical de Vladimir Jankélévitch," in *Présence de Vladimir Jankélévitch: Le charme et l'occasion*, ed. Françoise Schwab (Paris: Beauchesne, 2010), 88.

[29] Jankélévitch, *Gabriel Fauré et ses mélodies* (Paris: Plon, 1938), 249. "Fauré's art, on the contrary, is the walled garden (*le jardin clos*), the Other Nature, the magical space cloistered from worldly promiscuities, finally, the joyful island (*l'île joyeuse*) surrounded by high cliffs battered by the waves of life."

[30] Camille Saint-Saëns, "Une Sonate," *Le Journal de musique* (April 7, 1877), reprinted in Saint-Saëns, *Écrits sur la musique et les musiciens, 1870–1921*, ed. Marie-Gabrielle Soret (Paris: Vrin, 2012), 196–197.

from the political discourse of the Third Republic. Carlo Caballero took the same approach in *Fauré and French Musical Aesthetics* (Cambridge: Cambridge University Press, 2001), setting himself the task of identifying the central categories of French music reception between 1885 and 1925. His study focused on the issues of sincerity, originality, novelty, personal renewal, homogeneity, and religious faith. I shall focus on an alternative group of terms that accompanied the flowering of Fauré's works and their entrance into musical aesthetics. This group of terms is neither an exact repetition of the familiar vocabulary of French criticism nor are they newly minted ideas. They represent an intermediate situation: a more or less conventional vocabulary that has been adapted in an attempt to pinpoint the originality of music that stands on a threshold, neither breaking radically with the past nor simply continuing it. Fauré's contemporaries were conscious of the question of terminology, as Georges Servières' comment from 1898 reveals:

Despite his worldly success and the words that flow most often from the pens of those who study his works – languor, gentle grace, delicate harmonies, supple rhythms, etc. – one should not confuse this severe and conscientious composer with those fashionable musicians whose banal melodies and swooning cadences captivate shallow listeners. [Assuredly, Fauré] possesses charm in a high degree, and his gifts are rather those of grace and power.[31]

From this remarkable passage, let us observe for the moment that Servières could not avoid the familiar critical argot (languor, grace, delicacy, charm), because it indicates precisely the entry points to Fauré's work, and doubtless also because he was targeting the specific readership of the *Revue pour les jeunes filles*. But he endows those terms with a new intensity (as when he speaks of a "high degree"). It was normative in nineteenth-century journalism to comment on the charm of a melody, the grace of a musical phrase. One already finds a predilection in the Second Empire for whatever is charming, pleasing, sweet, cheerful, and so forth. During the Third Republic, as Jann Pasler has noted, diversity, eclecticism, and pleasure were prized.[32] This tendency, she explained, went hand in hand with a renewal of interest in feminine values and recent debates over the character of French music. An entire semantic field developed around the notion of grace as elegance and ease, and around the search for well-being through

[31] Georges Servières, "Compositeurs modernes. Gabriel Fauré," *Revue pour les jeunes filles* (April 5, 1898), 281–282.
[32] See Jann Pasler, *Composing the Citizen: Music as Public Utility in Third Republic France* (Berkeley: University of California Press, 2009), 358–400.

pleasurable sensations. Music described as "charming" was thus understood to be accessible and agreeable. At the height of the fin de siècle, with Wagnerism at its triumphant pinnacle, Massenet, Delibes, and Messager also carried on and helped to elaborate this French strain of grace and romance, of facility (for some) or strength (for others), of pleasure and sensuality.[33] It is not insignificant, then, that when Fauré listed some of his favorite musical compatriots in 1887 he included "certain light works by Delibes that have grace and charm."[34]

The return to the eighteenth century – an age idealized (and fantasized), where good taste radiated through the development of grace, elegance, and charm of an entirely French character – coincided with the historical revaluation of an aesthetic of pleasure. Debussy mocked this tendency in a letter of 1893 addressed to the devout Wagnerian Ernest Chausson: "I received a letter from Madame Sulzbach, perfumed like the toilette of a Turkish harem! She invites me to dine with Fauré, Bagès [an amateur tenor], and Monsieur Sulzbach. I did not judge it advantageous to accept this invitation, since God only knows what I should suffer there, perhaps a recital of eighteenth-century formulas newly refurbished by G. Fauré."[35] Many other critics have concluded, to the contrary, that for Fauré grace and charm are not marks of a superficial facility, or the effect of a naïvely pleasant character, but rather the expression of a truly musical nature; they are not the symptom of anodyne consumerism or a simpleminded score, but the goal and, as it were, the very substance of his art, imponderable and mysterious. *Le charme* and *la grâce* will be reworked and elevated thereafter into true aesthetic categories.

Charms or Charm?

In 1877, in a review cited above, Saint-Saëns introduced his student:

The appearance of Fauré's Sonata announces a new champion, perhaps the most formidable of all, for the work unites profound musical science with great melodic abundance and a sort of unconscious naïveté that is the most irresistible of all powers. This sonata contains all that can seduce a refined ear, formal novelty, the

---

[33] Massenet's heroines (Manon, Thaïs, Esclarmonde) exemplify this erotic vein.
[34] Letter to Hugues Imbert, August 1887, in Fauré, *Correspondance, suivie de Lettres à Madame H.*, ed. Jean-Michel Nectoux (Paris: Fayard, 2015), 128.
[35] Letter to Ernest Chausson of August 15, 1893, in Claude Debussy, *Correspondance: 1872–1918*, ed. François Lesure et Denis Herlin (Paris: Gallimard, 2005), 149.

search for fresh modulations and curious sonorities, surprising rhythms; above all, a pervasive charm envelops the entire work and makes the throng of average listeners accept as quite natural the most raging audacities. A stronger work has not appeared in France and Germany for many years, and none so charming.[36]

Fauré manages to reconcile opposites through the mysterious operations of charm at the levels of technique (science vs. melody), character of inspiration (power vs. naïveté), invention (audacities vs. naturalness), and reception (refined listeners vs. the throng). Appreciating Fauré's music thus demands that we accept this play of paradoxes and what would appear to be the reversal of values traditionally encoded as feminine (charm and naïveté) and masculine (power and audacity). Aguettant reminds us of this bond between femininity and language: "I shall leave to more learned professionals the task of studying Fauré's art of modulation and those harmonic procedures upon which so many flighty epithets and feminine metaphors have been squandered."[37] Aguettant, an advocate of Fauré's art, made use of this vocabulary, but without pejorative connotations. Writing in the same year, Debussy also cited the feminine quality of Fauré's music, but now to demean it. He penned a particularly malicious account of Fauré's Ballade, Op. 19, which had been performed at the Société nationale de musique:

We heard a Ballade for piano and orchestra by Fauré, the Master of Charms, a piece almost as pretty as Marguerite Hasselmans, who played the piano part while replacing a shoulder strap that tended to come off whenever there was a somewhat rapid scale. I do not know why I should feel an analogy between this sudden charming gesture and Fauré's music. Yet the graceful, fleeting play of lines that characterizes Fauré's music allows one to compare it to the gesture of a pretty woman, without fear of disparaging the one or the other.[38]

The accumulation of terms is striking – "charms" (plural), "charming," "charm" (singular), "pretty" (*jolie*, twice), "graceful." Debussy thus passes from music to feminine gesture and from the appearance of the pianist to the musical lines, to the point of dissolving the elements and turning them all into synonyms. We may schematize the parallels that Debussy draws between the feminine and musical realms:

[36] Saint-Saëns, "Une Sonate," 197.   [37] Aguettant, "Les mélodies de Gabriel Fauré," 77.
[38] Claude Debussy, *Monsieur Croche et autres écrits*, ed. François Lesure (Paris: Gallimard, 1987), 119.

Mme. Hasselmans (pretty)	Fauré's Ballade, Op. 19 (almost as pretty)
charming feminine gesture	pianistic gesture
the slipping shoulder strap	somewhat rapid scale
gesture of a pretty woman	gracefully fleeting musical lines
mistress of charms	Master of Charms

Describing Fauré as "the Master of Charms" is a way to relegate his music to the feminine space of the salon and demote it from the Beautiful to the Pretty, from serious art to entertainment. Larousse's nineteenth-century dictionary clearly distinguishes this usage: in the plural, we read, the word *charmes* denotes "allures, attractions, physical beauty, above all, in speaking of women."[39] For Debussy, Fauré occupies the same position as Madame Hasselmans (his mistress in real life), whom Debussy maliciously portrays as a veritable "mistress of charms."

Some critics accused Fauré of feminizing the genre of the Requiem Mass by rejecting the sublime terror traditionally associated with the funeral prose, the Dies irae. Similar reproaches abound in the critical literature. What stands out is the oscillation between, on the one hand, feminine and masculine, and, on the other hand, femininity as a specific quality and femininity as a weakness. Louis Aguettant returned to this question in his 1924 study. It would be erroneous, he explained, to confine Fauré to the "pretty" (the category Debussy used to snub Fauré), to see him as "a prisoner of his own charm." Aguettant then added, "This master of grace, sometimes imagined drowning irretrievably in '*l'odor di femmina*,' can be, when he wishes, a master of strength ... capable of the most manly vigor."[40]

In 1921 Kœchlin seemed to echo almost verbatim Debussy's moniker, calling Fauré "the musician of charm."[41] But in sliding from the plural (charms) to the singular (charm), he ennobled an aesthetic category that Debussy had dismissed as a worldly trait. Charm would become the indefinable movement by which music attracts, pleases, irresistibly fascinates, and produces a truly magical effect. Charm resembles that action described by Saint-Saëns as an "unconscious naïveté," that is, one lying beyond the domain of reason. Thus, at the meeting point of sundry schemas (critical, psychological, gendered) emerges one of Jankélévitch's central aesthetic categories – *le charme.*[42]

---

[39] Pierre Larousse, "Charme," *Grand dictionnaire universel du XIXe siècle*, Vol. 3 (Paris: Larousse, 1867–77), 1024.

[40] Aguettant, "Sur la mort de Gabriel Fauré," 90.   [41] Kœchlin, "Gabriel Fauré [1]," 222.

[42] See Marianne Massin, "Consentir au charme?" in *Présence de Vladimir Jankélévitch: Le charme et l'occasion*, ed. Françoise Schwab (Paris: Beauchesne, 2010), 35–55.

Hence, Jankélévitch both synthesized and extended his predecessors' language. In his culminating work, *Fauré et l'inexprimable* (1974), he seems to respond term by term to Debussy's critique, even as he forges a continuity with Louis Aguettant's writings. Those who show little affinity for Fauré's music, he wrote, "understand his charm as mechanical and manipulative and turn the Ballade in F♯ into an effeminate seduction; they cannot interpret this condition of power and softness, this amphiboly of *gentle force* that is the entire mystery of Fauréan charm."[43] Jankélévitch again cited the Ballade as an example of charm in his philosophical book, *Le Je-ne-sais-quoi et le Presque-rien.*[44]

To Formulate the Ineffable: Speaking Fauré through Oxymorons

Charm and the ineffable should be understood as the manifestation of an ambiguity, an "in-between," a passage between two terms (masculine–feminine), in short, as an oxymoron. Oxymoron is a figure of speech that yokes two apparently incompatible terms in a seeming contradiction, in order to evoke a new meaning through the very coexistence of the opposition. The *mélodie*, a genre in which Fauré excelled, can thus be regarded as an oxymoronic form that joins sound and sense, music and poetry, forging both into an amalgam that transcends their specific difference. All of Fauré's works showed him to be, in Alfred Cortot's words, "a great poet in sound."[45] The extraordinary union of Verlaine's verse with Fauré's music stems in part from these contrary qualities in the poetry of *Fêtes galantes* (1869), from which Fauré drew four songs. Verlaine's poetry mingles images, impressions, and emotions that are ceaselessly inverted, as in the opening poem, "Clair de lune." Sadness and fantasy, minor mode and happiness, triumphant love and incredulity, sobbing and ecstasy – simultaneously night and brightness, the moonlight fuses all oppositions. The famous poem unites calm and peacefulness: on the one hand, the fixity

---

[43] Jankélévitch, *Fauré et l'inexprimable* (Paris: Presses Pocket, 1988), 348–349. The gendered argument (feminine vs. masculine) that might seem limited to Fauré returns, in fact, in Jankélévitch's great aesthetic project *La musique et l'ineffable*, where he denounces the traditional equation of femininity with weakness (8–9).

[44] For example, see Jankélévitch, *Le Je-ne-sais-quoi et le Presque-rien, Vol. 1: La manière et l'occasion* (Paris: Seuil, 1980), 73–74.

[45] Letter to Fauré from February 1913, in *Correspondance*, 390.

of the painter's canvas, and on the other, a glimpse into the imagination and secret dream-world of the birds. This play of opposites, already noted by Saint-Saëns, also appears in Aguettant's writings on Fauré:[46]

grace	power
odor di femmina	masculine energy
elegant nonchalance	Racinian nobility
freshness	ardor
evasive harmony	stable harmony
natural	peculiar
refinement	simplicity
charm	strength
voluptuous detail	living unity

Aguettant pointed to a paradoxical alloy. "Fauré's music," as he put it an elegant turn of phrase, "is a site of reconciled oppositions."[47]

Many other contemporaries of Fauré detected the same ambiguities, the same foregrounding of paradoxes in his music: richness without weight (Pierre Lalo),[48] alliance of the old and modern (Julien Tiersot),[49] a fusion of the singing voice and the speaking voice, and of pleasure and intellect (André Beaunier).[50] Reviewing the Requiem, Camille Benoît ended with a summary of the paradoxical experience aroused by the music: "It is a precious science ... that teaches us to enjoy the intoxication of tears, to savor at length the voluptuousness of sorrow, to face without fear the fascination of our inevitable evanescence."[51] Émile Jaques-Dalcroze transposed the same nexus of oppositions into the domain of national musical identity when he described Fauré's contribution: "with an unequalled contrapuntal skill, fully aware of the old German masters, he was able to develop purely French ideas, endowing his works with an indeniably novel

[46] See Aguettant, "Les mélodies de Gabriel Fauré," and "Sur la mort de Gabriel Fauré," 90.

[47] Aguettant, "Sur la mort de Gabriel Fauré," 88, 93.

[48] Pierre Lalo, "La musique," *Le Temps*, July 13, 1906. The [First] Quintet is a "work without noise or weight, but rich in poetic and musical substance."

[49] J. T. [Julien Tiersot], "Revue des grands concerts," *Le Ménestrel* (May 6, 1906), 136. The Adagio of the First Quintet has a theme "of almost archaic tonality, in the manner of Bach, that an atmosphere of utterly modern harmonies somehow envelops."

[50] André Beaunier, "Histoire de la musique: Festival Gabriel Fauré," *Journal de l'Université des annales* (February 15, 1912), 285. In the songs, "two voices are joined in unison, the speaking voice and the singing voice, so as to reach more directly to the mind and heart"; "no one has put more thought into the pleasures of music" (289).

[51] Camille Benoît, "La messe de Requiem de Gabriel Fauré," *Le guide musical* 34, Nos. 32–33 (August 9 and 16, 1888), 197.

character."[52] Louis Vierne admired the subtlety, and the refinement underneath the simplicity;[53] Reynaldo Hahn an art that sounded at times
"voluptuously Gregorian"![54] Maurice Ravel cited a precise example of
the play of opposites between music and word in the song "Clair de
lune": "Have you noticed how the words 'sur le mode mineur' prompt
an arpeggio that paradoxically outlines a C-major chord, lending a sort of
melancholic allure to the moonlit landscape?"[55] Oxymoron broaches a
reality inaccessible to common sense; it expresses what seems inexpressible
or intractable to ordinary speech. Jankélévitch listed the methods of *le
charme* in Fauré's music: "feigned weakness" understood as "modesty in
strength," "Fauréan understatement [*litote*]," the *crescendo* that leads to a
piano, equivocation or ambiguity. Music, which ranks so high in Jankélévitch's philosophy, partakes of the poetics of oxymoron whose origins may
be traced back to Plato.[56]

Oxymoron emerges in Fauré's own writings as a key to understanding
his musical universe. In a remarkable letter to Winnaretta Singer, the
dedicatee of the *Cinq mélodies "de Venise,"* Op. 58, Fauré found no better
way to characterize the third song ("Green") than through a nexus of
oppositions. He began by calling Verlaine's poetic love-offering a "hymn
of adoration" [*cantique d'adoration*], thus uniting religious and amatory
realms, and then extended this combination of opposites into an imperative
for performance: "Slow movement and agitated expression, happy and
sorrowful, ardent and discouraged!"[57] In 1904, commenting on an article
commemorating the death of Henri Fantin-Latour, written by Arsène
Alexandre, his fellow critic at *Le Figaro*, Fauré turned to his own work:
"I have often been told that my music never quite expresses happiness or
sorrow."[58] In this light, oxymoron could also be understood more

---

[52] Émile Jaques-Dalcroze, "Gabriel Fauré," *La semaine littéraire* (November 10, 1894), 532.

[53] "The simplicity of his line is . . . only apparent, his means of realization are so subtle and refined
that we would have to linger over each detail to study its flavor before considering the whole."
Louis Vierne, "Silhouettes d'artistes: Gabriel Fauré," *L'écho musical* 1, No. 12 (December
1912), 1.

[54] Reynaldo Hahn, "Gabriel Fauré," *Journal de l'Université des annales* (July 15, 1914), 116. Messiaen
would note this union of modality and tonality in his preface to Françoise Gervais, *Étude
comparée des langages harmoniques de Fauré et de Debussy, La revue musicale* 272 (1971), 7.

[55] Ravel, "Les mélodies de Gabriel Fauré," 24–25.

[56] See the remarkable approach to a "poetics of the oxymoron" by Teresa Chevrolet, *L'idée de
fable: Théories de la fiction poétique à la Renaissance* (Geneva: Droz, 2006), 121–122.

[57] Letter to Winnaretta Singer (then the Princess de Scey-Montbéliard), July 1891, in Fauré,
Correspondance, 195.

[58] Letter to Arsène Alexandre, c. September 3, 1904, in Fauré, *Correspondance*, 303. See Arsène
Alexandre, "Souvenirs sur Fantin-Latour," *Le Figaro*, August 31, 1904. The following passage in

specifically as the weighing of extremes, a classical ideal of balance. "Might my music," Fauré continued, "wear that slightly veiled smile that 'alone is wise'?" The embedded quotation mixes in another text, which actually came from a retrospective on the eighteenth-century painter Maurice-Quentin de La Tour published the previous month by the literary critic André Beaunier, another friend and fellow critic at *Le Figaro*. Beaunier treated both the aesthetics and ethics of the smile, a manner of being in the world that discloses "the mystery of things" and a certain wisdom (the rejection of both despair and exuberance) – an aesthetic and ethic that Fauré's seems to accept as his own by his allusion to this quotation:

La Tour's little women teach us an attitude, which is to smile at the mystery of things, and to smile as simply as possible and without affecting too much joy; to smile unceasingly and not to laugh at all in order to show life that we do not expect more happiness, that we do not trust in its promises and that it will pass away. In despair there is the confession of a naïve credulity, and in exuberance, childishness. The smile alone is wise.[59]

Unsayable or Ineffable?

Parisian musical journalism of the later nineteenth century not infrequently refers to especially moving passages as "ineffable." Yet in Fauré's case, this theme underwent expansion, with a new level of intensity and corresponding variations. His music wore a halo of nebulous language: such terms as "ungraspable,"[60] "impalpable,"[61] "unsayable,"[62] "unanalysable,"[63] "inexpressible,"[64] and

---

particular must have struck Fauré: "he had also begun as an orchestrator of splendid tones and dreamy forms in *La Féerie*, famously rejected by the Salon of 1863."

[59] André Beaunier, "La Tour," *Le Figaro*, August 18, 1904.

[60] In the song "Jardin nocturne," "the writing dwindles to the limits of what can be grasped," as Émile Vuillermoz remarked in *Musiques d'aujourd'hui* (Paris: Crès, 1923), 7.

[61] See note 84.

[62] Louis Aguettant, "Sur la mort de Gabriel Fauré," 388. See also Louis Vierne, "Silhouettes d'artistes: Gabriel Fauré," *L'écho musical* 1, No. 12 (December 1912), 1: "A rare originality, a deep and muted sensibility, an unsayable charm, such are the principal qualities that emerge from Gabriel Fauré's personality."

[63] Concerning the Pie Jesu of the *Requiem*: "That cannot be analyzed, cannot be defined" (Camille Benoît, "La messe de Requiem de Gabriel Fauré," 196); "the art of Gabriel Fauré is not one to reveal its secrets to analysis" (Émile Vuillermoz, "Gabriel Fauré," *Revue illustrée*, July 1, 1905.)

[64] Fauré's songs have "an inexpressible tenderness" (Émile Jaques-Dalcroze, "*La bonne chanson*," *Gazette musicale de la Suisse romande* [November 1, 1894], 207–211).

"untranslatable"[65] circulated in contemporary writings that sought to appreciate his art. Moreover, the complicated question of musical expression and the inexpressible lay at the heart of Fauré's own reflections on music and his work as a composer – what to express, how to express it, how to bring forth through his music that which cannot be formulated in words. The composer explored these questions in a letter to his wife, in what reads almost like an inquiry into some unreachable absolute: "So often the point where you are, or the one you are aiming for is untranslatable. And how many times haven't I asked myself what music is for? And what it is? And what I am translating? What feelings? What ideas? How to express what I myself cannot account for!"[66] The inexpressible appears as that which simultaneously exists and escapes. In Jankélévitch, we pass from the observation of this inexpressibility to a reflection on its nature and meaning. And here, the philosopher finds an essential nexus of all his own philosophy. Put differently, there exists in music – and paradigmatically in the works of Fauré – an experience and a mystery that are the admirable expression of a more radically philosophical question that shines through all of Jankélévitch's writing. Fauré's music leads us to experience – and, for a philosopher, to ponder – a limit, an absolute degree of our humanity. Music is "a form of experience of the ineffable," and it enacts time itself for us. It places us in the presence of "the essentially temporal character of existence." Jankélévitch even wonders whether music might not be "a way to retrieve all the energies of sentient being and thus the entirety of human nature."[67]

In his first book on the composer (*Gabriel Fauré et ses mélodies*, 1938), Jankélévitch began with the scores but then abandoned them to engage in a more general reflection bearing the disconcerting title, "The Science of Loving Things." He took stock: "Now that we have taken analysis as far as we can, let us admit that we have allowed the essential element to escape, that residue irreducible to analysis that is none other than the inexpressible. The *je ne sais quoi*, the unsayable, the fragrance of the spirit … it is what we must call Charm."[68] Jankélévitch wished to approach "the

[65] "He is truly a master in this language of sounds that, for us anyway, cannot be compared to any other language, and to which alone is given the power to evoke within us feelings, sensations, and emotions utterly special and untranslatable into any other art" (Louis Vierne, "Salle Pleyel: Concerts Ysaye-Pugno," *Le monde musical* 17, No. 9 [May 15, 1906], 137).

[66] Letter to Marie Fauré, September 20, 1907, in Fauré, *Lettres intimes*, ed. Philippe Fauré-Fremiet (Paris: La Colombe, 1951), 78.

[67] Jankélévitch, with Béatrice Berlowitz, *Quelque part dans l'inachevé* (Paris: Gallimard, 1978), 297.

[68] Jankélévitch, *Gabriel Fauré et ses mélodies*, 248–249.

essential" lodged in "that irreducible residue."[69] Yet humans are speaking, thinking beings, and the philosopher a creature of concepts. Fauré led Jankélévitch to confront the inexpressible, whence the title of his *Fauré et l'inexprimable* (1974), the first book in the series *De la musique au silence* (*From Music to Silence*), whose baffling title in fact reveals the underlying enterprise: to explore the paths of silence. The philosopher Jean Lacoste has remarked, "The title is paradoxical since it treats silence not as the condition out of which music should emerge, but rather its real achievement."[70] Moreover, the idea of silence, as Simone Zacchini notes, "is at the center of every branch of Jankélévitch's philosophy."[71] Music of silence or silent music: we are back at the oxymoron.

In 1938, Jankélévitch spoke of the "unsayable" (*l'indicible*). He would increasingly favor the word "ineffable," and even oppose the two terms. In *La musique et l'ineffable*, he devoted an entire section to this question, which can be presented schematically:[72]

	Unsayable	Ineffable
Energy	negativity	positivity
Existential horizon	death	life
	sorrow	freedom
	nothingness	love

The unsayable (or unspeakable – now we may introduce a synonym whose vectors in English tend to be pejorative) is a negativity that issues from death, sorrow, nothingness.[73] The ineffable is positive, giving birth to hope; according to Jankélévitch, it is "the inexpressible that engenders life,

---

[69] Here is a lesson for musicology: to use analysis as a springboard for aesthetics; to explore musical scores, but also the lexicon applied to them in commentary through which they enter the space of reception and discourse.

[70] See Jean Lacoste, "La musique et la plénitude exaltante de l'être," *Critique* 500–501 (January–February 1989), 71. Lacoste also writes that for Fauré, "silence is inside music; it is a pause, an enchanted oasis amid the continuous din, a way, alongside motion toward flat keys and the *'forte con sordina,'* to attenuate, to subtract, to invite retreat into nocturnal intimacy" (101).

[71] Simone Zacchini, "Le 'logos' du silence: La philosophie de la musique de Jankélévitch," in *Vladimir Jankélévitch, l'empreinte du passeur*, ed. Françoise Schwab and Jean-Marc Rouvière (Paris: Édition le Manuscrit, 2007), 183.

[72] Jankélévitch, *La musique et l'ineffable*, Chapter 2, "L'Indicible et l'ineffable. Le sens du sens," 92–97.

[73] At the end of the twentieth century, the term "unspeakable" [*indicible*] continued in this new negative meaning, linked to reflection on recorded experiences of mass violence. See for example Luba Jurgenson, "L'indicible: Outil d'analyse ou objet esthétique," *Protée* 37, No. 2 (2009), 9–19.

liberty, and love."[74] Music stands to the side of life, but a life that perceives its own finitude. And while he insisted that we cannot speak of death (or of music, or of love), Jankélévitch devoted a 467-page book to the topic! In the course of the work, he evoked "the divine silence" that "resembles a supersensible *pianissimo* where the soul's ear discerns the musical secrets and mysterious bells of the invisible city."[75] Herein lies the origin of the general title *From Music to Silence*, mentioned above. This passage also recalls one of Fauré's most important letters, which now calls us to close study.

Fauré on the Source of Music

In a letter of 1908 to his wife Marie, Fauré confided that he did not generally think about anything concrete when he composed. He recalled an exceptional case, however, that lead him to wonder about the nature of music, or more precisely, the process by which music comes about:

It is only in the Andante of the Second Quartet that I can remember having translated, and almost involuntarily, the very distant memory of ringing bells, which at Montgauzy in the evenings ... would reach us from a village called Cadirac when the wind blew from the west. Over this drone a vague reverie goes aloft, which, like all vague reveries, would be untranslatable *by literary means*. Yet isn't it often that something external thus lulls us into thoughts of a sort so imprecise that in truth they are not thoughts, and yet they are something in which we take pleasure? The desire for nonexistent things, perhaps. And that is indeed the domain of music.[76]

These lines evince the distancing and removal from reality at the heart of Fauré's musical thought: not the direct transcription of a ringing bell, but a "memory of ringing bells"; not recent memory, but a "distant memory."[77] And this ringing itself, carried by the village breeze, is located far away in the west, itself a metaphor for remoteness. Finally, this same distancing movement affects the sound itself: it is no longer a matter of notes or timbres, but only a "drone." This experience sets in motion a reverie that

---

[74] Jankélévitch, *La musique et l'ineffable*, 92.

[75] Jankélévitch, *La mort* (Paris: Flammarion, 1966), 83.

[76] Letter to Marie Fauré, September 11, 1908, *Lettres intimes*, 132; translation by Carlo Caballero, from his *Fauré and French Musical Aesthetics*, 41.

[77] Jean-Michel Nectoux, *Gabriel Fauré* (Paris: Fayard, 2008), 149, notes evocations of bell-sounds in Fauré's piano music. For the phenomenology of the bells evoked in the Second Piano Quartet, see the discussion in Caballero, *Fauré and French Musical Aesthetics*, 41–45.

words cannot translate and transports the self into a state of in-between: thoughts so imprecise as not to be thoughts. At the moment when everything is almost fully evaporated, blurred, and unformed (time, space, sound, thought), music is born as motion toward that which no longer has any content: a "desire for nonexistent things."

This passage relocates music from something sayable to something unsayable (in the original sense of the term). It is not dissociated from all referents, but is born on the threshold where the referent dissolves. Music bursts forth when memory vibrates sympathetically: in our innermost state and with desires normally blocked from consciousness. Already in 1904, the composer openly acknowledged the possibility of an unconscious biography inscribed within his works.[78] Four year later, the letter to his wife cited above confirms the idea of subconscious activity within the work. At times, driven by an exceptionally powerful desire, music takes up this force that transcends us. Fauré conveyed something about this process in a letter to his mistress Marguerite Hasselmans, written in the exhilaration of their budding romance: "My D flat was badly shaken by travels, muffled by the clamor of all the relatives [that surrounded me]. But that note still lives on, and I hope that it will rise to a dignity so supreme that you will deign to receive it. I can hardly express how I long to be reunited with you! Words are useless: only D flat can translate them!"[79] A spectacular metamorphosis: unsayable desire become sayable through music! What interests Fauré is precisely that moment when the mind is freed from reason and gains access through sensation to the heart of the living object. Music is not a pure play of forms; through its "infra-semantic" origin, it comes into contact with our inner world; it does not say, but evokes.

Pure Music and Reverie

More than other artistic expressions, Fauré's music brings us into contact with the ineffable. His is not a poetics of lacuna, absence, a hollowing out of the real, or of the meaning revealed by this ineffability, but rather the mysterious presence and quality of a music that reveals itself as music, that

[78] "I would really be flattered, if it is true that we express ourselves unconsciously in our art, to think that I have seen life as you see it." Letter to Arsène Alexandre, September 1904, in Fauré, *Correspondance*, 304.

[79] Letter to Marguerite Hasselmans, early September 1901, in *Correspondance*, 583.

is, whose form and emotion flow from the work of composition and not from a program.

This happens as if Fauré, excited at some point by "thoughts that are not thoughts," arrived at a final detachment from all that is not music – an idea that Louis Vierne expressed rather awkwardly in his review of a 1906 performance of the First Piano Quintet: "We must now surely confess that analysis is useless in the presence of such a creation: the feeling we experience in hearing this score is that it is all music, nothing but music, always music."[80] Music that makes you feel you are listening to music! It has no recourse to external elements or demonstrative forms that would estrange it from itself. Hence, Fauré's avoidance of glaring virtuosity, or his rejection of traits prized in French Romanticism – characteristic and picturesque elements, local color, exoticism, or folklore. Hence, too, his indifference, if not repugnance, toward the contemporary movements of Impressionism, Naturalism, or Expressionism. The composer's artistic quest thus lay in the musicalization of music, a principle that he crystallized in 1891 after hearing three Beethoven symphonies, works whose power and grandeur remained intact despite the passage of time and banal repetitions in public concerts. Fauré sought to grasp how the energy of Beethoven's work, arising solely from the intrinsic nature of the music, proved impermeable to the vicissitudes of history and repertoire. Fauré then declared, "Music that truly contains *music* is rarer and rarer," before defining his own mission: "I am more resolved than ever to put it into every thing that I compose."[81] *To put music into music* means adhering to compositional logic and the lofty demand of an ideal fashioning sound from balance, fluidity, and refinement; it means composing "a work that lives entirely through itself."[82] For Fauré, art is born of craft; it requires hard work and training, not just inspiration, as he remarked to his younger son. Yet his work does not aim to reproduce a model perfectly, but rather to exceed it: "for me, art and above all, music, consists in lifting us as high as possible above what exists."[83] The act of musicalization aims to separate us from reality and provide access to a higher world by mining the language of music and fully working out its realization. Louis Schneider clearly understood what set Fauré apart from Debussy. While both composers had as their goal "the impalpable," their music differed profoundly.

---

[80] Louis Vierne, "Salle Pleyel: Concerts Ysaye-Pugno," *Le monde musical* (May 15, 1906), 137.
[81] Letter to Winnaretta Singer, October 1891, Fauré, *Correspondance*, 204.
[82] Letter to Marie Fauré, March 23, 1906, in Fauré, *Lettres intimes*, 118.
[83] Letter to Philippe Fauré-Fremiet, August 31, 1908, in Fauré, *Correspondance*, 346.

While Debussy's chief means for expressing *l'impalpable* was timbre, Schneider located the same quality in Fauré's treatment of harmony, as Ken Johansen has so magnificently demonstrated through the concept of "equivocation."[84]

Discussing his Piano Quintet in D Minor, Op. 89, Fauré reported to his wife the highly favorable judgment of violinist Eugène Ysaÿe, who found the style "more lofty" than that of the two piano quartets, "more fully purified of any search for effects: absolute music" – a position that, according to the composer, put him completely out of step with the times: "Right now, music is striving to be everything *but* music."[85] This is only one side of creative work, however: a different "human logic" must be joined to the logic of the craft, of composition, of music as music.[86] For Fauré, music remains bound to feelings or emotions, but in a higher form, just as the Symbolists sought the Idea rather than the object. Another oxymoron steps forward when he describes his intentions for an opera on the story of Mazeppa: "I shall do my best to translate human feelings with more-than-human values, if that's possible."[87]

What stands in the place of the tangible reality this art escapes? Reverie. Reverie was its origin, and reverie is the state the music produces in the listener. Music that offers itself as music – most obviously in chamber works – allows the listener's thought to roam freely, in harmony with the work. Let us return to Fauré's letter of 1908. The distant memory is simultaneously bound to a referent and detached from that referent to the point of losing touch with it. This act of distancing, upon which the composer insists, consists in the process by which the bells dissolve into droning, that is, in the passage from a concrete referent into almost formless material, the source of a reverie "untranslatable *by literary means*." This mental activity, which is directed not by conscious attention but rather through the passive influence of subjective and affective causes, and which overcomes the opposition between logic and intuition, places us in a perfect state of receptivity. It occupies the threshold between conscious and unconscious and conduces to the chance association of ideas, images

---

[84] Fauré "possesses the secret to notating the impalpable; with two chords he says more than many others can with an entire phrase." Louis Schneider, "Gabriel Fauré directeur du Conservatoire," *Gil Blas*, June 14, 1905. "M. Debussy is gifted, musically, with the notation of the impalpable. He makes a sonority out of the impalpable." Schneider, "Les concerts classiques," *Gil Blas*, October 16, 1905. See Ken Johansen, "Gabriel Fauré, un art de l'équivoque," *Revue de musicologie* 85, No. 1 (1999), 63–96.

[85] Letter to Marie Fauré, March 23, 1906, in *Lettres intimes*, 118.

[86] Letter to Philippe Fauré-Fremiet, August 31, 1908, in Fauré, *Correspondance*, 346.

[87] Letter to Paul Poujaud, September 3, 1885, in Fauré, *Correspondance*, 123.

and obsessions, memories and "thoughts that are not thoughts." Vuillermoz summarized it thus: "Pure music is really the accompaniment to a dream, the obedient commentary on the spectacle that unfolds in the imagination behind the curtain of closed eyelids."[88] The 1908 letter reveals the strong threads that music weaves between past and present by means of reminiscence, in the Proustian sense of the term.[89]

* * *

Music is encircled by a halo of words, notions, and ideas, which illuminate it or blur it, bear it up or crush it. Its sense and value do not reside solely in the score but emerge from the encounter between the work and the constellation of discourses that envelop it. Some notions become common-places, while others seek vainly to become keys to understanding. Thus, the idea of faith or optimism [*confiance*] put forth by Philippe Fauré-Fremiet has found no echo. Even so, he wrote: "The great secret of Fauré's thought is his *confiance*."[90] The history of the lexicon applied to Fauré's music testifies to the process through which an aesthetic line of thought crystal-lizes. There is nothing contrived in these concepts: fusion of opposites (oxymoron), pure music, the ineffable, charm, grace, the *je ne sais quoi*, or even of reverie. They reveal an understanding of music and a secret process described by the composer, perceived by the critics of his time, and explored in depth by Vladimir Jankélévitch.

Translated by Stephen Rumph

---

[88] Lecture by Vuillermoz delivered by M. Signoret on April 15, 1913 at the Comédie des Champs-Elysées, typescript, F-Pn, Vma. 5429. For a similar remark by Reynaldo Hahn, see "Gabriel Fauré," *Journal de l'Université des annales* (July 15, 1914), 116.

[89] For the idea of reminiscence, see Jankélévitch, *Quelque part dans l'inachevé*, 53–55.

[90] Philippe Fauré-Fremiet, *Gabriel Fauré*, second edition (Paris: A. Michel, 1957); Jankélévitch, *Gabriel Fauré, ses mélodies, son esthétique* (Paris: Plon, 1951). 136.

Appendix | Vladimir Jankélévitch's Writings about Fauré

Gabriel Fauré et ses mélodies (Paris: Plon, 1938).

"Pelléas et Pénélope," *Revue historique et littéraire du Languedoc* (1945), 123–130; reprinted in Chapter 17 of *Premières et dernières pages*, ed. Françoise Schwab (Paris: Seuil, 1994), 259–265.

"Marguerite Hasselmans et Gabriel Fauré," *Europe* 29 (1948), 138–139.

Gabriel Fauré, ses mélodies, son esthétique (Paris: Plon, 1951).

"Gabriel Fauré et le mystère," Concert program, Festival G. Fauré de Foix, April 20, 1958.

"Gabriel Fauré et son temps," Concert program, Festival G. Fauré de Foix, July 9 and 13, 1958.

"Gabriel Fauré et ses disciples," Concert program, Festival G. Fauré de Foix, July 21, 1958.

Fauré et l'inexprimable, first volume of the series *De la musique au silence* (Paris: Plon, 1974). The book consists of three essays, "Les mélodies de Gabriel Fauré" (reworked from the 1951 study), "Commentaire sur la musique de piano et sur la musique de chambre de Fauré" (new), and "L'ambiguïté, la tranquillité d'âme et le charme dans l'œuvre de Fauré" (derived from the Foix concert programs).

3 | Fauré as Student and Teacher of Harmony

ROBERT O. GJERDINGEN

Understanding the training of professional musicians in nineteenth-century France may require some conceptual adjustments. Words that seem to mean one thing for us today can actually have meant something rather different then. *Accompagnement*, for instance, meant practical keyboard harmony and thoroughbass, *harmonie* meant practical counterpoint, and *contrepoint* meant imitative counterpoint in the form of fugues and canons. As we shall see below, when Gabriel Fauré wrote a harmony exercise in which he provided the bass and a student was to add the implied tenor, alto, and soprano voices, he intended it to be completed as an informal type of fugue, the *locus classicus* of counterpoint. "Counterpoint" was a word deeply rooted in the practices of trained medieval monks who could improvise a series of points (= notes) against (Lat. *contra*) the notes of a Gregorian chant. Putting one point against another – *punctus contra punctum* – gave rise to the term counterpoint, which came to mean the art of combining separate melodies into a pleasing whole. Beginning in the eighteenth century, this intrinsically musical concept began to be replaced for the reading public by the general, layperson's term "harmony," which since antiquity had meant a combination or reconciliation of differing or opposed elements. In the period from Bach to Ravel, counterpoint, an artisanal craft learned through long apprenticeship, was never the subject of abstract theoretical flights of fancy. Harmony, by contrast, was a constant object of speculation by musical amateurs or by professional musicians who wrote books intended for sale to lay readers. In a nutshell, counterpoint was a craft, harmony was a speculative science. Crafts were learned through apprenticeships, sciences were learned through classes at colleges and universities. While the musicians who taught at conservatories may have been titled as professors, in truth they were master artisans who each supervised a small studio of apprentices.

An Apprenticeship in Counterpoint

Fauré began his long apprenticeship at the age of nine in October of 1854. From his home in southern France he was brought to Paris and enrolled in the École de musique classique et religieuse. This school had gone through a number of administrative reorganizations. It began as part of Alexandre Choron's many efforts to reestablish training in Catholic sacred music following the Concordat of 1801, the official rapprochement between Napoleon and the Church. The École Niedermeyer, as it came to be known in honor of its later director Louis Niedermeyer, focused on chant and early music to a greater extent than its more famous competitor, the Paris Conservatory. The École used its brand as nurturer of sacred music to win state bursaries for many of its students. As a residential school, it needed funds to house and feed its twenty or more wards and to pay for their instructors. In the manner of the old Naples conservatories, the École had a common practice room whose walls were lined with fifteen keyboards upon which the students played their individual lessons in simultaneous cacophony. This noisy institute would be Fauré's home for the next eleven years.

Details of Fauré's daily lessons at the École are sparse at best. Into that void have sprung a number of ideas about his training in harmony that may or may not withstand close scrutiny. Take, for instance, the idea that the institution's focus on serious religious music put Fauré on a different, more "modal" path than his contemporaries at the Conserva-toire.[1] A cautionary note comes from an observation of Henri Busser, a student at both institutions in the 1880s. He wrote, "It is curious to note that Niedermeyer, a school of classical religious music, has been a hothouse for composers of light music," mentioning, among many others, Fauré's close friend André Messager.[2] Messager, the successor to Offenbach in French operetta, wrote delightfully frothy music that at times may suggest the world of Fauré but hardly the world of "classical religious music." Ernest Guiraud, a composition professor at the Conservatory with no connections to the École, welcomed modal inflections in his students' music, and that attitude attracted the young Claude Debussy to his class. Thus, tastes for and against musical evocations of the antique could be found at either institution. It is nonetheless both possible and reasonable that the greater exposure to early music at the École was a factor in Fauré's development. Many nineteenth-century editions of early music came without the correct *musica ficta* and hence sounded more modal than necessary. But again, the picture is clouded because other composers with

[1] See, for example, the excellent study by James C. Kidd, "Louis Niedermeyer's System for Gregorian Chant Accompaniment as a Compositional Source for Gabriel Fauré" (Ph.D. dissertation, University of Chicago, 1973).

[2] Henri Busser, *De Pelléas aux Indes galantes – De la flûte au tambour* (Paris: Fayard, 1955), 38.

similar exposures at other institutions (e.g., Delibes with Renaissance dances) did not produce a sound anything like Fauré's.

In the same vein, the harmony book of Gustave Lefèvre has been cited as a special factor influencing the teaching of harmony at the École.[3] Both Lefèvre and Camille Saint-Saëns had ties to Pierre Maleden, whose teacher Gottfried Weber was an important figure in the history of theories of harmony. The problems with connecting Fauré's unique style to Lefèvre or Maleden are, nevertheless, many. Lefèvre became director of the school only in the year that Fauré graduated (1865), and his book on harmony was still twenty-four years in the future (1889). Henri Busser studied solfège, harmony, and counterpoint with Lefèvre and "never opened a book or method," since Lefèvre's teaching was "purely oral."[4] If that practice extended back to the days of Fauré's lessons, it is not surprising that few traces of the actual instruction survive. The real impact of Weber's best known treatise was in universities and, as its partial title – *zum Selbstunterricht* – suggested, in self-study, not in conservatories.[5] In Weber's own words, "it would be a great mistake to infer from the title prefixed to my work, namely, the *Theory of Composition*, that it is designed more for those who wish to become practical composers than for those who have the more limited purpose of securing an acquaintance with the principles of the Science."[6] "Science" is the operative word, and while conservatories did bow before it, they did not teach it.

The Revolution had extinguished music education in France. To rekindle it, the state established the Paris Conservatory (1795), allowed the rebuilding of cathedral choir schools (*maîtrises*), and supported Choron in setting up (1816) what would later become the École Niedermeyer.[7] In all these projects, it was taken as self-evident that music education in Italy, along with a repertory of Italian classics, should form the model. Choron's two major publications both highlighted "The Schools of Italy" in the course of reprinting practically the entire curriculum of the Naples conservatories.[8] Core lessons in those schools were the voice-and-

---

[3] Gustave Lefèvre, *Traité d'harmonie à l'usage des cours de l'École* (Paris: École de musique classique, 1889). See, for example, Jean-Michel Nectoux, "Fauré, Gabriel," *Grove Music Online*, ed. Deane Root. www.oxfordmusiconline.com.

[4] Busser, *De Pelléas*, 31.

[5] Gottfried Weber, *Versuch einer geordnete Theorie der Tonsetzkunst zum Selbstunterricht, mit Anmerkungeun für Gelehrtere* (Mainz: B. Schott, 1817–21).

[6] Ibid., 5.

[7] While a few scattered and clandestine attempts were made to continue education in sacred music during the Revolution, it was not until the mid-nineteenth century that the *maîtrises* were fully reestablished in all the major dioceses.

[8] Alexandre Choron, *Principes d'accompagnement des écoles d'Italie* (Paris, 1804); *Principes de compositions des écoles d'Italie* (Paris, 1808).

accompaniment duos known as *solfeggi*, and the keyboard works that featured fully notated left-hand parts meant to be completed by improvised right-hand parts, lessons known as *partimenti*. Large collections of Italian *solfeggi* had been published in Paris since 1772.[9] *Partimenti* circulated in manuscript form until the very early nineteenth century, when a series of Parisian publications began to appear, edited by Choron (1808), Imbimbo (1814), Fétis (1823), Colet (1846), Panseron (1855), Deldevez (1872), and doubtless many others.[10] Throughout the century, keyboard realization of *partimenti* remained a central part of the course in *accompagnement*, and it was in that course, improvising *partimenti* under the tutelage of Auguste Bazille, that Claude Debussy won his only course-related first prize at the Paris Conservatory (he would, to be sure, later win the Prix de Rome).

Partimenti, as the embodied experiences of apprentice musical artisans, were viewed by nineteenth- and early twentieth-century university scholars as records of manual labor, and thus beneath academic consideration. Only in the twenty-first century have scholars begun to imagine the implications of this daily physical practice on the mental development of future composers.[11] Lefèvre, for example, studied with Hippolyte Colet, whose 378-page edition of *partimenti* was cited above. For Colet, harmony was a practice learned by realizing *partimenti*. Lefèvre also studied with Michele Carafa, a student of the *partimento* master Fenaroli in Naples. Even Lefèvre's teacher Maleden had studied with Fétis, who advocated *partimento* training and, as cited above, published a *partimento* edition to aid his students. Given the ubiquity of this artisanal activity, it may be time to reevaluate notions about Fauré's training in harmony.

His primary harmony teachers were Niedermeyer and Pierre-Louis Dietsch. Niedermeyer had studied *partimenti* in Naples with Zingarelli, and Dietsch would have learned *partimenti* during the eight years (1822–30) he spent in Choron's Italian-influenced Institution royale de musique classique et religieuse, the predecessor to the École. Choron, as mentioned, was a pioneer in the French publishing of Neapolitan *partimenti* and the rules governing them. Niedermeyer, Dietsch, and other

---

[9] P. Levesque and L. Bèche, *Solfèges d'Italie avec la basse chiffrée* (Paris: Le Duc, 1772).

[10] Fedele Fenaroli, *Partimenti ossia Basso numerato*, trans. and ed. Emanuele Imbimbo (Paris: Carli, 1814); François-Joseph Fétis, *Méthode élémentaire et abrégée d'harmonie et d'accompagnement* (Paris: À la Nouveauté, au Magasin de musique et d'instrumens de Ph. Petit, succr. de P. Gaveaux, 1823); Hippolyte-Raymond Colet, *Partimenti, ou Traité spécial, de l'accompagnement pratique au piano* (Paris: Chabal, 1846); Auguste Mathieu Panseron, *Traité de l'harmonie pratique et des modulations à l'usage des pianistes, en trois parties: Traité d'Harmonie, L'Art de moduler, Devoirs à faire par les élèves* (Paris: Brandus, 1855); E. M. E. Deldevez, *Fenaroli, Cours complet d'harmonie et de haute composition* (Paris: Richault, 1872).

[11] See, for example, my *Music in the Galant Style* (New York: Oxford University Press, 2007).

masters trained in *partimenti* realization maintained artisanal traditions of harmonization (discussed below) that were largely unaffected by the more academic theories of harmony or tonality. Fauré's counterpoint teacher Xavier Wackenthaler was an organist from a conservative family of organists in Strasbourg. Since Wackenthaler died when Fauré had finished only his second year, other teachers like Saint-Saëns (who had also studied with Maleden) may have taken up that role. So the artisanal traditions of physical pattern memory that Fauré absorbed at the keyboard, as opposed to theories of harmony that he may or may not have read, were probably the major influence on his development in harmony. Fauré's mannerisms in manipulating those patterns, combined with his personal preferences for certain modulations and changes of diatonic scales, may account for a large measure of his unique sound. It may be worth noting that in none of the letters published in collections of Fauré's correspondence examined by this author does Fauré use the type of chord vocabulary that might have been expected had he wanted to discuss harmony in terms of the chord theories of Weber or Maleden. Indeed, judging by a 1906 letter to his younger son Philippe, Fauré used the term *harmonie* in reference to the titles of standard textbooks on the realization of given melodies and basses, not to an abstract chordal grammar distinct from counterpoint.[12]

Long after his student days, Saint-Saëns provided an encomium for Maleden's theories. His remarks seem at first glance to be quite significant:

Maleden was an incomparable teacher. He had gone, in his youth, to educate himself in Germany with a certain Gottfried Weber, inventor of a system that Maleden brought back and perfected. He had made it a wonderful tool to penetrate the depths of music, a light to shine into the most secret corners. In this system chords are not considered only by themselves – a 5-3 chord, a 6-3 chord, a 7th chord – but according to the scale degree on which they are placed; one learns that according to the place they occupy, they acquire different properties, and one thus can explain cases deemed inexplicable. This method is taught at the École Niedermeyer; I do not know if it is taught elsewhere.[13]

---

[12] See Fauré, *Correspondance*, 322 (letter to Philippe Fauré-Fremiet, August 1906). Fauré referred his son to François Bazin's *Cours d'harmonie théorique et pratique* (Paris: Léon Escudier, 1857) and Augustin Savard's *Cours complet d'harmonie théorique et pratique* (Paris: J. Maho, 1853), or various reprints. Bazin's lessons are named "partimenti" and require the student to realize them; in the 1870s Savard published a volume of partimenti for students and a companion volume of their realizations: *Études d'harmonie pratique. Partimenti progressifs, basses et chants donnés pour l'emploi des différents accords et des divers artifices harmoniques* (Paris: E. & A. Girod, ca. 1875). Both authors represented a conservative, Italianate approach to composition learned when they attended the Conservatoire in the 1830s. My thanks to Stephen Rumph for bringing this letter to my attention.

[13] Camille Saint-Saëns, *École buissonnière: Notes et souvenirs* (Paris: Pierre Lafitte, 1913), 8–9.

Saint-Saëns was likely unaware that he was describing the training of students at the old Naples conservatories, or for that matter almost anywhere in eighteenth-century Italy. The Rule of the Octave, which was one of the first things taught at the keyboard to young apprentices, was entirely couched in terms of scale degrees and direction.[14] A chord on the fourth scale degree, for example, would be built with the intervals 6/5/3 or 6/4/2 depending on whether the bass subsequently ascended or descended. Inasmuch as the Rule of the Octave continued to be taught at the Paris Conservatory, the remarks of Saint-Saëns are perhaps best taken as a well-intentioned attempt by a very famous musician to support the idea that his dear teacher had much to offer in spite of never having been hired to teach at the Conservatory. His generous but muddled praise for Maleden mispresents artisanal commonplaces as theoretical insights.

Documentary and anecdotal evidence is similarly contradictory concerning Fauré's standing as a harmonist at the École. On the one hand he won a first in harmony in 1860, but on the other hand Henri Busser recounts that "some students had to repeat one or two classes; in the annals of the École it was said that Gabriel Fauré, a particularly nonchalant pupil, remained at his echelon [bancs] for ten years, not being able to pass through to the top level. Let's admit that he did not turn out so badly!"[15] Because a boy (the École, unlike the Conservatory, admitted only boys) usually began at the bottom of the four levels of each of the common subjects – solfège, harmony, counterpoint and fugue, organ, piano – he would need to pass many contests with sufficiently high marks to progress to the next level in each subject. So some of Fauré's reported prizes might be associated with simple annual advancement. Whatever his actual progress, upon leaving the École he was judged a qualified chapel master and church organist.

The official mission of the École to produce fine church musicians was nowhere made clearer than in its house publication, *La Maîtrise*. This journal, founded by Niedermeyer and published in the late 1850s, gave helpful advice to church musicians and included for them numerous scores by Palestrina, Vittoria, and modern French composers like Niedermeyer and Gounod. In Fauré's fourth year at the École, Niedermeyer included his own organ work "Communion" in *La Maîtrise*.[16] After an initial passage on a tonic D pedal, Niedermeyer's piece continues as shown in Example 3.1. The grey bars placed in the first two measures (mm. 7–8)

---

[14] See Thomas Christensen, "The 'Règle de l'Octave' in Thorough-Bass Theory and Practice," *Acta Musicologica* 64 (1992), 91–117.

[15] Busser, *De Pelléas*, 30.

[16] *La Maîtrise* 2, No. 2 (1858). The scores printed with the journal were each paginated separately.

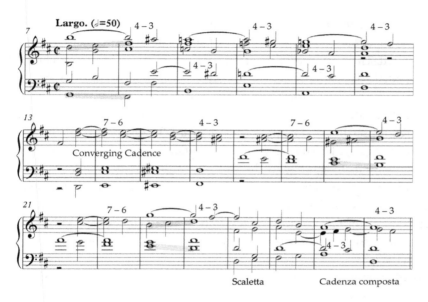

Example 3.1 Louis Niedermeyer, "Communion" for organ, in *La Maîtrise* 2, No. 2 (1858), mm. 7–28
Grey shading indicates 5–6–8 cadences; verbal annotations mark conventional *marches harmoniques*. Note the pervasive preparation and execution of 4–3 and 7–6 suspensions.

have been added to indicate the Renaissance discant-tenor cadence of a major sixth (imperfection) moving in contrary motion to an octave (perfection). The same cadence recurs twice more beginning in measures 19 and 23. A marker of the sacred style was the presentation of prepared suspensions. Niedermeyer places a 4-3 or 7-6 suspension in almost every other measure. I have marked "converging cadence" beginning in measure 13, the beginning of a stock eighteenth-century approach to a half cadence, one featuring a diminished octave (m. 15) much cultivated by, among others, J. C. Bach. Near the end of the excerpt you will see the terms *scaletta* ("little scale") and *cadenza composta*. These last two annotations are to show Niedermeyer's completely conventional approach to a cadence through a portion of the Rule of the Octave and one of the three cadence types taught in the Naples conservatories. If Fauré studied this piece or other pieces by Niedermeyer, he would have been exposed to a conservative, even archaic kind of counterpoint rather than any special approach to harmony. What, for example, could be more conventional that the harmonic circle of fifths in Niedermeyer's measures 8–12? The harsh dissonances in that passage result from the doubling of suspensions in thirds or sixths, not from any type of advanced chordal vocabulary.

In the *partimento* training typically found in preparatory harmony classes, one learned a large repertory of stock patterns to be played at the keyboard. There were cadences of the type just mentioned and a number of sequential bass patterns known in Italy as *moti del basso*. In the French context the *moti del basso* became known as *marches harmoniques*. This is often translated as "harmonic progressions," but the idea of a series of chords misses the true nature of the *marches*. The *marches harmoniques* were quite specific contrapuntal combinations of voices. A *partimento* lesson gave a student a given bass to play with the left hand and left its completion to an improvised right-hand part (or parts). The *partimento* bass served as a series of memory cues to the *marches*, and a good student could recall the upper voice(s) that matched the cues in the bass. This given bass or *basse donnée* was often paired with a *chant donné*, a separate exercise where a melody provided cues to its own series of *marches*. Whether improvised at the keyboard or notated, the solution of the problems posed by a given voice was termed a *réalisation*, indicating that the solution realized the *marches* and cadences implicit in the given voice.

Describing in words a nonverbal tradition of multivoice patterns can be difficult, which is perhaps why *partimento* training remained for centuries the guild knowledge of professional musicians.[17] Let us take just one bass pattern and explore its history and affordances, meaning the responses it invited from a trained student. In the Neapolitan terminology of the eighteenth century, one of the standard *moti del basso* went "down a third, up a step" (*cala di terzo, sala di grado*). Example 3.2a shows three measures of a simple presentation of this bass pattern in half notes. Within each measure the bass descends a third, and across each bar line it ascends a step. For an apprentice at one of the old conservatories, this stimulus could evoke the learned response of Example 3.2b, where an upper voice moves in contrary motion to the bass and alternates thirds and sixths above that bass. One of the attractions of this pattern was the call-and-response interplay that could emerge between melody and bass. Example 3.2c, measures 38–40 from the Kyrie of Fauré's *Messe basse* (*c.* 1881), shows, in its second measure, how easily the filled-in descending third in the bass (Gb–F–Eb) could be echoed in the melody (C–Bb–Ab), although Fauré avoids the cliché by shifting the melodic response forward one half-beat (the stars above the eighth notes C and Ab show the displaced

17 See Giorgio Sanguinetti, *The Art of Partimento: History, Theory, and Practice* (New York: Oxford, 2012).

Example 3.2 A schema for two-part counterpoint: a. Cue to the "down a third, up a step" schema; b. Addition of a stock upper voice; c. From Fauré's *Messe basse*, Kyrie, mm. 38–40 (*c.* 1881); d. From Fauré's *Pavane*, opening theme (1887)

tones of the alternating thirds and sixths). The opening of Fauré's *Pavane* (1887) represents a further disguising of the underlying scheme (see Example 3.2d). His bass clearly matches the "down a third, up a step" schema, but his melody delays the arrival of the alternating thirds and sixths (marked with stars), giving the passage, in its full orchestral coloring, that unique mixture of perceptual simplicity, wistfulness, and repressed desire that Fauré did better than almost anyone else. So in terms of the craft of composition taught at the École, Example 3.2a is a cue to a schema, Example 3.2b is a default two-voice realization of the schema, Example 3.2c is a rather obvious but still charming instantiation of the schema in a real musical context, and Example 3.2d is a crowning example of Beaux-Arts ideals applied to musical expression. Although these phrases are built on simple two-voice models of the type seen in Niedermeyer's "Communion" (Example 3.1), they can result in sonorities and chord successions that frustrate conventional harmonic analysis.

A Teacher of Counterpoint

Fauré completed his training at the École in the summer of 1865. After spending several years as a church organist in various locales, he briefly taught composition back at the École, which had decamped to Switzerland to avoid the chaos caused by the Franco-Prussian War. Returning to Paris, he was engaged as organist or choir director at increasingly prestigious churches, teaching private lessons in piano or harmony on the side. Exactly what he taught in those harmony lessons remains a subject of conjecture. He re-entered the realm of conservatories as an inspector of the provincial institutions in 1892, advancing to take over Massenet's chair as professor of composition at the Paris Conservatory in the summer of 1896. He attracted the top students to his studio (including Ravel and Enescu) and, after *l'affaire Ravel* resulting from the disputed Prix de Rome competition of 1905, ascended improbably to the directorship of the entire institution.

Without a thorough knowledge of the artisanal schemas of counterpoint, students of Fauré at the Conservatory would likely have been unable to compete successfully in the end-of-year harmony contests (*concours d'harmonie*) that determined advancement and the possible awarding of cash prizes. These tests were so difficult and specialized that even Henri Busser, a musician of great talent and later a professor of composition at the Conservatory, failed the entrance examination in harmony given by Théodore Dubois when he transferred to the Conservatory. It is possible that Busser's harmony training at the École (and by implication Fauré's) was more like the simple realizations of figured basses in the Conservatory class in *accompagnement*. In Busser's retelling, Dubois, in a sugared voice, said, "My friend, you did not learn very much at the École Niedermeyer: you will need to relearn your harmony book."[18] Unlike Busser, who tended to rely on his substantial natural gifts, wiser students would prepare for these entrance examinations by studying collections of *basses et chants donnés* printed in two versions, with and without four-voice realizations (the "answers"). An apprentice could write his own realizations and then compare the results with those written by masters.

One of the largest such compilations was edited by Albert Lavignac, a Conservatory professor of harmony from 1891 to 1916.[19] It contains 208 lessons, each with and without a realization, in three collections of increasing difficulty. The third collection presents specially composed *basses et chants donnés* by many of the most prominent Parisian masters – Barthe, Bazille, Chapuis, Delibes, Dubois, Duprato, Fauré, Franck, Guilmant, Guiraud, Lenepveu, Leroux, Marty, Massenet, Pessard, Rousseau, Taudou, Widor, and Vidal. It bears mentioning that Fauré is not specially set apart in this collection. He is presented as just one of many late nineteenth-century masters, rather than, in the words of Nadia Boulanger, "The first twentieth-century composer."[20] Apparently, the same set of skills that could lead to success in realizing a bass or melody by Widor, Massenet, or Delibes could lead to success with Fauré, though perhaps not to the extent of fully capturing Fauré's personal style.

[18] Busser, *De Pelléas*, 33.
[19] Albert Lavignac, *Collection complète des leçons d'harmonie*, 3 Vols. (Paris: Lemoine, 1899).
[20] Comment in a public lecture, retold by the pianist Paul Lyddon.

Example 3.3 Planning counterpoint and harmony for a Fauré melody: a. The subject of Fauré's *basse donnée*, in Lavignac, *Collection complète*, Vol. 3, 50; b. The subject treated as a circle of fifths; c. The subject treated as "down a third, up a step"; d. Fauré's countermelody; e. Fauré's three-voice realization

Example 3.3a presents the opening phrase of Fauré's *basse donnée* from the Lavignac collection. It is shown an octave higher than written and in treble clef to avoid ledger lines.[21] The overall key will turn out to be E minor, so the opening bass begins on the dominant tone B, ascends to the sixth degree C, and then slowly descends the E-minor hexachord C–B–A–G–F♯–E. This is a standard, even archaic, structure for a fugal theme, and it suggests many possible settings. Example 3.3b shows how a hypothetical countermelody could descend with the subject, only a third higher. The stars under notes in the bass indicate a circle of fifths (C–F♯–B–E–A). In the first complete measure, the E in the countersubject begins as a consonant third over the bass C, but this E becomes a dissonant seventh over the starred F♯ and will thus resolve downward to the D in the following measure. Example 3.3c shows another possible interpretation of the bass. As the starred notes indicate, the bass could be seen as a "down a third, up a step" *marche* (C–A–B–G–A–F♯–G), with the "down a third" notes delayed until the last quarter note of the measure. This reading of the

---

[21] Lavignac, *Collection complète*, Vol. 3, Realizations, 89–90.

bass suggests a different countermelody, where the upper voice alternates thirds and sixths with the bass. Example 3.3d can be heard as Fauré's reconciliation of Examples 3.3b and c. In its first full measure, his counter-melody holds the initial E long enough to create the dissonant seventh (the circle-of-fifths interpretation) but then leaps "up a step" before falling "down a third" (the interpretation of alternating thirds and sixths). Again, a simple two-voice framework can lead to unexpected harmonies. For instance, ordinarily, in the minor mode, one descends through the lowered versions of the sixth and seventh scale degrees (D♮, C♮). Fauré's counter-melody, by contrast, uses D♯ and C♯ descending. Moreover, the downbeat thirds of the first three full measures are all major thirds (C–E, B–D♯, A–C♯), and no single major or minor scale contains three adjacent descending major thirds (or four, counting the mid-measure G–B in the third full measure). So although his duo of bass and countermelody is completely diatonic, it forces subtle shifts in its perceived tonal orientation as it proceeds. It is not immediately obvious why Fauré chose these raised tones, though he may have felt that the lowered D and C led too strongly toward the key of G major.

In Example 3.3e, a third voice is added above the prior duo of Example 3.3d. Because the downbeat-to-downbeat structure of the duo involves descending parallel thirds, a standard third voice can be added a sixth above the bass. And if that third voice is delayed across bar lines, it can form a series of 7–6 suspensions above the bass. For example, the initial high A in the first complete measure is a consonant sixth above the bass's downbeat C. But at the beginning of the following measure it becomes a dissonant seventh above the bass's B. Note Fauré's elegant touch of using an ornamental resolution that mimics the "down a third, up a step" contours of the other voices. That is, instead of the high A merely descending a step to G, it descends a third to F♯ before rising a step to G. The complete three-voice combination results in counterpoint of great sophistication even though it is built upon the foundation of nineteenth-century fauxbourdon (improvised counterpoint in parallel 6/3 chords) taught to and performed by choirboys in the *maîtrises*.

Example 3.4 reproduces Fauré's complete realization of his *basse donnée*. The original was in open score with four voices in bass, tenor, alto, and soprano clefs. For ease of reading, those voices have been condensed onto a single grand staff in the example. The letters A, B, and C at the beginning are original and indicate the three contrapuntal components discussed above in relation to Example 3.2. Such letters figured prominently in sample realizations and may have been used by students in examinations.

Example 3.4 Fa015é's four-voice realization of his *basse donnée*, in Lavignac, *Collection complète*, Vol. 3, 112–113 (*c.* 1899)

When used in open score, they were followed by brackets that showed the temporal extent of a melodic subject or a fragment of a subject. Although not shown here for ease of readability, almost every measure of this *basse donnée* was marked by one or more letters and brackets. Lavignac's volumes are full of these letters, though interestingly none of the other masters who contributed to the third volume used them. Fauré's *basse donnée* was the most openly contrapuntal. Numbers over bar lines have been added to facilitate references to individual measures or particular passages, and the large letters S (subject), A (answer), P-I (tonic pedal point), and P-V (dominant pedal point) have been inserted to identify salient points in the plan of this informal fugue.

In the context of an E-minor fugue, the bass introduces the subject (S), which as mentioned above descends through the tonic hexachord after first intoning the dominant note B. As the subject finishes in measure 4, the answer (A) begins in the soprano. In standard practice, it first intones the tonic note E before descending through the hexachord of B minor. The *mutation* or change from the subject's initial half-step (B–C) to the answer's minor third (E–G) is normal for this class of tonal answers. Remarkably, Fauré changes the tonal profile of the first countersubject ("B") so that it descends like a normal melodic-minor scale, B–A–G, not the B–A♯–G♯ required if he had followed his practice with voice "B" of measures 1–3. Either version of this countersubject is contrapuntally acceptable with the answer, so this could either be an instance of oversight or an expression of a subtle preference for the more normal path in the four-voice, B-minor context. It does suggest that those seeking systematic explanations for Fauré's compositional choices may find many things to disappoint them.

Between the truncated end of the answer (m. 7) and the dominant pedal point (P-V, m. 11), Fauré returns to the key of E minor before initiating a lovely diatonic circle-of-fifths episode using chords with sevenths and ninths. Although it may not be immediately evident from the score, the series of chordal roots implied for the six half-note values of measures 9–10 is B–E–A–D–G–C. The regularity of this schema helps Fauré set a small stretto based on the third through sixth tones of the subject, a stretto whose entries cascade downward from soprano to alto to tenor to bass. Compared to the circle of fifths in Niedermeyer's "Communion" (see Example 3.1, m. 2), this circle of Fauré's is a small masterpiece of understatement and finesse.

The last pair of bass notes in measure 10 (B–C) cues a cadence in G major. B is the third scale degree, and from the Rule of the Octave, which was known to every musician in Paris, that degree takes a 3 and a 6 (the D and G above B). Fauré leaves out the G, which had just sounded in the bass. Then the bass B ascends stepwise to C, where D and B are held over from the previous chord to create a 9/7 double suspension in relation to the bass C and alto E. This pre-cadential gesture had been popular since the days of Mozart and Paisiello, but in its form with parallel sixths (here the soprano and alto, mm. 10–11) it was a Romantic favorite much loved by Schumann and Brahms. Where those composers would have had the bass continue rising to the dominant D to finish a cadence in G major, Fauré lets his texture sink down a third so that the same chord, now cueing an E-minor context, occurs on the second quarter note of measure 11. That bass, A, then rises to B to introduce a dominant pedal (P-V) in E minor.

At the end of measure 12, the subject returns in the opposite mode (major) with a tonic G. It is modified to connect with the preceding context (the subject in G major should begin D–E, not B–D) and reharmonized without the previous countersubjects to create a brighter, more cheerful tone. And at the moment when the subject would cadence in G major (the downbeat of m. 16), the answer enters in the bass to effect a modulation to C major. This begins the section typical of an advanced *basse donnée* where remote modulations were expected, and Fauré does not disappoint. Only with the augmented sixth chord (m. 22) leading to the second dominant pedal point (mm. 23–27) does the tonality stabilize as the three-voice contrapuntal combination of the opening measures returns, played over the pedal-point B.

The final entry of the subject (m. 27, bass) is likewise shorn of the full countersubjects and given a markedly darker tone. The repeated fragments of the subject that precede the concluding tonic pedal point (fragments in mm. 31–34, pedal point in mm. 35–38) shift back and forth between C-major contexts with F♮s and E-minor contexts with F♯s and optional D♯s. The situation here is not unlike that described by Fauré with reference to the "Air de danse" from his *Caligula* (*c.* 1888). Fauré wrote to his son Philippe, who was arranging *Caligula* for piano solo.[22] He described his "Air de danse" as combining G major and B minor, and wrote out a scale resembling G Lydian, that is, a G-major scale with C♯. The passage in question from Fauré's *basse donnée* (mm. 31–34) has a similar dual nature, but with G major and B minor replaced by C major and E minor.

[22] Jean-Michel Nectoux, *Gabriel Fauré: Correspondance, suivie de Lettres à Madame H.* (Paris: Fayard, 2015), 323–324.

Example 3.5 Fauré's four-voice realization of his *chant donné*, in Lavignac, *Collection complète*, Vol. 3, 114–115

Like the *basse donnée* just examined, Fauré's *chant donné* is a small masterpiece in his mature style (see Example 3.5). *Chants donnés* were considered more difficult than *basses données*, perhaps because training in *accompagnement* and *marches harmoniques* focused on basses and built multivoice sonorities from the bottom up. Whatever the reasons, it is generally true that for a given melody–bass pair used in the harmony contests, the given melody was harmonically simpler and in a more popular style. Fauré's melody is not fugal, as was his bass, and it is laid out in broader phrases. For the student harmonizer, however, the shifting of keys without the typical cues in the melody and the extended chromaticism in the middle section would likely pose great challenges.

As mentioned above, Fauré himself had described his "Air de danse" as having a mixed mode of major and minor keys a major third apart. In the "Air de danse," the pair was G major and B minor; in the closing section of the *basse donnée* (see Example 3.4) the pair was C major and E minor; and in the opening of the *chant donné* (see Example 3.5) the pair is A major and C♯ minor. This last pairing results in a number of D♯s, which do not, as they more normally would, signal a modulation to the dominant, E major. These D♯s figure prominently in the melody in measures 6–7, where a pedal point on C♯ gently anchors that key against the more modal upper voices.

Fauré's melodic opening, which a student would scrutinize for hints about its intended harmonization, begins similarly to his *basse donnée*. That is, it sounds the fifth scale degree (E) before rising to the sixth (F♯) and then falling sinuously through the other notes of the tonic hexachord (F♯–E–D–C♯–B–A). A common harmonization would set a cadence in A to conclude measure 2, followed by a move to an E-major chord at the end of measure 4 as a type of half cadence. Fauré, as could be predicted, was more subtle and indirect. Measure 1 begins with an A-major harmony, but the potential cadence in measure 2 rises to an F♯-minor chord at the beginning of measure 3 – a weak deceptive cadence. The subsequent chromatic descent of minor thirds between tenor and alto (F♯/D♯ in m. 3, F♮/D♮ in m. 4, E/C♯ in m. 5) does deflect toward E major, but only in an implied circle of fifths that returns to A major at the beginning of measure 5.

It is at the second half of measure 5 leading into measure 6 that we encounter one of Fauré's signature pairings of sonorities, one which I hope to demonstrate has a contrapuntal origin, or at least an origin deriving from his youthful experience with early music and its contrapuntally determined cadences. In Examples 3.6a and 3.6b, one sees the two versions of the same discant-tenor cadence used by Niedermeyer shown earlier (Example 3.1). This standard Renaissance cadence features a move from imperfection to perfection (using the old categories), meaning a major sixth expands to an octave by half-step and whole step, or a minor third

Example 3.6 Cadences old and new: a. Two-voice Phrygian cadence; b. Two-voice clausula vera; c. Cadence from Fauré's *basse donnée* (transposed), in Lavignac, *Collection complète*, Vol. 3, 50; d. Cadence from Fauré's *chant donné*, in Lavignac, *Collection complète*, Vol. 3, 51; e. *Marche harmonique* and cadence by Jean Gallon, in La Presle, *Soixante leçons*, 38; f. Reharmonization by La Presle and Colet of Gallon's passage, in La Presle, *Soixante leçons*, 40 (c. 1939); g. Reharmonization by La Presle and J. Gervais of Gallon's passage, in La Presle, *Soixante leçons*, 42; h. Cadence in "Modus Phrygius" by Kufferath (1876)

contracts to a unison by the same intervals. If the half-step move is at the bottom of the sixth, as in Example 6a, it is today called a Phrygian cadence. If the half-step move is at the top of the sixth, as in Example 3.6b, it is sometimes called a *clausula vera*.

Example 3.6c shows the cadence from Fauré's *basse donnée* found at the end of measure 34 leading to the beginning of measure 35 (transposed in

Example 3.6c to conform to Examples 3.6a and b). What is characteristic of many Renaissance cadences is that the octave or unison to which the imperfect interval expands or contracts is not necessarily the keynote. In the case of Example 3.6c, the cadence ends with a C♯-minor triad, though the F♯–D♯ major sixth expands, as a *clausula vera*, to an E octave (the lower E gets shifted to the soprano voice). Similarly, the cadence in Example 3.6d is found in Fauré's *chant donné*, from the second half of measure 5 to the beginning of measure 6. Compared with the cadence in Example 3.6c, the octave E of "resolution" clearly results from the expansion and contrary motion of the alto and soprano voices.

A Legacy

In the late 1930s, another harmony teacher at the Conservatory, Jacques de La Presle, began a project to illustrate alternative realizations of *basses et chants donnés*.[23] He was at that period a professor of "*harmonie (femmes),*" meaning the separate women's class in harmony. Two of his prize students worked with him to create alternative realizations of a passage from a *basse donnée* by Jean Gallon, a harmony teacher at the Conservatory from 1919 to 1949. The original by Gallon is given in Example 3.6e, and the alternate version of Example 3.6f is by La Presle and Colette Boyer, a first-prize winner in harmony in 1938. The version of Example 3.6g is by La Presle and Jacqueline Gervais, another top student from the late 1930s.

The passage selected is from measures 6–8 of Gallon's realization (transposed to match the cadences of Examples 3.6a–d). For a student sitting the harmony examination this excerpt would have two obvious parts. The first is the *marche harmonique* of descending fourths and ascending steps, sometimes associated with the basso ostinato known as *La romanesca* (or Pachelbel's *Canon in D*). The second pattern is a cadence. In Gallon's realization the Romanesca passage is decorated with various suspensions and passing tones that conceal the underlying 5/3 chord (*accord parfait*) above every note in the bass. So constraining is this schema that both of the young women who reset it made only slight changes. But at the cadence, the younger generation recast Gallon's more traditional cadence – the sixth D♯–B♯ expanding to the octave of the keynote C♯, with the leading tone or *note sensible* in the upper voice – into

---

[23] Jacques de La Presle, *Soixante leçons d'harmonie*, 2 Vols. (Paris: Leduc, 1945).

Example 3.7 Opening of an alternate realization by La Presle and F. Gervais of Fauré's *chant donné*, in La Presle, *Soixante leçons*, 16 (cf. Example 3.4)

the Fauré-style cadence where D♯ and F♯ contract to E♯, the third of the chord, and the *note sensible* B♯ is replaced by B♮. These are slight changes, to be sure, but their immediate aural association with Fauré shows what a long shadow he cast at the Conservatory in the years between the wars.

Example 3.6h shows a cadence in "Modus Phrygius" taken from the textbook on chorales by Ferdinand Kufferath,[24] professor of counterpoint at the conservatory in Brussels. According to Roger-Ducasse,[25] Fauré would on occasion direct students to study Kufferath's book, and we might therefore assume that its take on modality, only loosely aligned with Renaissance practice, was in some way congenial to Fauré. Kufferath's cadence (Example 3.6h). transposed to match the prior examples) contains two 6-to-8 cadences. The first, bass and tenor, expands the sixth G♯–E♯ to the octave F♯s. The second, also bass and tenor, has an F♯–D♯ sixth whose upper note rises to E♯, third of the chord, while the lower tone F♯ leaps to C♯. The result is not dissimilar to the Fauré-style cadences just discussed.

A thorough analysis of Fauré's efforts in *basses et chants donnés* (and of those inspired by him) would extend far beyond the confines of this chapter. The delicate balance that he achieved between independent vocal lines and composite sonorities warrants careful examination. To this end, a brief excerpt from an alternate harmonization by La Presle and Françoise Gervais of Fauré's *chant donné* may serve as an aid to further study (see Example 3.7).[26] The La Presle–Gervais realization differs in many

[24] For example, H. Ferdinand Kufferath, *École pratique du choral. Praktische Choral-Schule* (1876; reprinted in French in Brussels: Schott frères), 192.

[25] Jean-Michel Nectoux, *Gabriel Fauré: A Musical Life*, trans. Roger Nichols (Cambridge: Cambridge University Press, 2004), 264.

[26] Françoise Gervais, possibly the sister of Jacqueline who realized the Gallon bass of Example 3.6g, became an important figure at the Conservatory after the war. She won a Prix de Rome, wrote a dissertation titled "Étude comparée des langages harmoniques de Fauré et de Debussy" (Sorbonne, 1954), and became a professor at the Conservatory.

respects from Fauré's. The long A at the opening in the tenor, for instance, is a cliché of academic *chant donné* realizations. Yet even if this alternate realization takes different paths, they almost always lead through the same musical garden cultivated by the master. To understand the choices made and not made is to begin to appreciate what harmony meant to Fauré and his many admirers.

4 | Romancing the *mélodie*, or Generic Play in the Early Hugo Settings

STEPHEN RUMPH

Gabriel Fauré's long career as a song composer, which stretched from 1861 to 1921, divides conveniently in half. Until 1890, he wrote individual *mélodies*; thereafter, he composed all but a handful within six carefully integrated cycles. (The lone outlier is *Poème d'un jour*, a short cycle composed in 1878.) Fauré's turn to cyclic composition comes as little surprise as he had always tended to concentrate on individual poets. He confined himself to Victor Hugo in his early years, and then moved systematically through Charles Baudelaire and Théophile Gautier before immersing himself in the poets of the Parnassian school. With single-minded focus, he would set ten poems by Armand Silvestre (1878–84), seventeen by Paul Verlaine (1887–94), and eighteen by Charles van Lerberghe (1906–14). Far more than Debussy, Ravel, or Poulenc, Fauré conceived his song cycles as integrated works rather than mere sets. He reordered poems creatively and used thematic recollections, key schemes, and even leitmotives to unify the songs.

Fauré's earliest songs, written at the École Niedermeyer between 1861 and 1865, already give a taste of the cyclic impulse that would come to dominate his song composition. This premonition does not appear in musical devices like thematic recollection or tonal planning; these features would come and go across his seven song cycles. Nor can we locate it in a narrative, for three of those cycles lack any story line. The telltale element in Fauré's student songs is a common poetic vision, a reading that transcends the individual author and poems and engages deeper artistic concerns. As in his later song cycles, Fauré grasped poetry not merely as a source of evocative texts, but as a nexus of technical and aesthetic issues bearing on his historical moment. And the issue that unites his earliest songs is genre.

Fauré's student songs demonstrate his lifelong penchant for focusing on a single poet, indeed, a single collection. All six have texts by Victor Hugo, and five come from *Les chants du crépuscule* (1835). Fauré mined Hugo's volume for "Le papillon et la fleur," "Puisque j'ai mis ma lèvre," "Mai," "L'aube naît," and "S'il est un charmant gazon" (published as "Rêve d'amour"). "Puisque j'ai mis ma lèvre" remained unpublished and "L'aube naît" has vanished entirely, although it is mentioned alongside the other songs in a letter from 1864.[1] Fauré set yet another poem from *Les chants du crépuscule*, "L'aurore s'allume," toward the end of the decade.

In studying Fauré's adolescent songs, we immediately face the question of genre. No single category existed for French art song in the 1860s equivalent to the Austro-Germanic *Lied*. Since the late eighteenth century, the native *romance* had dominated song production in France. Elegant and unpretentious, the *romance* featured sentimental or characteristic texts set in strophic form with an unobtrusive piano accompaniment.[2] During the second quarter of the nineteenth century, a new genre emerged alongside the *romance*, the highbrow *mélodie*. Inspired by Schubert's *Lieder*, composers of *mélodies* gave the piano a more independent role, experimented with non-strophic forms, and enriched the expressive palette. Guided by Frits Noske's classic study *La mélodie française de Berlioz à Duparc* (1954), histories of French song have tended to trace an evolutionary narrative in which the *mélodie* inevitably usurps the place of the *romance* and reigns supreme after 1870.[3]

Fauré himself seems to ratify this narrative in a letter from 1870. The composer agrees to send an old schoolmate "the little *mélodie* that you asked for" (most likely "Lydia") as well as "a copy of my *romance* 'S'il est un charmant gazon.'"[4] The letter appears to cordon off Fauré's student songs from later and more ambitious compositions like "Lydia" or his three Baudelaire settings. And indeed, his adolescent Hugo songs are lightweight by comparison with their pastoral texts, simple accompaniments, and

[1] Paul Meurice wrote to the poet concerning the copyright of the song texts: "A young man, a pupil of Niedermeyer's, M. Gabriel Fauré, has set some of your poetry to music; he is prepared to pay you for the rights to the poor things, but I know that several pieces have rights reserved, and I am sending you the titles of those he has chosen so that you can tell me whether they are reserved: *La fleur et le papillon* [sic], *Puisque mai tout en fleurs, S'il est un charmant gazon, Puisqu'ici bas toute âme, L'aube naît, Puisque j'ai mis ma lèvre.*" Paul Meurice to Victor Hugo, May 1864, in *Correspondance entre Victor Hugo et Paul Meurice*, ed. Eugène Fasquelle (Paris: Bibliothèque-Charpentier, 1909), 187. "Puisqu'ici bas toute âme" is a duet drawn from Hugo's *Les voix intérieures* (1837). All translations from French in this chapter are my own.

[2] See David Tunley, *Salons, Singers, and Songs: A Background to Romantic French Song, 1830–1870* (Aldershot, England; Burlington, VT: Ashgate, 2002), which complements his Garland anthologies of French Romantic song.

[3] Frits Noske, *La mélodie française de Berlioz à Duparc: Essai de critique historique* (Amsterdam: North-Holland Publishing Co., 1954); translated by Rita Benton as *French Song from Berlioz to Duparc: The Origin and Development of the Mélodie* (New York: Dover Publications, 1970).

[4] "Je t'enverrai la Gavotte un de ces jours avec la petite mélodie que tu me demandes. J'y joindrai un exemplaire de ma romance *S'il est un charmant gazon* qui va paraître bientôt." Fauré to Julien Koszul, June 1870, in Gabriel Fauré, *Correspondance suivie de Lettres à Madame H.*, ed. Jean-Michel Nectoux (Paris: Fayard, 2015), 29.

strophic form. Fauré's critics have found it easy to follow his lead and retrace the history of French song across his early career. Charles Kœchlin brushed past the Hugo settings, dismissing one as a "slight *romance*," and rejoiced at Fauré's emancipation from strophic form.[5] Jean-Michel Nectoux entitled his fine chapter on the early songs "From the *romance* to the *mélodie*," while Roy Howat and Emily Kilpatrick hailed Fauré's "transition from the *romance* to the *mélodie*" during the 1860s.[6]

Like all evolutionary narratives, however, this account of Fauré's early songwriting downplays the role of the historical agent. It ignores the way in which the composer himself understood and navigated the genres available to him. The evolution of French song into the *mélodie* was by no means preordained in the early 1860s. Composers continued to label songs both *romance* and *mélodie* until the end of the decade, titles that reflected real differences in form and style.[7] Nor did Fauré lack for Germanic models of song composition during his student years. His tutor Camille Saint-Saëns was a champion of Liszt, Schumann, and Mendelssohn, while his teacher and headmaster Louis Niedermeyer had virtually founded the *mélodie* genre with his 1820 song "Le lac." Niedermeyer cast Alphonse de Lamartine's elegiac poem in the form of an operatic *scène* in which three stanzas of obbligato recitative introduce the lyric set piece, three strophes entitled "Romance." As Saint-Saëns attested, Niedermeyer "broke the mold of the tired old French *romance* and, inspired by the beautiful poems of Lamartine and Victor Hugo, created a new genre, a superior art analogous to the German *Lied*."[8]

Fauré's setting of Hugo's "Tristesse d'Olympio" (*Les rayons et les ombres*), written around 1865, demonstrates how easily he could adopt this elevated style. His song emulates Niedermeyer's "Le lac" just as Hugo's poem emulates Lamartine's elegy. A recitative-like *Grave* built over an operatic *lamento* bass leads into two stormy strophes with a notably free phrase structure. This serious *mélodie*, written just a year or two after "S'il est un charmant gazon," muddies the image of a linear evolution from *romance* to *mélodie*. Indeed, Fauré circled back to his lighter manner in his

[5] Charles Kœchlin, *Gabriel Fauré (1845–1924)*, trans. Leslie Orrey (London: Dennis Dobson Limited, 1946), 18.

[6] Jean-Michel Nectoux, *Gabriel Fauré: A Musical Life*, trans. Roger Nichols (Cambridge: Cambridge University Press, 1991), 64–78; Roy Howat and Emily Kilpatrick, "Editorial Challenges in the Early Songs of Gabriel Fauré," *Notes* 68, No. 2 (2011), 246.

[7] See Kitti Messina, "Mélodie et romance au milieu du XIXe siècle: Points communs et divergences," *Revue de musicologie* 94, No. 1 (2008), 59–90.

[8] Introduction to Louis Alfred Niedermeyer, *Vie d'un compositeur moderne (1802–1861)* (Paris: Fischenbacher, 1893), vii–viii.

next Hugo settings, "Dans les ruines d'une abbaye" and "L'aurore" – as one would expect from their lighter pastoral texts.

Yet Fauré perhaps learned a deeper lesson about genre from "Le lac." In Niedermeyer's song the young composer found a strophic *romance*, labeled as such, embedded within a *mélodie* of Teutonic scope and gravitas. Niedermeyer's song does not renounce the *romance* but deploys it artfully within the larger form of the operatic *scène*. Dramaturgically, the *romance* becomes a site of memory, the timeless lyric moment in which the bereaved poet finds consolation. Fauré's "Tristesse d'Olympio" frames the *romance* even more clearly as a retrospective utterance. The introductory *Grave* recounts the poet's return to the site of his lost love, ending as the poet begins his lament:

Il se sentit le coeur triste comme une tombe,
Alors il s'écria:

His heart felt as sad as a tomb,
So he cried out:

The following strophes render the poet's elegy, enclosed within quotation marks. The strophic *romance* again provides a locus of memory and nostalgia, a role that reflects its historical position as a conservative, backward-looking genre.

The evolutionary view of Fauré's early songwriting, then, is not merely dubious history. It also leads to an impoverished reading of his early songs. As "Tristesse d'Olympio" demonstrates, Fauré did not abandon the *romance* in favor of the *mélodie* but combined both in a sophisticated dialogue. And it was Hugo's poetry that inspired this play between genres. To read Fauré's songs in this manner requires that we view genres as more than taxonomic categories. Musical genres function instead as codes shared by composers, performers, and listeners, which activate expectations and shape the reception of individual works. Indeed, a composer can evoke multiple genres within the same work to produce a complex, resonant utterance.[9] This essay explores the dialogue of genres within Fauré's surviving songs from *Les chants du crépuscule*, showing how he manipulated the generic codes of the *romance* and *mélodie* in response to Hugo's poetry. As we shall see, the student songs not only demonstrate an urbane grasp of poetic art but also show clear signs of the synthetic

---

[9] For examples of this dialogic approach to genre, see Jeffrey Kallberg, "The Rhetoric of Genre: Chopin's Nocturne in G Minor," *19th-century Music* 11, No. 3 (1988), 238–261; and James Hepokoski, "Genre and Content in Mid-century Verdi: 'Addio del passato,' *La traviata*, Act III," *Cambridge Opera Journal* 1, No. 3 (1989), 249–276.

imagination expressed so magnificently in *Poème d'un jour*, *La bonne chanson*, *La chanson d'Ève*, or *L'horizon chimérique*.

An Anacreontic Cycle

In *Les chants du crépuscule*, as in the preceding *Feuilles d'automne*, Hugo grappled with the new energies unleashed by the July Revolution of 1830. His title plays on the twin meanings of *crépuscule*, both dawn and dusk, to express the uncertainty of the times. As he mused in the preface, "Society waits to see if what lies on the horizon will be fully illuminated or whether it will be absolutely extinguished."[10] The cluster of texts set by Fauré begins midway through the thirty-nine poems of Hugo's collection (see Table 4.1). An envoi to the *Feuilles d'automne* (No. 18) closes the first half, which consists of political odes and meditations. "L'aurore s'allume" (No. 20) heralds a new dawn, lit not by human events but by the eternal truths of nature:

Livre salutaire
Où le coeur s'emplit!
Où tout sage austère
Travaille et pâlit!
Dont le sens rebelle
Parfois se révèle!
Pythagore épèle
Et Moïse lit!

Salutary book
Where the heart is replenished!
Where every austere sage
Labors and grows pale!
Whose recalcitrant meaning
Sometimes reveals itself!
Pythagoras deciphers
And Moses reads!

The short five-syllable lines signal a shift toward the lighter *chanson* genre. The succeeding poems, from which Fauré drew his early song texts, abandon politics for pastoral verse and meditations inspired by nature. Fauré set Nos. 22, 23, 25, 27, and 31, and later, "L'aurore s'allume" itself.

---

[10] Victor Hugo, *Œuvres poétiques de Victor Hugo, Vol. 1. Avant l'exil, 1802–1851*, ed. Pierre Albouy (Paris: Éditions Gallimard, 1964), 812.

Table 4.1 Contents of Victor Hugo, *Les chants du crépuscule* (1835), with dates of Fauré's settings

---

Préface

Prélude

I. Dicté après juillet 1830

II. À la colonne

III. Hymne

IV. Noces et festins

V. Napoléon II

VI. Sur le bal de l'Hotel-de-Ville

VII. *O Dieu! Si vous avez la France sous vos ailes*

VIII. À Canaris

IX. *Seule au pied de la tour d'où sort la voix du maître*

X. À l'homme qui a livré une femme

XI. A M. le D. d'O.

XII. À Canaris

XIII. *Il n'avait pas vingt ans. Il avait abusé*

XIV. *Oh! N'insultez jamais une femme qui tombe!*

XV. Conseil

XVI. *Le grand homme vaincu peut perdre en un instant*

XVII. À Alphonse Rabbe

XVIII. Envoi des *Feuilles d'automne* à Madame ***

XIX. *Anacréon, poète aux ondes érotiques*

XX. **L'aurore s'allume (c. 1868–70)**

XXI. *Hier, la nuit d'été, qui nous prêtrait ses voiles*

XXII. **Nouveau chanson sur un vieil air (1864)**

XXIII. **Autre chanson (c. 1862–4)**

XXIV. *Oh! pour remplir de moi ta rêveuse pensée*

XXV. **Puisque j'ai mis ma lèvre à ta coupe encore pleine (1862)**

XXVI. À mademoiselle J.

XXVII. **La pauvre fleur disait au papillon céleste (c. 1861–2)**

XXVIII. Au bord de la mer

XXIX. *Puisque nos heures sont remplies*

XXX. Espoir en Dieu

XXXI. **Puisque mai tout en fleurs dans les prés nous réclame (c. 1862–4)**

XXXII. À Louis B.

XXXIII. Dans l'église de ***

XXXIV. Écrit sur la première page d'un Pétrarque

XXXV. *Les autres en tous sens laissent aller leur vie*

XXXVI. *Toi! sois bénie à jamais!*

XXXVII. À mademoiselle Louise B.

XXXVIII. Que nous avons le doute en nous

XXXIX. Date lilia

Between the two halves of the volume, preceding "L'aurore s'allume," comes a short ode to Anacreon, the Ionian poet of wine, love, and song (No. 19):

Anacréon, poète aux ondes érotiques
Qui filtres du sommet des sagesses antiques,
Et qu'on trouve à mi-côte alors qu'on y gravit,
Clair, à l'ombre, épandu sur l'herbe qui revit,
Tu me plais, doux poète au flot calme et limpide!
Quand le sentier qui monte aux cimes est rapide,
Bien souvent, fatigués du soleil, nous aimons
Boire au petit ruisseau tamisé par les monts!

Anacreon, poet of the erotic waters,
You who filter ancient wisdom from the summit,
Which we find midway up the mountain as we climb,
Bright in the shade, diffused over the reviving grass,
You please me, sweet poet of the calm and limpid stream!
When the path that ascends to the heights is steep,
How often, weary from the sun, we love
To drink from the little brook filtered by the mountains!

Anacreon's modern reception had peaked during the eighteenth century. A handful of surviving odes (now known to be wrongly attributed) were translated and imitated and gained currency in France through Pierre de Ronsard's sixteenth-century versions. Most recently, Charles-Marie René Leconte de Lisle had translated nine Anacreontic odes in his *Poèmes antiques* (1852), the last of which Fauré would set in 1890 ("La rose"). The author and critic Léo Joubert reviewed Leconte de Lisle's translations in 1863, giving an intriguing description of the Anacreontic genre:

The gaze effortlessly embraces a bounded field that displays familiar and alluring objects; the hyacinth blooms there; the rose spreads its purple robe beside the green ivy; the swallow babbles from break of dawn; the dew-drunk cicada sings on the high branches; reclining on the fresh myrtle and green lotus, an old man with white temples but a youthful heart drains his cup and watches the young girls dance to the sound of the zither. This little landscape, invented for the express pleasure of the eyes, is so lively, so brilliant, that we never think to count the artificial flowers in the decorative garlands; the little scenes of this *mascarade galante* succeed one another too quickly to weary us.[11]

---

[11] Léo Joubert, *Essais de critique et d'histoire* (Paris: Firmin-Didot, 1863), 192.

Joubert's vignette summons all the Anacreontic commonplaces – idyllic nature, wine, revelry, erotic desire, old age. Yet it also evokes the pleasure parks of the *fêtes galantes*, the fantastic eighteenth-century landscapes of Antoine Watteau that were enjoying a vogue in French poetry.[12] Joubert fashioned his Arcadia as a theater, adorned with silk roses, where maskers play their stock roles. His essay celebrates the deliberate artifice of the Anacreontic genre, its play between surface convention and lyric depth.[13]

No poem in *Les chants du crépuscule* better demonstrates this equivocation than the lyric subtitled "S'il est un charmant gazon." The poem bears the title "Nouvelle chanson sur un vieil air" – roughly, new words to an old tune. Hugo wove pastoral imagery into an intimate romantic confession, using a complex rhyme scheme and tortuous syntax. Yet his artful poem is haunted by the specter of the lost air. The anonymous folk relic hides beneath the modern poet's verses, mutely reminding us that Hugo's jasmine, rose, and honeysuckle are but painted copies of nature. Liszt, Saint-Saëns, Massenet, Franck, and many other composers set "S'il est un charmant gazon," but as we shall see, only Fauré found the irony in Hugo's title.

The poems that Fauré chose from *Les chants du crépuscule* exemplify both the erotic tone of the Anacreontic genre and its delicate artifice. "La pauvre fleur disait au papillon céleste," in which a flower chides her unfaithful butterfly, is a sly allegory by the priapic Hugo with an envoi dedicated to his mistress Juliette Drouet. Notably, Fauré chose the only two *chansons* in Hugo's collection, songs in which lyric expression is distanced as performance. "Autre chanson" (subtitled "L'aube naît") even originated as a stage song in Hugo's play *Angelo, tyran de Padoue*. While we can only guess at Fauré's treatment of "L'aube naît," the autograph score of "S'il est un charmant gazon" imitates a serenader's mandolin with an accompaniment in broken *staccato* chords. Fauré used a similar piano figuration in "Puisque j'ai mis ma lèvre," despite the poem's more elevated register (he was perhaps tempted by Hugo's racy opening line, "Since I placed my lips to your still brimming cup"). Fauré left a motivic signature on these *chanson* accompaniments. The piano ritornellos of "Puisque j'ai mis ma lèvre" and "S'il est un charmant gazon" trail off with the same descending

---

[12] Watteau's canvases had inspired poems by Hugo, Gautier, Banville, and Baudelaire, as well as Charles Blanc's *Les peintres de fêtes galantes: Watteau, Lancret, Pater, Boucher* (Paris: Jules Renouard et cie, 1854) and Edmond and Jules de Goncourt's *L'art du dix-huitième siècle* (Paris: E. Dentu, 1859–75). They would also inspire Paul Verlaine's *Fêtes galantes* (1869), which Fauré discovered in 1887.

[13] See Marshall Brown, "Passion and Love: Anacreontic Song and The Roots of Romantic Lyric," *ELH* 66, No. 2 (1999), 373–404.

Example 4.1 Common pentatonic motive in Fauré's settings from Hugo, *Les chants du crepuscule*: a. "Puisque j'ai mis ma lèvre," m. 8; b. "Mai," m. 34; c. "S'il est un charmant gazon," m. 8. Based on the critical edition by Howat and Kilpatrick, *Gabriel Fauré, Complete Songs, Vol. 1: 1861–1882* (London: Peters Edition, 2015)

pentatonic figure, as does the ritornello in the autograph of "Mai" (see Example 4.1). This naïve coda, which follows passages of real harmonic complexity, sets an appropriately arch tone for poems presided over by the spirit of Anacreon.

"Anacréon aux ondes érotiques" advertises the titillating nature of the genre, but it offered Fauré another clue as well. The protagonist finds the refreshing waters "mi-côte," midway up the mountain. Similarly, Hugo's ode arrives midway through *Les chants du crépuscule* as a respite from his odes to the Greek patriot Canaris or his diatribe against the Chambre des députés. The Anacreontic ode, or *odelette* as poets from Ronsard to Gautier called it, occupies a middle register between the sublime ode and the lower forms of satire and comedy. In short, an educated reader would not have mistaken the turn to pastoral love poetry in the second half of *Les chants du crépuscule* as a stylistic regression, but would have understood it as a self-conscious modulation between genres.

Neither should the simplicity of Fauré's adolescent songs imply a lack of maturity, technique, or ambition. Read within the context of Hugo's collection, their unpretentious charm suggests a deliberate artistic choice. Fauré's student songs are not lacking in sophistication, but they mask it behind a faux-naïf manner that matches Hugo's artful simplicity. What distinguishes these songs from truly naïve *romances* is the keen awareness of Hugo's poetic craft: in apparently systematic fashion, Fauré concentrated on a different aspect of the poet's art in each song, whether prosody, syntax, rhetoric, or genre. This astute reading should come as no surprise in a pupil of Niedermeyer's school who studied literature as part of the curriculum and won prizes in 1858 and 1862.[14] The following discussion, based on the autograph scores, looks closely at Fauré's craftsmanship in his student songs. As we shall see, the young composer was not simply tossing off individual songs but was already exploring a single idea from different angles, generating a set of songs unified neither by musical features nor by a story line, but by a common poetic ideal.

Do Fauré's settings from *Les chants du crépuscule*, then, constitute a hidden cycle? To answer this question, we must recapture the horizon against which he was writing in the early 1860s. French composers had as yet no native models equivalent to Beethoven's *An die ferne Geliebte*, Schubert's *Die schöne Müllerin*, or Schumann's *Frauenliebe und -leben*. Not until 1866 did Jules Massenet compose *Poème d'avril*, the first French song cycle with a unified narrative and thematic recollections. Fauré could only look back to Hector Berlioz's *Les nuits d'été* (1841) and Félicien David's *Les perles d'Orient* (1846).[15] Apart from its evocative title, Berlioz's work coheres solely through its poetic source, Gautier's *La comédie de la mort*, while David's songs have four different poets and share only an exotic theme. By these standards, Fauré's five songs would indeed qualify as a cycle had he published them together. The common piano motive certainly argues for a unified conception. The autograph of "Mai"

---

[14] See Nectoux, *Gabriel Fauré*, 7–9.
[15] For a complete list of French song cycles from 1841 to 1962, see Ulrich Linke, *Der französische Liederzyklus von 1866 bis 1914: Entwicklungen und Strukturen* (Stuttgart: Franz Steiner Verlag, 2010), 293–298.

provides another possible clue: Fauré entitled the folio "No. 4/Mai!/à Madame H. Garnier," suggesting that he originally ordered the five songs from *Les chants du crépuscule* as a set ("Mai" was indeed the fourth song composed). Unfortunately, the composer's intentions must remain uncertain, especially without the autograph of "L'aube naît."

Prosody and Rhythm

Fauré's first song, "Le papillon et la fleur," does not at first appear to reach very high. The breezy tone, unremarkable harmonies, and waltz accompaniment might tempt us to dismiss the song as a Second Empire bonbon. Yet a closer look reveals a surprising level of craftsmanship. Fauré paid special attention to Hugo's prosody as he addressed the knotty relationship between French verse and musical meter. Unlike musical meter, French prosody is not governed by accentual pattern but solely by syllable count. The second page of Louis Quicherat's popular *Petit traité de versification française* (second edition, 1850) instructs the student that "since French poetic lines have a fixed number of syllables, one must learn, above all, to count the syllables of the constituent words, or of those that one wishes to include."[16] Hugo's quatrains alternate lines of twelve and three syllables (this does not include the final mute *e*'s, which are not counted although composers set them):

```
1    2    3    4        6   7  8  9   10  11  12
La pau-vre fleur di-sait au pa- pi- llon cé-lest(e):
                    1    2    3
              —Ne fuis pas!
1     2    3   4   5   6     7   8  9   10   11   12
Vois com- me nos des-tins    sont dif- fé-rents. Je rest(e),
                    1    2    3
              Tu t'en vas!
```

---

[16] Louis Marie Quicherat, *Traité de versification française*, second edition (Paris: Hachette, 1850), 2.

Fauré had a striking predilection for such heterometric stanzas in his early songs, including "L'aube naît" (8 + 4 syllables), "S'il est un charmant gazon" (7 + 5), "Tristesse d'Olympio" (12 + 6), "Dans les ruines d'une abbaye" (7 + 3), and "Seule!" (8 + 4).[17] In practice, these early heterometric settings fall rather flat. Fauré struggled with the short lines, which tend to sound padded and inert. Not until "Au bord de l'eau" (1875) and "Nell" (1878) are the uneven lines convincingly integrated within the phrase structure. Nevertheless, Fauré made an imaginative stab at the problem in "Le papillon et la fleur."

The waltz topic helped Fauré negotiate this prosodic challenge. The song imitates not only the typical accompaniment of the waltz, but also one of its most distinctive melodic features, an offbeat dotted rhythm introduced in measure 11 that permeates the vocal line (see Example 4.2). The lilting figure pervades nineteenth-century waltzes and provided the signature rhythm for Ravel's *La valse*. Waltzes evoke glittering entertainment, care-free pleasure, Second Empire frivolity, all connotations that suit the flighty butterfly. Yet the waltz topic also helped Fauré to integrate the twelve- and three-syllable lines. Fauré fitted each pair of unequal lines into a four-measure musical phrase but subdivided the phrases asymmetrically (2½ + 1½ measures), thereby reducing the need to pad the short lines. The waltz topic, with its lilting rhythm, provides the glue to connect the unequal lines: in each strophe, the long lines end with the offbeat rhythm, which the short lines immediately echo (see mm. 12–14 or 20–21). The syncopated figure thus unites Hugo's unequal lines in the infectious, gyrating rhythm of the waltz.

Fauré has suffered much criticism for his apparent mangling of word accent in the early songs.[18] In "Le papillon et la fleur," for example, the first phrase places the weak second syllables of "pauvre" and "papillon" on strong beats, resulting in "pau-*vre*" and "pa-*pi*-llon." Such critiques, how-ever, assume an equivalence of musical and poetic meter that is antithetical to French prosody. In fact, Fauré seems deliberately to have separated musical and poetic accent in "Le papillon et la fleur." Each phrase starts on the second eighth note of the measure, ensuring that the first syllable is not stressed. The first two phrases begin with an almost chant-like inton-ation and, and aside from the dotted waltz rhythm, the entire vocal melody consists of a stream of equal eighth notes. Each phrase of "Le papillon et la

[17] See Noske, *French Song from Berlioz to Duparc*, 257–259.
[18] See, for instance, Mimi Daitz, "Les manuscrits et les premières éditions des mélodies de Fauré: étude préliminaire," *Études fauréennes* 20, No. 21 (1983–4), 19–28.

Example 4.2 Fauré, "Le papillon et la fleur," mm. 1–25 (autograph version)

fleur" begins *in medias res* and flows smoothly toward the final accented syllable. Fauré's first crack at French prosody shows an almost exaggerated concern for its distinctively syllabic, non-accentual structure.

Indeed, musical and poetic accents line up only twice in Hugo's verses, at the end of each line and at the caesura of each twelve-syllable alexandrine. In the first two phrases of each strophe, Fauré marked the caesura

Example 4.2 (*cont.*)

with an upward leap on the sixth syllable, while in the third and fourth phrases he subdivided the line with a descending sequence. His opening phrase is perfectly tailored to Hugo's prosody: the monotone melody leaps a minor third on the sixth syllable, "di-*sait*," then descends to linger over an accented passing tone on the twelfth syllable, "cé-*leste*." The musical phrase hugs the arching contour of Hugo's alexandrine as it rises to the caesura and falls to the final syllable.[19]

Moreover, Fauré respected the subdivisions within each hemistich. The alexandrine offers a rich variety of internal divisions.[20] In Hugo's first line, for examples, both hemistichs subdivide into 4 + 2 syllables:

1   2   3   4   1   2 ‖ 1   2   3   4   1   2

Le pau-vre *fleur* | di-*sait*   au pa-pi-*llon* | cé-*lest(e)*

Fauré's melody fastidiously marks these subdivisions dipping a half-step on "fleur" and elongating the third syllable of "pap-i-*llon*." If we disregard the metrical accents and attend only to the rhythm and contour of Fauré's melody, we find that he has indeed set the word "papillon" in perfect accordance with the prosody. Howat and Kilpatrick have noted that the vocal line of "Le papillon et la fleur" falls into an implicit 3/4 meter (on the alexandrines), and the reason for the hemiola lies in Hugo's first line.[21] Unfortunately, the shortcomings of Fauré text-setting emerge during the succeeding strophes where he automatically repeats the rhythm of the first line even where it conflicts with the prosody. (Following the conventions of the *romance*, Fauré's autograph provides only the vocal line of the second and third stanzas, duplicating the rhythm of the first stanza.) The second strophe, for example, begins with a 3 + 3 + 3 + 3 line better suited to 6/8 meter:

2   3 | 1   2   3 ‖ 1   2   3 | 1   2   3

Mais hé-*las*, l'air t'em-*porte*   et la *ter*-re m'en *chain(e)*

The third strophe, on the other hand, scans as 2 + 4 + 4 + 2:

[19] David Hunter has discussed the characteristic arch shape of the alexandrine in *Understanding French Verse: A Guide for Singers* (New York: Oxford University Press, 2005), 30–31.
[20] See Clive Scott, *French Verse-Art: A Study* (Cambridge: Cambridge University Press, 1980), 29–60.
[21] Howat and Kilpatrick, "Editorial Challenges in the Early Songs," 265.

```
1    2  | 1    2   3    4   || 1    2   3    4 | 1    2
```
Tu *fuis,*   puis tu re- *viens,*   puis tu t'en *vas*   en- *cor(e)*

In his early songs, alas, Fauré's attention to prosody often ends with the first line.[22]

Did Fauré really attend so closely to Hugo's verse structure? Are we perhaps imputing too much to the adolescent composer? The piano ritornello provides the answer. The first four measures consist of a little dialogue in the right hand, with soaring scales for the flighty butterfly and short chromatic responses for the dejected flower. The sequential melody that follows in measures 5–8 is an ornamented version of the singer's third phrase; given the primacy of the vocal line in the *romance*, we may assume that Fauré composed the strophes first and then derived the ritornello from the third phrase. The "butterfly" scales in measures 1–4 derive in turn from the sequence in measures 5–8, beginning on the second beat and inverting exactly the first four notes of the descending scale. We may conclude, then, that Fauré composed the opening dialogue last of all, as an afterthought. Now, there are twelve notes in the "butterfly" scale and three notes in the chromatic "flower" response in measures 1–2. The same pair of twelve- and three-note motives repeats up an octave in measures 3–4. Taken together, the note count of the piano melody in measures 1–4 comes to 12 + 3 + 12 + 3 – the precise syllable count of Hugo's stanzas! With this erudite wink, the novice composer reveals that he is already an astute reader of French prosody.

Syntax and Harmony

Fauré confronted a different poetic technique in "Puisque j'ai mis ma lèvre." The most noticeable feature of Hugo's poem is the insistent repetition of "puisque" ("since") in the first twelve lines. This litany results in a striking instance of hypotaxis, or nesting of subordinate clauses within a sentence. In parataxis, the opposite syntactic principle, clauses are strung together additively as in "I came, I saw, I conquered." A hypotactic version of Caesar's sentence might read, "After I came, because I saw,

---

[22] For an alternative reading of musical and prosodic interplay in "La fleur et le papillon," see Roy Howat's essay in this volume, pp. 172–174.

I conquered." The first two clauses no longer stand alone but must await completion by the main clause. Hugo exploited hypotaxis artfully in "Puisque j'ai mis ma lèvre" to project the poem's meaning. While Fauré's setting does not fully align with Hugo's rhetorical design, it shows a keen awareness of his syntactic structure.

The five stanzas of "Puisque j'ai mis ma lèvre" divide into two groups based on syntax. The first three stanzas belong to a single complex sentence and consist of nine subordinate clauses:

> Puisque j'ai mis ma lèvre à ta coupe encor pleine;
> Puisque j'ai dans tes mains posé mon front pâli;
> Puisque j'ai respiré parfois la douce haleine
> De ton âme, parfum dans l'ombre enseveli;
>
> Puisqu'il me fut donné de t'entendre me dire
> Les mots où se répand le coeur mystérieux;
> Puisque j'ai vu pleurer, puisque j'ai vu sourire
> Ta bouche sur ma bouche et tes yeux sur mes yeux;
>
> Puisque j'ai vu briller sur ma tête ravie
> Un rayon de ton astre, hélas! voilé toujours;
> Puisque j'ai vu tomber dans l'onde de ma vie
> Une feuille de rose arrachée à tes jours;

> Since I placed my lips to your still brimming cup;
> Since I rested my pale brow on your hands;
> Since at times I breathed the sweet breath
> Of your soul, perfume hidden in the shade;
>
> Since I was blessed to hear you speak
> Words that spill over from a mysterious heart;
> Since I beheld tears, since I beheld smiles,
> Your mouth on my mouth, and your eyes on my eyes;
>
> Since I beheld, shining on my joyful head,
> A ray of your star, alas! always veiled;
> Since I beheld falling into the stream of my life
> A rose leaf torn from your days;

The accumulation of dependent clauses strains the limits of the sentence, whetting the desire for closure.

The fourth stanza discharges this pent-up energy in a flurry of exclamatory sentences:

Je puis maintenant dire aux rapides années:
—Passez! passez toujours! je n'ai plus à vieillir!
Allez-vous en avec vos fleurs toutes fanées;
J'ai dans l'âme une fleur que nul ne peut cueillir!

I can now say to the rushing years:
—Pass on! pass on forever! I shall age no longer!
Go forth with your withered flowers;
I have a flower in my soul that none may pluck!

The long-awaited main clause introduces two imperatives – "Passez!" and "Allez-vous en!" – that call the syntax to order like twin trumpet blasts. (Note how Hugo has marked the turn by inverting "Puis-que" to "Je puis.") The fourth stanza consists almost entirely of simple sentences, with only one subordinate clause. The fifth stanza, finally, concludes with a pair of sentences in which the subordinate clause follows the main clause. The poem thus ends by reversing the syntactic order of the sprawling opening sentence:

Votre aile en le heurtant ne fera rien répandre
Du vase où je m'abreuve et que j'ai bien rempli.
Mon âme a plus de feu que vous n'avez de cendre!
Mon coeur a plus d'amour que vous n'avez d'oubli!

The blow of your wings shall not dislodge it
From the vase where I drink and which I have filled up.
My soul has more fire than you have ashes!
My heart has more love than you have oblivion!

Hugo's syntax complements the theme of the poem, the victory of love over time and mortality. The first three stanzas dwell on the beloved, lingering over her hands, her breath, her eyes, her mouth. The massive prolongation of the sentence immerses the reader in the lover's experience of time, his sense of desire and unsatisfied longing. In the fourth stanza, the lover asserts his triumph over time as he issues commands to the passing years. Having tasted of the beloved, he no longer fears decay and oblivion, and the stabilized syntax reflects his newfound peace. The last lines of the poem, finally, encapsulate the entire progression of thought, reversing the structure of the opening sentence. Each antithesis begins with a main clause exalting immortal love and ends with a subordinate clause mocking Father Time.

Fauré's setting shows little concern with the overall form of Hugo's poem. The composer chose a *da capo* form that obscures the crucial turn between the third and fourth stanzas:

Section:	A	B	A′
Stanzas:	1–2	3–4	5
Key:	C major	A minor	C major

The modulation to A minor does not correspond to any break in Hugo's text and the turn to the fourth stanza is buried within the B section, marked only by a brief feint toward F major. The *da capo* form also imposes a symmetry at odds with Hugo's dynamic trajectory. Fauré's setting of "Puisque j'ai mis ma lèvre" makes a shapely lyric piece but largely misses the point of Hugo's poem.

Nevertheless, at the local level, "Puisque j'ai mis ma lèvre" shows a keen awareness of Hugo's syntax. Fauré's vocal melody is an exercise in unfulfilled yearning worthy of Wagner (see Example 4.3). The phrases rise insistently, crest on aching dissonances, then sink back to the starting point. The singer's first eight measures push insistently against the upper tonic and third, but fall back each time to the dominant. The following eight measures break through this ceiling with a leap to high A, but the melody again descends to the dominant, lingering deliciously over several dissonant passing tones. To enhance the upward surge of the melody, Fauré began each phrase of the song with an upbeat. This means that the vocalist sings "puis-*que*" eight times, an apparent gaffe that surpasses anything in "Le papillon et la fleur." As in the previous song, however, Fauré's concern lies with the larger shape of the line: by denying the natural trochaic rhythm ("*puis*-que"), he allowed the melody to flow restlessly toward its unattainable goals.

Fauré's phrase structure projects the same sense of deferred resolution. The first sixteen measures form a sentence, as Arnold Schoenberg and Erwin Ratz dubbed this thematic type: after a pair of identical four-measure phrases, an eight-measure continuation leads to a half cadence.[23] Unlike the period (ABAB'), with its balanced antecedent and consequent, the AAB sentence creates a sense of propulsion and dynamic movement. Indeed, Fauré's sentence perfectly matches Hugo's first stanza, which also begins with two parallel clauses (lines 1 and 2) and continues with an expanded clause (3–4). Moreover, the sentence belongs to a larger compound form, functioning as the antecedent of a thirty-two-measure period that does not reach a full cadence until almost halfway through the song. This massive deferral of harmonic closure creates a sense of postponed

[23] See William Caplin, *Classical Form: A Theory of Formal Functions for the Instrumental Music of Haydn, Mozart, and Beethoven* (New York: Oxford University Press, 1998), 35–48.

Example 4.3 Fauré, "Puisque j'ai mis ma lèvre," mm. 1–40

Example 4.3 (*cont.*)

Example 4.3 (*cont.*)

desire that perfectly matches Hugo's syntactic strategy, at least in his first
three stanzas.

As in "Le papillon et la fleur," Fauré left a clue to his reading in a short
piano prelude that again seems to gloss Hugo's poetic structure. The
eight-measure prelude is a duet in imitative counterpoint supported by
pizzicato chords in the left hand. The melody and harmony derive from
the continuation of the singer's melody (mm. 17–18), indicating that
Fauré again composed the vocal strophes first and wrote the prelude as an
afterthought. The harmony of the prelude is a model of hypotactic
construction. Instead of beginning on the tonic, it descends gradually
through the circle of fifths, beginning on vii, the most distant point. The
subtonic triad is also the most dissonant in the diatonic collection with its
diminished fifth. Until the final cadence, moreover, the prelude consists
entirely of seventh chords that heighten the harmonic instability. The
tonality itself remains in doubt through the first four measures, whose
oscillation between $b^{\o 7}$ and E^7 implies a resolution to A minor. Clarity
emerges gradually in measures 5–8, which complete the descent through

the cycle of fifths (a^7-d^7-G^7-C). Fauré's prelude thus creates a neat harmonic analogue to Hugo's hypotactic design. Like the poem, it begins from a point of instability and uncertainty, with the harmonic equivalent of subordinate clauses, and generates maximal tension before resolving. Once again, we perceive an urbane grasp of Hugo's art beneath the naïve veneer of the *romance*.

Rhetoric and Motive

Fauré responded alertly to another facet of Hugo's craft in "Mai": rhetorical expression. Of the five settings from *Les chants du crépuscule*, only "Mai" employs direct lyric address. "Le papillon et la fleur" is a monologue quoted by a narrator, "L'aube naît" and "S'il est un gazon charmant" are *chansons*, and the mandolin accompaniment also seems to frame "Puisque j'ai mis ma lèvre" as a performed song. "Mai" bears no trace of the *chanson* genre nor is it even prefaced by a piano ritornello. In Hugo's poem, Fauré found a paragon of lyric expression, a direct and exuberant invitation to the beloved. Indeed, the composer faced the challenge of containing Hugo's vigorous rhetoric within the genteel confines of the strophic *romance*.

The poem achieves its headlong effect through the rhetorical figure of *enumeratio*, piling noun upon noun, phrase upon phrase:

Puisque mai tout en fleurs dans les prés nous réclame,
Viens! ne te lasse pas de mêler à ton âme
La campagne, les bois, les ombrages charmants,
Les larges clairs de lune au bord des flots dormants,
Le sentier qui finit où le chemin commence,
Et l'air et le printemps et l'horizon immense,
L'horizon que ce monde attache humble et joyeux
Comme une lèvre au bas de la robe des cieux.
Viens! et que le regard des pudiques étoiles
Qui tombe sur la terre à travers tant de voiles,
Que l'arbre pénétré de parfum et de chants,
Que le souffle embrasé de midi dans les champs,
Et l'ombre et le soleil et l'onde et la verdure,
Et le rayonnement de toute la nature,
Fassent épanouir, comme une double fleur,
La beauté sur ton front et l'amour dans ton coeur!

Since May, full of flowers, calls us to the meadows,
Come! do not weary of mingling your soul

With the countryside, the woods, the pleasant shade,
The wide moonlight on the banks of the sleeping waters,
The path that ends where the road begins,
And the air, and the springtime, and the vast horizon,
The horizon that the world attaches, humbly and joyfully,
Like a lip at the hem of heaven's robe.
Come! And may the gaze of the chaste stars,
Which fall to earth through so many veils,
May the tree infused with perfume and songs,
May the breeze inflamed with noontime in the fields,
And the shade and the sun and the wave and the greenery,
And the resplendence of all nature
Cause to blossom, like a double flower,
Beauty on your brow and love in your heart!

The poem unspools in two long sentences into which Hugo has crowded a jumble of nature imagery. The phrases tumble out breathlessly, overwhelming the syntax as if straining toward a mystical union with the cosmos. The landscape is imbued with religious meaning – chaste stars gaze down through their veils, the earth kisses the edge of heaven's robe like the hem of Christ's garment. The poem plunges headlong into an animistic nature and ends with a triumphant fusion of body and soul, outward beauty and inward love.

The form of Hugo's poem produces the same cumulative effect. It does not divide into stanzas, but consists of an unbroken stream of rhyming couplets. This stichic form is typically found in epics and discursive poems where the poet sacrifices concentration of thought to flexibility. In this case, the continuous form heightens the sense of impetuosity as if the deluge of emotion had burst the banks of the stanza. The absence of interlocking rhymes drives the poem onward, pressing from one couplet to the next.

Comparing Hugo's poem with Fauré's setting can easily lead to disappointment. As Graham Johnson remarked, "the problem faced by the interpreter of this song is that Hugo's over-the-top romantic enthusiasm (whereby he seems to embrace the whole of nature) is ill-suited to Fauré's less extrovert temperament."[24] Yet Fauré found his own quiet answer to Hugo's virile rhetoric. "Mai" wastes no time on a piano prelude, but plunges the singer in after two measures of arpeggios. Fauré filled out

---

[24] Graham Johnson, *Gabriel Fauré: The Songs and Their Poets*, with translations of the song texts by Richard Stokes (Farnham, Surrey: Ashgate Publishing, 2009), 41.

Hugo's rolling alexandrines with another broad melody without rests, yet the form is even more spacious than that of "Puisque j'ai mis ma lèvre." The two strophes begin with a sixteen-measure period, but the consequent closes on a half cadence, extending the period into a thirty-two-measure lyric form (A₁A₂BA₃) that does not reach tonic closure until the end of the strophe. The B section wanders far afield, modulating to C♭ major (♭III) before reaching an apparent cadence on G♭ major. The augmented triad in measure 24 frustrates the cadence, however, and pivots back to V⁷ for the final A phrase. Even then, a deceptive cadence undercuts the reprise, deferring tonic closure until the final measure. With its breathless urgency, formal breadth, and harmonic twists, Fauré's setting responds ably to Hugo's rhapsodic poem. The composer also nodded to the poet's religious imagery with the modal cadence of the first phrase (m. 10) and the *fauxbourdon* 6/3 chords leading into the reprise (m. 25).

Fauré found an even more direct analogue to Hugo's accumulative rhetoric. As Frits Noske pointed out, the four phrases of "Mai" spin out different versions of the opening two-measure motive (see Example 4.4).[25] This ebullient melodic idea bounds up a fifth, outlining the tonic triad like a trumpet fanfare. Indeed, the singer's triadic melody seems to spring directly from the pianist's arpeggios, absorbing the energy of the surging accompaniment.[26] The third and fourth phrases reiterate the two-measure figure, compressing and intensifying the motivic development across the second half of the song. The fourth phrase ends by leaping a fifth to the climactic high A♭, unleashing the full energy of Fauré's heraldic figure. The "Mai" motive also acquires fresh harmonic colors with each new variation. In the first phrase, it perches atop a tonic triad, colored by a descending inner line. In the second phrase, a subdominant inflection shades the harmony deliciously. The third phrase ventures into more distant keys as the motive repeats, depicting Hugo's image of "The path that ends where the road begins." Finally, the fourth phrase presents the motive in the relative minor with a faintly modal coloration.

With his persistent, subtly varied motive, Fauré captured something of Hugo's verve. New versions of the motive continually sprout from the melody like the poem's cornucopial imagery. This sort of concentrated motivic development is absent from Fauré's other Hugo settings and does

[25] Noske, *French Song from Berlioz to Duparc*, 256.

[26] The triadic accompaniment figure in "Dans les ruines d'une abbaye" also generates the singer's opening motive, as Klaus Strobel noted in *Das Liedschaffen Gabriel Faurés* (Hamburg: Verlag Dr. Kovač, 2000), 46.

Example 4.4 Fauré, variation of a head motive across the first strophe of "Mai": a. First phrase, mm. 3–4; b. Second phrase, mm. 11–12; c. Third phrase, mm. 19–22; d. Fourth phrase, mm. 27–31

not resurface until the 1870s, when the composer turned to more serious verse. The motivic work in "Mai" exceeds the polite norms of song composition, gesturing toward the chamber and symphonic genres. We catch another glimpse of an elevated style behind the façade of the salon *romance*.

Genre and Counterpoint

In "S'il est un charmant gazon," his fifth song from *Les chants du crépuscule*, Fauré explored the expressive potential of counterpoint. Counterpoint here signifies not only the combination of melodic lines but also the relationship between the two performers. For the first time in Fauré's songs, the piano ritornello plays a truly integrated role, becoming an inseparable part of the musical-poetic design. At a deeper level still, "S'il est un charmant gazon" presents a counterpoint of genres that crystallizes a particular moment in the history of French song.

Motivically, the ritornello and strophes of "S'il est un charmant gazon" are closely interrelated (see Example 4.5). The piano and vocal melodies both fall into two-measure subphrases that descend to an accented passing tone, a sighing figure that permeates the entire song. The rising arpeggio in measure 2 also resembles a similar figure in the second half of the vocal strophes (see mm. 19 and 21). Yet the pentatonic piano arpeggio is obviously related to the common motive from "Puisque j'ai mis ma lèvre" and "Mai" that follows at the end of the ritornello. Clearly, Fauré did not compose the piano ritornello of "S'il est un charmant gazon" as an afterthought, as in the earlier songs. The ritornello develops material from previous songs and is integrated motivically with the vocal strophes.

The ritornello and strophes share another less noticeable structural feature. Fauré wrote the entire ritornello in strict four-part counterpoint, paying close attention to voice leading. The first measure contains a voice exchange between the melody, which descends from f' to d', and the tenor voice in the left hand, which ascends from d to f in even quarter notes. The same voice exchange returns twice, each time a fifth higher, as the two-measure model repeats sequentially. The inner voice also returns at the cadence, where the alto line rises from d' to f'.

We might overlook this voice-leading detail did it not return so strikingly in the strophes. The first two phrases begin with a voice exchange between the descending vocal line (c″ to a') and the ascending alto line in the piano (a to c'). The bass line, meanwhile, rises in contrary motion against the voice as it falls from c″ to f'. The bass only climbs a fourth in

Example 4.5 Fauré, "S'il est un charmant gazon," mm. 1–24

Example 4.5 (*cont.*)

the first phrase, reversing direction on B♭, but in the consequent phrase it reaches c, mirroring the singer's fifth descent. This contrapuntal "consummation" immediately precedes the rhapsodic arpeggios, as if the rising bass line had released a new energy in the melody.

The expressive meaning behind this contrapuntal design becomes clear in the third stanza, where Fauré departed from the strophic form. In the first two strophes, the *staccato* accompaniment consists of a bass line and offbeat chords, imitating a mandolin or guitar. In the third strophe, an emphatic new voice joins the serenade (see Example 4.6). This inner voice begins with a series of descending octaves leaps, foregrounded with heavy accents. The falling interval is, of course, an inversion of the vocalist's octave leap, which follows immediately in the fifth measure. The contrary motion introduced in the piano ritornello has thus expanded from a third to a fifth to a full octave. During the modified consequent phrase, the new tenor voice descends chromatically, shadowing the singer's melody in parallel tenths (mm. 65–68). Fauré clearly wanted to call attention to the

Example 4.6 Fauré, "S'il est un charmant gazon," mm. 57–68

counterpoint in this stanza, but why? The answer lies in the fifth and sixth lines:

Un rêve que Dieu bénit
Où l'âme à l'âme s'unit …

A dream that God blesses
In which soul with soul unites …

The contrapuntal lines depict this union of souls as they crisscross, mirror, and parallel one another. This is no facile pictorialism or isolated effect. Fauré has baked the contrapuntal design into every measure of the song, in both the piano ritornello and vocal strophes.

Yet the poetry and music of "S'il est un charmant gazon" are hardly soulmates. In fact, poetic and musical syntax are at loggerheads in Fauré's peculiar setting. Hugo's poem has a markedly hypotactic structure like that of "Puisque j'ai mis ma lèvre." Each stanza consists of a single complex sentence that begins with a series of subordinate clauses and does not reach closure until the last two lines:

S'il est un charmant gazon
  Que le ciel arrose,
Où naisse en toute saison
  Quelque fleur éclose,
Où l'on cueille à pleine main
Lys, chèvrefeuille et jasmine,
J'en veux faire le chemin
  Où ton pied se pose!

If there is a pleasant lawn
  That heaven waters,
Where at each season spring
  Blossoming flowers,
Where one gathers abundantly
Lily, honeysuckle, and jasmine,
I would make a path
  Where your foot might tread!

The rhyme scheme also has a nested structure, *ababcccb*, in which the *b* rhyme encloses the whole stanza. Moreover, Hugo used the same *b* rhyme (*-ose*) in all three stanzas, knitting together the entire poem. If the construction of "Mai" suggests headlong enthusiasm, "S'il est un charmant gazon" has the effect of a tautly organized argument.

In his setting of "Puisque j'ai mis ma lèvre," Fauré responded to Hugo's hypotaxis with music that vividly represents the prolongation of desire – yearning melodic lines, unstable harmonies, a broad and complex phrase structure. His setting of "S'il est un charmant gazon," on the other hand, could hardly be more complacent. The strophes begin squarely in the tonic with a melody that descends from ^5 to ^1 like a cadential formula. The harmony sticks doggedly to the tonic and, most remarkably, the antecedent phrase ends with a full cadence. Fauré seems bent on defusing any harmonic or melodic tension, setting Hugo's tortuous sentences to remarkably bland music.

Yet Fauré has by no means overlooked Hugo's syntax. Let us turn again to the piano ritornello. The theme is an eight-measure sentence, like the prelude to "Puisque j'ai mis ma lèvre," with a pair of sequential two-measure phrases followed by a four-measure continuation. Each of the three phrases starts on a remote harmony with the melody poised on the dissonant seventh degree. The first phrase begins on a startling V^7 of V and moves elliptically to I^6. This uneasy resolution is undercut by the second phrase, which begins a fifth higher on vi^7 and resolves to ii. The third phrase ratchets the tension still higher, rising another fifth and beginning abruptly on V of vi before working back around to the tonic. The piano thus supplies the harmonic tension and sense of prolonged resolution absent from the vocal part. In fact, there is a precise parallel between the harmonic structure of Fauré's eight-measure ritornello and the syntax of Hugo's eight-line stanzas. Both consist of a single complex sentence that begins with three unstable clauses and reaches closure in the final two measures/lines.

A strange division of labor! The piano ritornello realizes Hugo's rhetorical structure while the vocal strophes blithely ignore the poet's complicated syntax. In fact, other than the shared motivic and contrapuntal features, the ritornello and strophes seem to belong to different songs. The ritornello strikes a serious tone with its strict four-part writing, rhapsodic gestures, and *espressivo* marking. The melody of the strophes, on the other hand, exudes a naïve, almost folk-like simplicity, while the *staccato* accompaniment evokes the modest *chanson* genre, the realm of serenades, barcarolles, and drinking songs. Not only do the vocal strophes ignore Hugo's syntax, but they fit poorly with the word accents. Of all Fauré's early songs, "S'il est un charmant gazon" is plagued by the most discrepancies of text-setting across sources, including editions. It almost seems as if Fauré had grafted Hugo's poem onto the melody of a discarded song . . .

Nouvelle chanson sur un vieil air. "New words to an old tune." Hugo's title, we recall, hints at an anonymous folksong beneath the new poem. Fauré seems to have taken the title seriously. His naïve vocal melody sounds very much like a *vieil air* to which new words have been awkwardly fitted. The sophisticated piano ritornello, on the other hand, suggests the perspective of the modern poet as he toys with his folk artifact. Given the carefully fashioned musical connections between the piano and vocal parts, it seems entirely plausible that composer intended this duality. It is an ingenious conception that should banish forever the notion of Fauré as a naïve reader.

Yet there is still more involved in this counterpoint of piano and voice. Fauré has staged a dialogue between national styles. The ritornello is pure German Romanticism, lifted from the pages of Schumann's *Dichterliebe*; the strophes, on the other hand, tap the limpid vocalism of Fauré's native tradition. As "S'il est un charmant gazon" demonstrates, Fauré did not need to graduate from the *romance* to the *mélodie*. His student songs already draw the two genres into a dialogue that engages stylistic register, social function, and national identity. Fauré clearly intended to publish these songs, since he approached Victor Hugo in 1864 for the rights to the poems.[27] We may thus view Fauré's dialogue of genres as his fashioning of a compositional voice as he prepared to set himself before the public eye: the early Hugo settings align him with the traditions of the salon *romance*, even as they bid for the prestige of the Germanic *mélodie*. They make a remarkable debut for the composer who more than any other would shape the course of French art song into the twentieth century.

---

[27] See note 1.

5 | Lux aeterna

Fauré's *Messe de Requiem*, Op. 48

BYRON ADAMS*

To the memory of my mother

Upon learning of Gabriel Fauré's death, his patron Leo Frank Schuster (1852–1927) raced across the Channel to attend the grandiose state funeral in Paris. The reason for this hectic journey was twofold: Schuster sought to mourn a departed friend, but he also hoped to hear Fauré's *Messe de Requiem*, Op. 48, which was being sung for the occasion. As the Requiem had not yet been performed in Great Britain – it would not be heard there until 1936 – Schuster did not want to miss this opportunity.[1] Prejudice was partly to blame for this state of affairs during Fauré's lifetime: as late as the 1930s, clergy in the Church of England frowned on the performance in their churches and cathedrals of liturgical music by living Roman Catholic composers.[2]

Even then, long after its composer's death, Fauré's score did not attain widespread popularity outside of France and Belgium. The reasons for this slow progress were varied and sundry. After all, Fauré's Requiem is an outlier in the repertory: it does not sit easily on concert programs beside the symphonies of Beethoven or Mahler. For that matter, it does not rub elbows comfortably with the tone poems of Richard Strauss or the ballets of Stravinsky. Fauré's Requiem is in no way "symphonic" or overtly contrapuntal like Brahms' *Ein deutsches Requiem*, Op. 45. Nor is it filled with the shuddering dread and venomous flame that permeates the

* The author gratefully acknowledges the assistance of the following: Carlo Caballero, Lauren Cowdery, Marcus Desmond Harmon, Mark Inchoco, Larisa Lucaci, Nathan Vail, Jann Pasler, Stephen Rumph, Carolyn Shuster Fournier, the staff of the Bibliothèque nationale de France, and the clergy and staff of L'Église de la Sainte-Marie-Madeleine, Paris.
[1] Robert Orledge, *Gabriel Fauré*, revised edition (London: Eulenburg Books, 1983), 31.
[2] A contemporary instance of Anglican intransigence in the face of Roman Catholicism was the stubborn refusal of the cathedral clergy to allow Elgar's oratorio, *The Dream of Gerontius*, Op. 38, to be performed in Gloucester Cathedral until a decade after its première in 1900; they especially objected to its text by St. John Henry Newman. See Charles Edward McGuire, "Vaughan Williams and the English Music Festival: 1910," in *Vaughan Williams Essays*, ed. Byron Adams and Robin Wells (Aldershot: Ashgate Press, 2003), 260.

requiems of Berlioz and Verdi. Yet Fauré's modest music gradually achieved as great a fame as any of these portentous nineteenth-century choral frescoes.

How did Fauré's Requiem rise to its present eminence? How did it come to be composed in the first place, and for whom? Meditating upon these and other questions provides insights into the score's genesis, even if the answers must be partial at best. Certainly, there is no need here to restate the exacting work of such musicologists as Jean-Michel Nectoux, Mutien-Omer Houziaux, Carlo Caballero, or Vincent Rollin. This chapter is designed in part to open pathways that may lead to further research. The course of this essay might best be likened to a *flâneur* strolling through the 8th arrondissement of Paris who finds his steps leading him up the stairs into L'Église de la Sainte-Marie-Madeleine, that neoclassical edifice where Fauré spent decades of his career in the at times reluctant service of the church, its clergy, and its parishioners (see Figure 5.1).

Figure 5.1 Unknown artist, photochrome of the Madeleine and Rue Royale, *c.* 1890–1900. Library of Congress Prints and Photographs Division, LC-DIG-ppmsc-05184

Fauré was not always so conflicted about La Madeleine, as Parisians colloquially call it, as he became toward the end of his tenure there. His lifelong friend, the distinguished organist and composer Eugène Gigout (1844–1925), who, like Fauré, studied at the École Niedermeyer, recalled to Alfred Bruneau that as the two ambitious young organists planned their careers, Gigout said, "I shall have Saint-Augustin," and Fauré declared, "I shall have La Madeleine."[3]

There were good reasons for a student of the École Niedermeyer to covet a position at La Madeleine, not the least of which was the history of the church and its signal position in Parisian life. La Madeleine is one of the most idiosyncratic churches in Paris, if not in all of France. The present building superseded an earlier church of the same name, into the graveyard of which were dumped the headless corpses, mixed with quicklime, of Louis XVI and his queen Marie Antoinette.[4] This church was razed in 1799. Napoléon decided to erect in its stead a great temple dedicated to the French army, but both the architectural plans and the construction of the building were hindered by a series of impediments. Upon the Bourbon Restoration, Louis XVIII decided to build a church on the site incorporating what had already been completed, but the building went through several phases before being consecrated in 1842. In 1845, Aristide Cavaillé-Coll (1811–99) completed the installation of a superb grand organ – perhaps the finest of his earlier instruments – featuring particularly beautiful flute stops. Two years later, the brilliant organist and mediocre composer Louis James Alfred Lefébure-Wély was appointed *organiste titulaire*. In 1858, Camille Saint-Saëns, a paragon of musical rectitude, succeeded the easygoing Lefébure-Wély. Saint-Saëns quickly disconcerted both the clergy and the congregation at La Madeleine with his austere musical taste.

Given that the present building was originally intended to be a national memorial, and that it is both capacious and centrally located, La Madeleine has long been chosen for the funerals of prominent individuals: French statesmen, including President-Marshal Patrice de MacMahon; members of the Légion d'honneur, the Institut, the Académie française, and other such noted organizations; the nobility, including the Duchesse de Polignac; celebrities, including Josephine Baker and Johnny Hallyday; and lauded

---

[3] Alfred Bruneau, "La vie et les œuvres de Gabriel Fauré. Notice lue par l'auteur à l'Académie des Beaux-Arts" (Paris: Charpentier et Fasquelle, 1925), 17.

[4] In 1815, the remains of the hapless king and queen were exhumed and reinterred in the Basilique royale de Saint-Denis.

composers, including Chopin, Gounod, Saint-Saëns, and Fauré himself. During the nineteenth century, its parishioners included some of the most aristocratic and wealthy members of the Parisian *beau monde*.[5] This affluent parish supported a musical establishment that boasted a substantial choir of boys and men, a *maître de chapelle* and his assistant organist, and the *organiste titulaire*, who played at High Mass.[6]

Fauré's first appearances at La Madeleine most likely took place on those occasions when he deputized for Saint-Saëns, who had been Fauré's most influential teacher at the École Niedermeyer.[7] Upon Saint-Saëns' resignation from the post in April of 1877, another noted composer, Théodore Dubois (1837–1924), was appointed *titulaire* in his stead, and Fauré assumed the position that had hitherto belonged to Dubois, that of *maître de chapelle*. Fauré succeeded Dubois as *titulaire* at La Madeleine in 1896, thus achieving his youthful ambition; he remained there until he was unexpectedly appointed Director of the Conservatoire de Paris in 1905.

A month or so after becoming *maître de chapelle*, Fauré sketched out a setting for solo baritone and organ of the text Libera me, the responsory that is sung after the Requiem Mass as part of the Office of the Dead.[8] This Libera me was a glimmer of greater things to come, but at the time Fauré seems to have paid it little regard. This setting languished unpublished, and there is no record of its performance at that time, like so many projects that Fauré attempted during the unsettled decade from 1877 to 1887. In 1877, he became engaged, disastrously, to the great diva Pauline Viardot's daughter Marianne. In the wake of the emotional tumult that followed Marianne's breaking off their engagement later that year, Fauré composed the powerful short song cycle, *Poème d'un jour*, Op. 21 (1878, published

---

[5] Among the aristocratic parishioners of La Madeleine was one of Fauré's patrons, Vicomtesse (later Comtesse) Élisabeth Greffulhe, who commissioned his *Pavane*, Op. 50, in 1887. Her cousin, Comte Robert de Montesquiou, took on the unenviable task of providing a text *après la lettre* for the *Pavane*. See Caroline Weber, *Proust's Duchess* (New York: Alfred A. Knopf, 2018), 49, 352, 368, 389.

[6] The number of singers in the choir was approximately thirty-six to forty, of whom thirty were boys.

[7] Jean-Michel Nectoux states that Fauré began deputizing for Saint-Saëns in January 1874, in *Gabriel Fauré: A Musical Life*, trans. Roger Nichols (Cambridge: Cambridge University Press, 1991), 19.

[8] In June 1877, Romain Bussine, the noted singing-teacher, wrote to Marie Clerc that Fauré had played for him "a *Libera me* for a Mass for the Dead." Quoted in Nectoux, *Gabriel Fauré*, 567, note 32. The Libera me traditionally is sung during the Rite of Absolution that is performed while the body is present but after the Requiem Mass has ended; after prayers, aspersion, and incensation, the body is carried out to the In Paradisum. Fauré retained the basic responsorial format of the Libera me in his setting.

1880), and played piano for the 1880 première of his First Piano Quartet, Op. 15, with its funereal third movement. Fauré discarded the score's original finale and wrote a new one in 1883; this revision of the First Piano Quartet was published by Hamelle in 1884.[9]

While it is certainly true that this decade saw the publication of such wonderful works as the Second Piano Quartet, Op. 45 (1885–86, published 1887), and the original piano solo form of the delectable Ballade in F♯ Major, Op. 19 (1877–79, published 1880), these years were also littered with the detritus of projects that were left unfinished or deemed unsuccessful by their creator.[10] Fauré began a violin concerto in 1878, but it remained unfinished. The next year a comic opera, *Barnabé*, was begun and abandoned after the completion of a single sextet. Even the heart-rending *Élégie* for cello and piano, Op. 24 (1880, published 1883), another score that bears the scar of his dashed matrimonial hopes, is a fragment of a projected sonata.[11] While Fauré did complete a Symphony in D Minor in 1884 that was performed twice the following year, the dissatisfied composer discouraged further performances and destroyed the score completely sometime after 1889.[12]

This troubled symphony, furthermore, was finished during the first year of Fauré's ill-considered marriage to the high-strung and unprepossessing Marie Fremiet, the daughter of a distinguished sculptor. Aside from his domestic adjustments, the gradual understanding that he was temperamentally unsuited to the post-Beethovenian rhetoric that his teacher Saint-Saëns exploited with such panache must have disheartened Fauré further. When he was young, he had sought to write opera, but after his marriage, this was out of the question for practical reasons: he needed to support his family by toiling as a choirmaster and teaching private lessons. In 1885, amid the wreck of his hopes as a composer of larger genres, Fauré could not have recognized that the Libera me that he had composed casually in 1877 was the hidden key of promise, a key that would unlock an unsought treasure chest that held an imperishable gem glimmering darkly.

When he chose, Fauré could appear quite straightforward about the genesis of his lapidary Requiem. Responding to Louis Aguettant during the course of an interview conducted in July 1902, the composer touched upon the creation of this score, placing it squarely at the heart of his experience

---

[9] Julien Hamelle (1836–1917) founded his music-publishing house in 1877 and published the music of d'Indy, Franck, and Saint-Saëns, as well as that of Fauré.
[10] An orchestrated version of the Ballade was published in 1881.
[11] Nectoux, *Gabriel Fauré,* 88.   [12] Ibid., 539.

as a church musician: "Concerning my Requiem, perhaps I instinctively sought to depart from the established path, after all those years of accompanying funerals on the organ! I knew it all by heart." He continued pointedly, "I wanted to write something different."[13] Furthermore, in a letter to Maurice Emmanuel posted in March 1910, Fauré confided, "My Requiem was composed *for nothing in particular* . . . for the pleasure of it, I dare say!"[14]

How could the composition of a Requiem bring its composer pleasure? Both in public declarations and private letters, Fauré sought to deflect any question from people who would only be satisfied with pious answers. Certain commentators have noted that Fauré composed a substantial amount of the Requiem between his father's death on July 25, 1885, and that of his mother on December 31, 1887, and these writers are content to lay the Requiem on the graves of Fauré's parents as a tribute. This hypothesis seems admirably filial until one recalls Fauré's uneasy relationship with his parents. As the sixth, youngest, and unplanned child of a schoolmaster, Fauré was sent away to a peasant wet-nurse in a nearby village until he was four years old, only returning to his family in 1849.[15] Just five years later, in October 1854, the child was enrolled at the École Niedermeyer, an institution in distant Paris that was dedicated to the reform of French church music.[16] His visits home grew increasingly rare; Fauré seems to have found dealing with his punctilious father a trial. Nectoux has characterized Fauré's father as "a strict and dignified man, the archetypal dedicated government servant." Nectoux points out that Toussaint-Honoré Fauré was an "energetic conformist."[17] Fauré's mother is rarely mentioned in his extant published correspondence, and then only in passing as one of his parents. In a particularly wistful passage found in a letter written in 1907, he confided to his wife, "Even as a child . . . as my

---

[13] See Louis Aguettant, "Rencontres avec Gabriel Fauré," *Études fauréennes* 19 (1982), 4.

[14] Gabriel Fauré, *Correspondance, suivie de Lettres à Madame H.*, ed. Jean-Michel Nectoux (Paris: Fayard, 2015), 360.

[15] Nectoux, *Gabriel Fauré*, 4.

[16] The founder of this school was a Swiss Protestant, Louis Niedermeyer (1802–61). Niedermeyer wrote several operas with varying success, but was best known for his religious music. The school opened in 1853, but existed as an institution devoted to the reform and propagation of religious music only until 1884, when, as Katherine Ellis notes, "anticlerical government directives forced it to become a more general, ostensibly secular, conservatoire"; Ellis, *Interpreting the Musical Past: Early Music in Nineteenth-Century France* (Oxford and New York: Oxford University Press, 2005), 71.

[17] Nectoux, *Gabriel Fauré*, 2.

parents said, I was silent and self-absorbed."[18] It therefore seems unlikely that sorrow over the deaths of his parents played a significant role in the creation of the Requiem.[19]

Neither was the Requiem an expression of its composer's piety. Like many church musicians, Fauré harbored a pronounced anti-clerical streak and was skeptical of clerical interference in musical matters. He deplored, for instance, the strictures of the *motu proprio* "Tra le sollecitudini," which was promulgated by Pope St. Pius X on November 22, 1903.[20] In reminiscences published by *La revue musicale* in 1922, Fauré, who, it should be remembered, had been the *titulaire* of a major Parisian church in 1903, disagreed with the spirit of the *motu proprio* in no uncertain terms: "What music is religious? What music is not? To try to resolve the question is rather risky when you consider that however sincere religious feeling may be in a musician, it is through his personal sensibility that he expresses himself and not according to laws that cannot be made to stick. All classification in this field of thought has always seemed arbitrary to me."[21] That Fauré could dispute a papal *motu proprio* is perhaps unsurprising: after the first performance of his Requiem, he was reportedly rebuked by the Curé of La Madeleine, who allegedly remonstrated, "Monsieur Fauré, we don't need all these novelties; the Madeleine's repertory is quite rich enough, just content yourself with that."[22] If this anecdote is true, one suspects that the Curé's comment was only one salvo in a long-standing exchange.

In quiet defiance of whatever musical taste was evinced by his clergy, Fauré's Requiem is parochial in the truest sense: a work for the parishioners of La Madeleine tailored to that specific time and place. As Vincent Rollin's detailed research has revealed, far from being a personal selection of the liturgy, as some writers have claimed, Fauré's Requiem fits

---

[18] Gabriel Fauré, *Lettres intimes*, ed. Philippe Fauré-Fremiet (Paris: Grasset, 1951), 147 (my translation).

[19] Typical of such speculation is Robert Orledge's statement that the death of Fauré's mother on December 31, 1887 "may have spurred him on to complete the *Agnus Dei, Sanctus,* and *In Paradisum* in the early days of 1888 for the first performance on 16 January"; Orledge, *Gabriel Fauré,* 14.

[20] Pope St. Pius X, *Motu Proprio,* "Tra le sollecitudini" (Vatican City: *Acta Sancta Sedis* 36, 1903–04), 325–339.

[21] Fauré, "Souvenirs," *La revue musicale* 4 (October 1922), 197; quoted in Carlo Caballero, *Fauré and French Musical Aesthetics* (Cambridge: Cambridge University Press, 2001), 184.

[22] Armand Vivet, "La musique sacrée en France depuis la révolution," in *Congrès international de musique sacrée* (Paris: Desclée de Brouwer, 1937), 147–153; quoted in Nectoux, *Gabriel Fauré,* 116.

seamlessly into the liturgical practice of La Madeleine. For example, Fauré did not omit the Dies irae sequence to make a personal theological point; the practice at La Madeleine, as in all large Parisian churches of the time, was to chant the Sequence in "fauxbourdon."[23] (This style of fauxbordon was a chordal formula accompanied by the organ in a manner similar to Anglican chant.) Another example is the absence of the Benedictus and second iteration of the Osanna from Fauré's Sanctus, as these sections of the liturgy were chanted during Requiem Masses.[24] Finally, it was the custom at La Madeleine for memorial Requiem Masses to have both the Libera me and In Paradisum from the Office for the Dead sung in the church itself at the conclusion of the service.[25]

Fauré tailored the Requiem for La Madeleine in other ways as well, especially in the way that he took the church's peculiar and diffuse acoustic into consideration. Given the acoustic space within which the music was to be heard, Fauré finely judged the rate of harmonic change in the score. As Jeanice Brooks observes of the Requiem, "Within this basic tonal framework, Fauré uses modal inflections and an expanded tonal palette to suggest frequent and rapid modulation, often to remote areas, and unexpected routes of return. This inventive manipulation of local harmonic events is the most striking element of his musical style."[26] While Brooks correctly notes the frequency of modulation in the Requiem, especially when contrasted with the relatively static liturgical music of Fauré's contemporaries such as Théodore Dubois or Alexandre Guilmant, the harmonic rhythm of the Requiem is much less rapid than in much of the

[23] Hector Berlioz provides an eyewitness account of the use of fauxbordon at La Madeleine. In a letter to his sister, Berlioz describes Chopin's funeral at La Madeleine, which took place on October 29, 1849. In this letter, begun the same day but finished and posted the next, Berlioz mentions the use of fauxbordon and by contrast, remarks on the ineffectual performance of Mozart's Requiem on that solemn occasion: "And some notes from the organ, and the De profundis sung in fauxbourdon moved the listener more than the so celebrated and so incomplete score of the great master." Quoted in Jeffrey Kallberg, "Chopin's March, Chopin's Death" in *19th-Century Music* 25, No. 1 (Summer 2001), 26, note 72.
[24] See Vincent Rollin, "Chants et musiques des cérémonies de funérailles à Paris sous le régime concordataire," *Revue de musicologie* 99, No. 2 (2013), 259–263. I must thank Professor Rollin for his generosity in sharing this and other parts of his important research with me. It should be noted that the Sanctus found in Fauré's *Messe basse* (1906) includes a Benedictus but omits the repeat of the Osanna in excelsis.
[25] In the case of a memorial Requiem Mass, such as the one said for Lesoufaché, the Libera me and In Paradisum would have been sung in the church out of necessity, as the person in whose memory the Mass was being offered had been buried the year before. On such occasions, a catafalque represented the body of the faithful departed.
[26] Jeanice Brooks, *The Musical Work of Nadia Boulanger: Performing Past and Future between the Wars* (Cambridge: Cambridge University Press, 2013), 51.

composer's own piano and chamber music written during the late 1880s.[27] The modulations in the Requiem are structural rather than coloristic, and all changes of key are carefully prepared. Concerning the conclusion of the Introït et Kyrie, Nadia Boulanger observed, "The return to the principal tonality after curves that resemble modulations, and modulations that are nothing but contrapuntal arabesques, is of a completely Fauréan grace."[28] The scoring of the original five-movement "petit Requiem" for organ, violas, violoncellos, double basses, solo violin (in the Sanctus and In Paradisum), harp, and timpani, is admirably suited to support and amplify a choir of boys and men in the vast spaces of La Madeleine.[29] Fauré gauged the harmonic successions, vocal writing, and instrumental sonority with such expertise that the music seems to float through the extended nave of the church toward the listener as if coming from a distant, otherworldly realm.

As is well known, the original form of the Requiem consisted of these movements: Introït et Kyrie, Sanctus, Pie Jesu, Agnus Dei, and In Paradisum. Fauré directed the première of this "petit Requiem" at La Madeleine during a memorial High Mass that began precisely at noon on January 16, 1888.[30] This Mass was offered for the repose of the soul of Joseph-Michel-Anne Lesoufaché (1804–87), who had died at Bruz exactly one year before.[31]

In the 1910 letter to Maurice Emmanuel quoted above, Fauré vaguely recalls that he conducted the first performance of the Requiem "for the funeral of some member of the parish." He then gives the year as 1890, two years after the fact. In a postscript to this short letter, obviously dashed off

---

[27] The liturgical music of Théodore Dubois, who was Fauré's predecessor both as *titulaire* at La Madeleine and as Director of the Conservatoire, is so unadventurous harmonically as to make Fauré's own minor religious works – the settings of Saint Thomas Aquinas' hymn "Tantum ergo" and the Ave Maria, Op. 67 – seem luxuriant, even daring, by comparison.

[28] Nadia Boulanger, "La musique réligieuse," *La revue musicale* 4, No. 11 [special issue on Fauré] (1922), 110; translated and quoted by Brooks, *The Musical Work of Nadia Boulanger*, 51.

[29] It is evident from the manuscript score that the timpani were part of the composer's original orchestration of the Introït et Kyrie. The bassoon parts added to the Sanctus were notated in black ink, and may well have been included in an early performance, if not the first one (MS 411, Fonds Conservatoire, Bibliothèque nationale de France).

[30] For the hour at which the funeral began, see Fauré's note to Paul Poujaud in Fauré, *Correspondance*, 139. Fauré himself referred to the original five movements as "le petit Requiem" in the note to Poujaud.

[31] There are several variant spellings of the deceased's name. The spelling used here is the one found in the catalogue of the collection of books that he willed to the École des Beaux-Arts. See Eugène Münitz, *La Bibliothèque Lesoufaché a l'École des Beaux-Arts* (Paris: D. Dumoulin, 1892).

in haste, Fauré remembers that the name of the deceased was "M. Le Soufaché," and comments wryly, "which is not a common name!"[32]

In fact, Lesoufaché was an architect of distinction who may or may not have been a parishioner at La Madeleine. Lesoufaché attended the École des Beaux-Arts in Paris, where he won two prizes. He worked as a successful "architecte privé" building grand houses for the rich as well as modernizing and restoring old chateaus. By so doing, he amassed a fortune, and he used part of that fortune to endow an annual medal awarded to outstanding architects in his branch of the profession. In an obituary tribute, *L'Univers illustré* lauded Lesoufaché as "one of the masters of our time, who was exceedingly eminent in his art, as well as one of the most truly sympathetic personalities of Paris."[33] For his work as an architect and an administrator, Lesoufaché was named a Chevalier de la Légion d'honneur in 1862, which decoration added an official dimension to his memorial Requiem Mass at La Madeleine.

Like Fauré's father-in-law, the eminent sculptor Emmanuel Fremiet (1824–1910), of whom he was an older contemporary, Lesoufaché was a diligent and successful product of the École des Beaux-Arts.[34] Given that both men were honored alumni of that august institution, it is inconceivable that Fremiet and Lesoufaché were not at least passing acquaintances. Furthermore, Fauré and Lesoufaché moved in the same circles. For example, Lesoufaché had designed the *hôtel particulier* that was built for the family of Fauré's patron Comte Robert de Montesquiou.[35]

The four movements of the "petit Requiem" that are preserved in Fauré's hand – the Introït et Kyrie, Sanctus, Agnus Dei, and In Paradisum – suggest that they were not written for "nothing in particular." Rather, the composer seems to have been working against a firm deadline, which may have been urged upon him by his father-in-law.[36] Fauré was prone to

---

[32] Fauré, *Correspondance*, 361. It is interesting that Fauré spells the name of the deceased precisely the way it was spelled in the entry for Lesoufaché's funeral in the Registre des actes de décès kept by La Madeleine: "Le Soufaché." French churches were required to keep such records at the behest of the government; it should be recalled that there was no separation of church and state in France until 1905.

[33] *L'Univers illustré*, January 29, 1887, 71 (my translation).

[34] Fremiet was named a Chevalier de la Légion d'honneur in 1860, two years before Lesoufaché was awarded his rosette; the sculptor was named a Grand-Officier de la Légion d'honneur in 1878. At Fremiet's state funeral, which was held in Passy on September 10, 1910, the Pie Jesu from his son-in-law's Requiem was performed; see *Journal des débats politiques et littéraires*, "Les obsèques de Fremiet," September 10, 1910.

[35] The *hôtel particulier* of the Montesquiou family is now the Chinese Cultural Center in Paris, 1 Boulevard de la Tour-Maubourg.

[36] MSS 410, 411, 412, 413, Fonds Conservatoire, Bibliothèque nationale de France.

procrastination, and he would have known months in advance that Lesouf-aché's "première classe" memorial Requiem Mass was scheduled for January 16, 1888 (see Figure 5.2). The manuscript itself suggests a race against time. The Introït et Kyrie and the In Paradisum were finished first. Both movements are exquisitely notated on twenty-two-stave manuscript paper using black ink and a single narrow pen nib, resulting in precise and fastidious notation. Neither movement bears its date of completion.[37] By contrast, the Agnus Dei, which is dated January 6, and the Sanctus were written later on twenty-stave manuscript paper with a noticeably broader pen nib than the one used for either the Introït et Kyrie or the In Paradisum. Fauré traded precision for speed. He notated both the Introït et Kyrie and In Paradisum with unruffled elegance, but the notation of both the Agnus Dei and the Sanctus betray signs of haste, such as less than perfect alignment, changes in scoring (especially the original harp part of the Agnus Dei), and crossings-out.

As noted on the score, Fauré completed the Sanctus of the Requiem on January 9 for a performance just seven days later. Since all choral and instrumental parts had to be copied by hand before a piece could be rehearsed, the tight deadline snaps even more sharply into focus. This may also explain in part why the Sanctus is the least difficult movement for the chorus to learn.[38] As there was no vocal score at this point, choristers sang from music containing only their own voice part written on a single line with the text underneath. Furthermore, the existing parts for strings, harp, and timpani that were most likely prepared for the first performance (along with a single surviving rudimentary part for choral alto), were the work of several hands, possibly including Fauré's own. With their occasionally haphazard spacing of the music on the page and crossed out, corrected mistakes, it is clear that these parts were not produced at leisure, but were copied under the shadow of a looming deadline. "Première classe" funerals were commonplace at La Madeleine, which meant that composer and copyists alike would have no other reason for such haste. It is therefore highly likely that the score was intended specifically for M. Lesoufaché's memorial Requiem Mass.

[37] Edward R. Phillips identifies this paper as being made by Lard-Esnault. However, the twenty-two-stave manuscript paper is markedly different from the twenty-stave paper. See Edward R. Phillips, *Gabriel Fauré: A Research and Information Guide*, second edition (New York and London: Routledge, 2011), 54–55.

[38] This date on the manuscript is unquestionably in Fauré's hand. See Sanctus, MS 411, Fonds Conservatoire, Bibliothèque nationale de France. For a listing of the surviving parts, see Phillips, *Gabriel Fauré*, 54–55, 77–80.

If the Curé did indeed rebuke Fauré after Lesoufaché's obsequies, his objections were ignored, as his *maître de chapelle* continued to perform the Requiem at La Madeleine. Indeed, the second iteration took place just a few weeks later.[39] A glance at the holograph manuscript sources that survive reveals that the composer considered his Requiem a work in progress rather than a finished composition. Just as Proust compared the sketches of his fictional composer Vinteuil in *À la recherche du temps perdu* to the experiments of a "chemist of genius," so the existing, currently accessible movements of the Requiem in Fauré's orthography can be likened to the notebooks of a scientist that record the ways in which each small discovery enhanced and transformed the original experiment. La Madeleine was Fauré's laboratory for the Requiem, of course; assisting him were the choir of boys and men that he himself had trained, as well as the instrumentalists brought in for the especially elaborate funerals.

The first enhancements to the score seem to have been the trumpet and horn fanfares added to the Sanctus that the music critic Camille Benoît (1851–1923) mentioned hearing at La Madeleine on May 4, 1888. These appear at the bottom of the page of the manuscript. The brass parts added to the Introït et Kyrie are sketched lightly and – it is quite evident – hastily in graphite pencil at the top of the score of that movement.[40] The well-worn condition of the holograph manuscript overall, as well as the worn instrumental parts, all of which were accessible on a shelf at La Madeleine for decades, might well caution scholars against the temptation to make the tidy assumption that there was ever an established "1893 version" that incorporated the Offertoire and Libera me and which permanently super-seded the original 1888 Requiem. As a practical *maître de chapelle*, Fauré surely chose from a variety of options when conducting his Requiem. He may well have made a selection among a host of configurations depending on the elaborateness of the Requiem Mass to be celebrated, the social position of the deceased, and the money available to hire additional players.[41] The surviving manuscript offers mute testimony to repeated usage in the smudged and tattered lower right-hand corners where the pages

---

[39] According to a reference in a letter sent by Fauré to Eugène d'Eichthal (1844–1938) (Fauré, *Correspondance*, 139), the second performance of the Requiem seems to have taken place on February 1, 1888. See Mutien-Omer Houziaux, *À la recherche "des" Requiem de Fauré* (Liège: Revue de la Société liégeoise de musicologie, 2000), 11.

[40] See Introït et Kyrie, MS 410, Fonds Conservatoire, Bibliothèque nationale de France.

[41] For an exegesis of the ways in which degrees of funereal pomp were apportioned by class – rather like the sumptuary laws in Tudor England – during the Concordat between France and the Vatican (1801–1905), see Rollin, "Chants et musiques," 236–241. However, there were occasional exceptions to these strictures, such as Chopin's funeral at La Madeleine in 1849: the Polish composer had no official status whatsoever in French society.

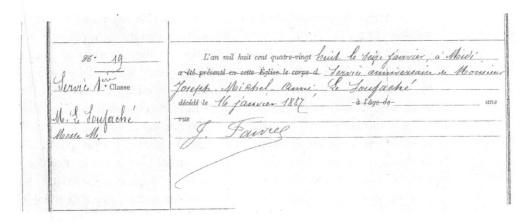

Figure 5.2 Registre des actes de décès Lesoufaché.

were turned over by the conductor. Furthermore, it is unclear whether Fauré's successor as *maître de chapelle*, the Abbé Auguste Chérion, who espoused the severe aesthetics of Solesmes, ever performed the Requiem for burial Masses once Fauré was appointed *titulaire* in 1896.[42]

What is clear, however, was that by 1887, Fauré was fed up with the music that he had had to endure during funerals at La Madeleine. Emboldened by the knowledge of an approaching service of the "première classe" for Lesoufaché, Fauré seized the chance to offer an alternative to the dire operatic repertory that in his opinion usually blighted burial services: "[P]erhaps I have instinctively sought to depart from the established path, after all those years of accompanying funerals on the organ!"[43] Fauré did not exaggerate the number of burial services that he played over his forty years as a church musician. The Registre des actes de décès kept by the Paroisse Sainte-Marie-Madeleine contains 327 entries for 1888, including that for Lesoufaché; the volume for the preceding year has 353.[44] These parish registries, which all Roman Catholic churches in France were required to maintain during the period of the Concordat (1801–1905), are sober public records of private heartbreak, especially as they include a sizable number of entries for children whose early deaths and burial

[42] Abbé A. Poupin, *Notice biographique sur l'abbé A. Chérion, maître de chapelle de la Madeleine, à Paris, chanoine honoraire de la cathédrale de Moulins, 1854–1904* (Arras: Procure générale de musique religieuse, 1907), 33. In a 1904 interview in *Musica*, Fauré dryly mentions his late successor as one who had tried unsuccessfully to impose unaccompanied plainchant and Palestrina at La Madeleine; see Orledge, *Fauré*, 117.

[43] Aguettant, "Rencontres," 4.

[44] Paroisse Sainte-Marie-Madeleine (Paris, France): "Registre des actes de décès 1887" and "Registre des actes de décès 1888." These volumes are held in a metal cabinet in the church's parish office.

Masses are recorded between their black covers. Like any Parisian church musician of the fin de siècle in the days before antibiotics, Fauré's working life was pervaded by funeral services. Revolted by the repertory used at La Madeleine for burial Masses, Fauré took pleasure – pleasure in the profoundest sense of the word – in providing "something different" at the same time as he clearly suggested a more humane approach to mourning.

Fauré did not restrict his Requiem to the hearing of either parishioners or mourners, however. From the beginning, he invited friends and critics to attend occasions of its performance at La Madeleine. He invited Paul Poujaud (1856–1936) and Prince Edmond de Polignac (1834–1901) the first time it was performed, for example, and notified Eugène d'Eichthal of what seems to have been the second iteration on February 1.[45] In addition, several of the composer's aristocratic patrons had organs designed by Cavaillé-Coll installed in their *hôtels particuliers*; his patroness the Princesse de Polignac (née Winnaretta Singer, 1865–1943) had a Cavaillé-Coll in her capacious music room, for example.[46] How often Fauré presented the Requiem, in whole or in part, in such salons is not easily determined. One performance in a salon, however, has been documented. Fauré conducted the score at Madame Paul Poirson's *hôtel particulier* at 18, place Malesherbes, on April 8, 1895. The organist on that occasion was Fauré's friend and colleague Léon Boëllmann (1862–97) who played on Madame Poirson's Cavaillé-Coll.[47] (In an uncanny twist of fate, Madame Poirson's husband died on April 28, exactly twenty days after this performance.)

As the Requiem's reputation spread beyond both La Madeleine and the salons, Fauré's publisher Hamelle pressured him to produce a "definitive" score designed for the concert hall. Fauré had signed a publishing contract

---

[45] For the attendance of Poujaud and d'Eichthal at the Requiem, see Fauré, *Correspondance*, 139. Polignac wrote to Montesquiou about the Requiem, describing the music as "deeply moving." See Sylvia Kahan, *In Search of New Scales: Prince Edmond de Polignac, Octatonic Explorer* (Rochester NY: University of Rochester Press, 2009), 60.

[46] Sylvia Kahan, *Music's Modern Muse: A Life of Winnaretta Singer, Princesse de Polignac* (Rochester: University of Rochester Press, 2003), 62, 86. The Princesse de Polignac arranged for the Requiem to be performed at a high society charity concert in the Salle d'Harcourt on May 17, 1894; see ibid., 84. For further discussion of the Princesse de Polignac's music room with her Cavaillé-Coll, see Jeanice Brooks, "Nadia Boulanger and the Salon of the Princesse de Polignac," *Journal of the American Musicological Society* 46 (1993), 415–468.

[47] By the time the performance took place at Madame Poirson's salon, the Requiem had twice been performed at Saint-Gervais and once in the aristocratic Théâtre La Bodinière; see Houziaux, *Requiem de Fauré*, xiv. The performance at Madame Poirson's salon used only the organ; see Carolyn Shuster Fournier, "Les orgues de salon d'Aristide Cavaillé-Coll," *L'Orgue: Cahiers et mémoires* 57–58 (1997), 71. Madame Poirson (1846–1931, née Seymourina Suzanne Vincente Cuthbert) was the wife of Paul Poirson (1836–95), friend and sometime collaborator of Charles Gounod. Madame Poirson, who was an accomplished musician, was the subject of a splendid portrait by John Singer Sargent, who was a friend of the Poirson family.

with Hamelle for the Requiem on September 16, 1890, but the work did not appear in print until a decade later.[48] David Gilbert has claimed that publication "was delayed, however, due to Fauré's general dilatory nature in business matters as well as the reluctance on the part of Hamelle to publish a significant, large-scale work with such a strange accompanying ensemble."[49] Hamelle shrewdly realized that the Requiem would be most profitable as a choral work with full orchestra.

At this point, however, something astonishing occurred: perhaps reluctant to end his musical experiments, the composer declined to be involved in the Requiem's publication. Consumed in 1900 with the creation of his lyric tragedy *Prométhée*, Fauré assigned the preparation of the vocal score to his student Jean Roger-Ducasse (1873–1954). There had been performances before 1900 of the Requiem with organ accompaniment, such as the one in 1895 that took place in Madame Poirson's salon. If, as was likely, there was only one extant full score from which the composer conducted, what kind of reduced score did Boëllmann use on that occasion? Did Boëllmann or Fauré make a reduction for chorus and organ, and did Roger-Ducasse have access to this reduction? Certain musicologists have also pointed to unusual features and errors in the full score of the Hamelle edition as evidence that Fauré had little or no hand in the expanded orchestration. In a prescient 1963 article, Malcolm Boyd opined, "The only serious criticism of Fauré's Requiem which might be raised on technical grounds is of the orchestration ... while I might hesitate at providing extra notes for the trombones and kettledrums, I should certainly not allow my four flute and clarinet players the embarrassment of having to sit still for forty minutes in order to play a mere eleven bars of unimportant music." Boyd concluded with a pertinent question: "Was he, indeed, solely responsible for the full score of the Requiem?"[50]

The answer to this query is almost certainly "no." To identify the person who expanded the orchestration of the Requiem, be it Roger-Ducasse, as

---

[48] As it transpired, the vocal score was published in 1900 and the orchestral score a year later. See Nectoux, *Gabriel Fauré*, 117.

[49] David Gilbert, Review of Requiem, pour soli, choeur et orchestre de chambre, op. 48. Version 1893, ed. Jean. Michel Nectoux and Roger Delage, *Notes* 54, No. 2 (December 1997), 574. Gilbert does not provide any documented sources for his assertions.

[50] Malcolm Boyd, "Fauré's Requiem: A Reappraisal," *The Musical Times* 104, No. 1444 (June 1963), 409. See also Gilbert, "Review of Requiem," 374–375 and Nectoux, *Gabriel Fauré*, 118. Houziaux argues that Fauré did not orchestrate the 1900 version of the Requiem himself; see Houziaux *A la recherche "des"* Requiem de Fauré, 57–61. On December 3, 1901, Roger-Ducasse wrote to a friend, "Fauré has just come to bring me the orchestration of his Requiem (35 frs .50, Hamelle edition) whose music ... seems to me to avoid nicely the profoundly liturgical." Jean Roger-Ducasse, *Lettres à son ami André Lambinet*, ed. Jacques Depaulis (Sprimont, Belgium: Editions Mardaga, 2001), 16.

Nectoux and others have cautiously posited, or someone else, is perhaps less important than recognizing that Fauré did *not* complete this task – rather, he chose to abdicate his responsibility as composer at a crucial juncture. If, however, Fauré himself orchestrated the 1900 full score of the Requiem, the state of that edition as published by Hamelle is a testament to its composer's deep discomfort with that endeavor. Under these circumstances, Fauré's complaints to Hamelle and others about the edition's many egregious errors are puzzling. An afternoon spent proofreading the vocal and full scores would have provided enough time to correct most of these mistakes, such as errors in text underlay and obvious wrong notes. Perhaps the grasping and careless Hamelle was to blame. Whatever the reasons, the "third version" of the Requiem published in 1900 represents a failure of imagination on the part of its publisher and, perhaps, a failure of nerve on the part of its composer.

It is also possible, however, that Fauré may have felt a pang of regret at permanently moving what started out as his gift to the parishioners of La Madeleine – and possibly to his father-in-law – into the concert hall. Even as he accustomed himself to performances of this "symphonic" version in secular venues, Fauré never repudiated the earlier configurations of his Requiem: as *titulaire* of La Madeleine until 1905, he could easily have destroyed all of the scores and parts for the versions that predated 1900, considering how much of his music he did repudiate. Finally, Fauré may well have realized that to move the Requiem from church to concert hall had irrevocably transformed – even betrayed – the score's essentially introspective nature.

Once the Hamelle edition premièred on July 12, 1900 in the vast hall of the Palais du Trocadéro during the Exposition Universelle, the Requiem was programmed with increasing frequency throughout France and Belgium. However, audiences in Great Britain and the United States had to wait until after Fauré's death. (See Table 5.1 for a select list of early performances in Great Britain and the United States.) First among the conductors who championed the Requiem in these countries was Fauré's pupil Nadia Boulanger (1887–1979), who by conducting the work often in concert as well as making several recordings, unquestionably widened its appreciation.[51] Still, even during most of Boulanger's lifetime, Fauré's work was placed in the domain of connoisseurs. In 1979, when Robert Orledge

---

[51] See Brooks, *The Musical Work of Nadia Boulanger*, 48–52, 141–143. Concerning Boulanger's studies with Fauré, see Jean-Michel Nectoux, "Nadia Boulanger: La recontre avec Gabriel Fauré," in *Nadia Boulanger et Lili Boulanger: Témoignages et études*, ed. Alexandra Laederich

Table 5.1 Early performances of Fauré's Requiem in the United States and Great Britain

---

Select list of early performances of the Requiem in the United States

March 16, 1930: First Baptist Church, Newton Center, Massachusetts. Choir, organ, strings; conductor unknown. First documented American performance. (John N. Burk alludes to this performance eight years later in his program note for the first performance of the Requiem by the Boston Symphony Orchestra conducted by Nadia Boulanger, February 17 and 18, 1938.)

April 19, 1931: Museum of Art, Philadelphia, under the auspices of the Curtis Institute of Music, Louis Bailly, conductor. Generally cited as the first American performance using the Hamelle Edition of 1900.

January 29, 1932: Carnegie Hall, New York. Performers from the Curtis Institute of Music, Louis Bailly, conductor. First recorded performance in New York.

February 17, 1937: Jordan Hall, New England Conservatory. Bach Cantata Club and members of the Boston Symphony Orchestra conducted by Richard Burgin.

February 17 and 18, 1938: Symphony Hall, Boston. Bach Cantata Club and The Boston Symphony Orchestra conducted by Nadia Boulanger.

Select list of early performances of the Requiem in Great Britain

November 24, 1936: Queen's Hall, London. Oriana Madrigal Society and London Symphony Orchestra conducted by Nadia Boulanger. Generally cited as the first British performance, certainly the first performance in London.

December 16, 1937: Royal Academy, London. Handel Society conducted by Reginald Goodhall; Gisèle Peyron, soprano.

September 6, 1938: Three Choirs Festival, Worcester, Great Britain. Festival Chorus and London Symphony Orchestra, conducted by Ivor Atkins; Isobel Baillie, soprano, and Harold Williams, baritone.

February 27, 1947: BBC Radio Broadcast. BBC Singers and the Boyd Neel Orchestra conducted by Nadia Boulanger. First broadcast by the BBC.

---

wrote that hearing "Fauré's *Requiem* as he originally intended it to be performed would be a revelation to most people," the seeds of its exalted status had been sown.[52] In 1967, the Choir of King's College Chapel, Cambridge, conducted by David Willcocks, made a recording that, although performed in the idiosyncratic style of English boy choirs, nevertheless offered a male sonority resembling Fauré's original singers.[53]

(Lyons: Symétrie, 2007), 33–47. For Boulanger's recordings of the Requiem, see Brooks, *The Musical Work of Nadia Boulanger*, 102, 277–328.

[52] Orledge, *Fauré*, 112.

[53] Fauré might have been puzzled by the lack of vibrato in the British choir, a style first promulgated by R. R. Terry and perfected by Boris Ord, and the style of the boys on this recording; French boy choirs have never eschewed vibrato.

This recording, which used the 1900 orchestration, was acclaimed by reviewers and sold very well.

In 1983, John Rutter published a sparsely annotated edition of Fauré's score that he claimed to base on the supposed "1893 version" of the Requiem. As Gilbert observes, "Rutter's premises are somewhat slippery, however, and the manuscript score serving as Rutter's primary source is difficult to untangle." Gilbert also notes, "Rutter evidently had access only to the autograph manuscript deposited in the Bibliothèque nationale and not to the manuscript parts."[54] Indeed, in the preface to his edition of the full score of the "1893 version," Rutter cites only the surviving 1888 manuscript as his source and makes no mention of any other. Rutter reconstructed the original orchestration of the Offertoire and Libera me from the 1900 full score.[55] At a time when the most affordable editions available offered the latest, largest version for full orchestra, Rutter's performing edition restored something of the flexibility of instrumental forces that Fauré had doubtless employed at La Madeleine. Rutter's canny handiwork became popular as a result.

Practical and fiscal considerations aside, a scholarly edition of the putative "1893 version" was published in 1995 by Hamelle, prepared by Jean-Michel Nectoux and Roger Delage. This edition, which does take the manuscript parts into consideration, is scrupulous in its scholarship. For performances of the 1900 version, the vocal score published circa 1978 by Edition Peters and edited by Nectoux and Rainer Zimmerman is the soundest choice. For the full score there is Nectoux's conscientious edition published by Hamelle in 1998. None of these editions is immaculate, however, which is unsurprising given the complexity and the fragmentary condition of the source materials. As Gilbert remarks, the

---

[54] Gilbert, Review of Requiem, 575.

[55] In the preface to his edition, Rutter mentions consulting only the four movements of the "petit Requiem." His edition certainly does not incorporate all of the parts that survived from the versions of the Requiem performed at La Madeleine, as there are three trombone parts for the Libera me that he blithely calls "dispensable" and so simply omits them. Clearly the trombones were used for performances at La Madeleine: on the recto of the first trombone part is stamped "Église de la Madeleine." For information on the instrumental parts, see Phillips, *Gabriel Fauré*, 54–55, 77–80. Of the Libera me, Nectoux notes, "In its final version for solo, choir, and orchestra (including three trombones) it was heard separately in a concert given under the auspices of the Société nationale in the church of St-Gervais on 28 January 1892, with Louis Ballard as soloist. In all probability, despite the claims made on the programme that this was a first performance, the Libera me had already been heard at the Madeleine as the parts were copied there"; Nectoux, *Gabriel Fauré*, 117.

Requiem still "harbors mysteries."[56] Nectoux sensibly recommends the 1900 full score for large concert halls, while suggesting that the versions performed at La Madeleine are best suited for intimate spaces such as churches.[57]

The question lingers still: why did Fauré resist finishing the Requiem himself, leaving that task to others? One answer might be found in the composer's own metaphysical beliefs or the lack thereof. In a program note published for the first performances of the Requiem by the Boston Symphony, Boulanger observed: "He seems to have conceived religion rather in the manner of St. John or St. Francis of Assisi than St. Bernard, or Bossuet. He looks for and finds in it a source of love and not of fear. This must be accepted if he is to be understood."[58] Yet even Boulanger equivocates here: she does not know for certain. Others have claimed that Fauré was a Hellenist, or a pagan, or a sensualist, or an atheist. He was all of these at different times of his life.

A deeply private man, Fauré did not disclose his beliefs publicly, except to hint at what he did *not* believe. While he made it clear that he dissented from Roman Catholic doctrine, Fauré alluded several times to his belief in the existence of a more beautiful realm beyond this one. He might well be described as a tender agnostic, who at certain times hoped for a transpersonal "something." Even at his most skeptical concerning metaphysics, Fauré believed in love. Nectoux reports the eyewitness account of the author Eugène Berteaux (1876–1948): "For him – and I have heard it from his own lips – the word 'God' was merely the imposing synonym for the word 'Love.'"[59] Nor should it come

---

[56] For critical assessments these editions, see Robert Orledge, "Fauré Revised," *The Musical Times* 121, No. 1647 (May 1980), 327; Gilbert, "Review of Requiem"; and Andrew Thomson, "Requiem (1893 version) by Jean-Michel Nectoux, Roger Delage, Fauré" *The Musical Times* 136, No. 1834 (December 1995), 670–671.

[57] Nectoux, *Fauré*, 118–119. The availability of the Requiem in the reduced orchestration has led to the score being once again performed liturgically during Requiem Masses, especially on All Souls' Day, in Anglo-Catholic parishes and those Roman Catholic parishes that use the Extraordinary Form of the Mass.

[58] Concert Bulletin of the Boston Symphony, Fifty-Seventh Season, 1937–8, 735. At the head of Boulanger's note about the Requiem, the editor of the program bulletin – probably John N. Burk, the regular annotator – parenthetically remarks, "The following is a quotation in part from the contribution of Nadia Boulanger to the 'Gabriel Fauré' number of La Revue Musicale, 1922." Neither the redaction of Boulanger's article nor its English translation is credited in the program.

[59] Eugène Berteaux, *En ce temps-là: souvenirs* (Paris: Edition du Bateau ivre, 1946), 237–238; quoted in Nectoux, *Gabriel Fauré*, 112. Eugène Hippolyte Adolphe Berteaux was a distinguished civil servant and a man of letters who was made a Chevalier de la Légion

as a surprise that the composer of the song cycle *La chanson d'Ève*, Op. 95 (1910), filled as it is with music that flickers between voluptuousness and chastity, made no distinction between corporeal and supernal love: "Did not the faith of Saint Theresa [Teresa of Ávila] express itself in words so ardent, so passionate, that they are at times licentious? And yet she was a saint and no one thinks of tossing her out of the church."[60]

On his deathbed, Fauré referred to a world to come, however indistinct. His son Philippe recorded his father's last words: "When I am no longer here you will hear it said of my works, 'After all, that did not amount to much!' People will become indifferent, perhaps. You must not let that trouble or depress you. It's fate: it happened to Saint-Saëns and others. There is always a moment of oblivion. But that is of no importance. I did the best that I could ... now ... God will be my judge!"[61]

Even *in extremis*, Fauré remained modest: as he lay dying, he simply commended his sincerity and industriousness to God. His Requiem, forever uncompleted except by each listener, is permeated by this radiant modesty. Fauré's compassionate music transforms even those sections of liturgy that tell of pain and judgment in such a way that many listeners, whatever their own convictions or lack thereof, are comforted, as if a kind and generous friend has come to share in their sorrow and to offer the consolation of beauty.

Fauré resisted finishing his Requiem definitively because its multivalent state allows for continual reinterpretation by both performers and listeners. Leaving behind multiple variants of his Requiem, Fauré embraced that sense of openness to manifold possibilities, both terrestrial and, perhaps, celestial, that had always marked his aesthetics, pedagogy, and his life-enhancing skepticism. In the final years of his career, Fauré composed a

---

d'honneur. I am grateful to M. Thierry Lange-Berteaux, his grandson and a noted jazz drummer, for this information.

[60] Fauré quoted by Auguste Mangeot, "La réforme de la musique religieuse," *Le monde musical* (February 15, 1904), 35; quoted in Caballero, *Fauré and French Musical Aesthetics*, 182–183. Concerning the source of Fauré's opinions to Mangeot, see ibid., 293–294, note 53.

[61] Philippe Fauré-Fremiet, *Gabriel Fauré*, second edition (Paris: Albin Michel, 1957), 129–130. The musicologist Paul Landormy (1869–1943) relays this anecdote from Philippe Fauré-Fremiet at the conclusion of an obituary article published by *The Musical Quarterly* in 1931. Presumably on the authority of Philippe Fauré-Fremiet, who later wrote about this moment in a biography of his father, Landormy writes that Fauré's words were uttered "in his last moments." See Paul Landormy, "Gabriel Fauré (1845–1924)," trans. M. D. Herter Norton in *The Musical Quarterly* 17, No. 3 (July 1931), 301.

mélodie that can be considered his final testament, music whose radiance echoes the serene D major of the Requiem's In Paradisum. Cast in the same key as the In Paradisum and evincing the same deliberate rate of harmonic change, the final song, "Vaisseaux, nous vous aurons aimés" from Fauré's last song cycle, *L'horizon chimérique*, Op. 118 (1921), ends with a stirring call to adventure that surely expresses its elderly composer's courage and deepest convictions: "Car j'ai de grands départs inassouvis en moi."[62]

[62] "For I have great departures unassuaged within me."

6 | From Homer's Banquet to Fauchois' Feast

The *Odyssey*'s Odyssey

SANDER GOLDBERG[*]

The tragedian Aeschylus is said to have called his plays slices from Homer's banquet, by which he presumably meant slices from what Homer had left behind on the table.[1] It is much easier, as Aeschylus knew (and so famously did), to develop stories that Homer probably knew but did not tell or (as Roman poets eventually did) to weave new stories using Homeric techniques than it is to rework in an artistically effective way what Homer had already done in the *Iliad* and *Odyssey*. A change of genre may certainly make that task easier, and the aim of this essay is to look specifically at what happens when a slice from Homer's own platter becomes a libretto and then, in turn, a performable opera. The specific process in question involves the self-styled *poème lyrique* of the prolific dramatist, librettist, and actor René Fauchois and *Pénélope*, the opera made from it by Gabriel Fauré.[2] The work's recasting of familiar material is interesting in its own right, but the easiest way to appreciate its creative process is to begin with Homer, partly to recall the character of Odysseus and the story that the *Odyssey* made from his return from Troy to Ithaca, but especially to identify the challenges and the opportunities that the epic exemplar presents to later authors working with the same material. So let us start with Odysseus.

---

[*] I am grateful to Stephen Rumph and Carlo Caballero for the invitation to contribute to the conference "Effable and Ineffable: Fauré and the Limits of Criticism" and to its participants, who did so much to deepen my appreciation of Fauré and his music. What follows is but a small repayment for that experience in the one currency available to me.

[1] Athenaeus, *The Learned Banquet* 8.39 (τεμάχη ... τῶν Ὁμήρου μεγάλων δείπνων).

[2] The opera had a successful debut at Monte Carlo in March 1913, then in May moved to the Théâtre des Champs-Élysées Paris, where it alternated with (and was ultimately eclipsed by) Stravinsky's *Le sacre du printemps*. There were revivals at the Opéra-Comique in 1919 and several times in the 1920s and 1930s, but its American premiere was not until 1993 (Opera Manhattan). Good survey discussions of the work are provided in Robert Orledge, *Gabriel Fauré* (London: Eulenburg, 1983), 155–165; Jean-Michel Nectoux, *Gabriel Fauré, A Musical Life*, trans. Roger Nichols (Cambridge: Cambridge University Press, 1991) 313–336; Carlo Caballero, *Fauré and French Musical Aesthetics* (Cambridge: Cambridge University Press, 2001), 159–164; and a brief mention in Edith Hall, *The Return of Ulysses: A Cultural History of Homer's "Odyssey"* (Baltimore: Johns Hopkins, 2008), 66–68 (heavily indebted to Nectoux).

Priam, seeing him from the walls of Troy and wondering who he is, describes him this way:[3]

Shorter than Atreus' son Agamemnon, clearly,
but broader across the shoulders, through the chest ...
... the man keeps ranging the ranks of fighters like a ram –
yes, he looks to me like a thick-fleeced bellwether ram
making his way through a big mass of sheep-flocks,
shining silver gray.

(Il. 3.193–198)

This is, replies Helen, "Laertes' son, the great tactician Odysseus ... quick at every treachery under the sun, the man of twists and turns" (*Il.* 3.200–202). That is at least the start of a fair description, and subsequent events will reveal him also to be murderous, vengeful, egotistical, a congenital liar, and, above all, a survivor who owes that survival as much to friends in the highest of places as to his own resources. He is much more a man you might want to be than a man you want to be with, since those around him generally wind up fully and gruesomely dead. He seems to learn nothing from start to finish, and it is no great surprise to realize that his character becomes increasingly villainous and unprincipled in later Greek tradition until he winds up, via Vergil's *Aeneid*, among the evil counselors in Dante's *Inferno* (Canto 26).[4]

Yet the *Odyssey* is also immensely richer than the *Iliad* in the variety of perspectives it represents, in the range of characters it portrays, and in the moral dilemmas it presents, which not only play themselves out on a human scale but also reflect something very like the world of recognizable human experience. In later antiquity, the anonymous critic writing *On the Sublime* likened the poem to a comedy of manners (κωμῳδία τίς ἐστιν ἠθολογουμένη). He considered that a fault, the inevitable product of a great poet in his dotage ("like the setting sun: the grandeur remains without the intensity"), but we could instead say that the poem is more attuned to the multifaceted nature of human existence than its more belligerent partner in the canon, more willing to pay attention to domestic arrangements and to the situation of characters of "lower" status like the nurse Eurykleia and the

---

[3] Translations of Homer are from Robert Fagles, *The Iliad* and *The Odyssey* (New York: Viking, 1990, 1996), but the line numbers used throughout refer to the standard Greek texts of T. W. Allen, *Homeri Opera*, Vols. 1–4 (Oxford: Oxford University Press, 1908).

[4] Though the interpretation of individual instantiations has since varied, the generally downward trend in the characterization of Odysseus traced by W. B. Stanford, *The Ulysses Theme* (Oxford: Blackwell, 1954), 90–158 remains accurate.

swineherd Eumaios.[5] It thus tells a story redolent of human experience, and the significance of its narrative emerges as a natural consequence of the way that story is told.

One consequence of its origin in an oral tradition of storytelling is that the poem as we have it is an amalgam of narrative possibilities, and once we start looking for them, it is not hard to spot moments when the oral poet could decide in the course of performance whether or not to take the repeat, to embellish, to show off, or to skip the cadenza entirely. The decision-making process is a phenomenon especially familiar to modern collectors of oral poetry who, like Dwight Reynolds, are attuned not simply to a poet and his poem but to the dynamics of the individual performance: "As one poet stated regarding a lengthy sequence of battles between one of the main heroes and the seven kings of an opposing tribe, 'I can kill them off in half an hour or take a whole night doing it!'"[6] So in Book 21 of the *Odyssey*, when Eurykleia touches Odysseus' scar and starts up in recognition, does he silence her at once or do we first hear the story of how he got that scar while boar-hunting on Mount Parnassus? By classical times a full repertoire of possibilities for narrative twists and turns, digressions and economies had codified into a fairly well stabilized written text,[7] but its origin in oral tradition has two important consequences for the authors of successor texts: (1) that the *Odyssey* is particularly rich in narrative possibilities and (2) that the desire to choose, to rework, and to revalue elements of its narrative has a very long history.

This complexity is at once clear from the sequence of its episodes. Popular culture readily conflates the ideas of the epic poem and the voyage,

---

[5] [Longinus] *On the Sublime* 9.14–15. The ancient sense that the *Odyssey* postdates the *Iliad* has since been confirmed by more objective stylistic analysis, e.g. Richard Janko, *Homer, Hesiod and the Hymns: Diachronic Development* (Cambridge: Cambridge University Press, 1982). Once Odysseus reaches Ithaca disguised as a beggar, the narrative directs increasing attention toward characters of lower status and the details of their lives. See e.g. A. M. Bowie (ed.), *Homer: Odyssey, Books XIII and XIV* (Cambridge: Cambridge University Press, 2013), 16–23, and Hall, *The Return of Ulysses*, 4, where it is suggested that "one reason for the poem's enduring popularity must be that its personnel is so varied that every ancient or modern listener, of any age, sex or status, seaman or servant, will have found someone with whom to identify."

[6] Dwight Reynolds, "Epic and History in the Arabic Tradition," in *Epic and History*, ed. David Konstan and Kurt Raaflaub (Malden, MA: Wiley-Blackwell, 2010), 404. Reynolds was reviewing the modern Egyptian epic tradition studied at length in his *Heroic Poets, Poetic Heroes: The Ethnography of Performance in an Egyptian Oral Epic Tradition* (Ithaca: Cornell University Press, 1995). See also Ruth Scodel, "The Story-Teller and His Audience," in *The Cambridge Companion to Homer*, ed. Robert Fowler (Cambridge: Cambridge University Press, 2004), 46 on the storyteller's task as "selecting his story, telling it at the level of detail appropriate to the occasion, and deploying the familiar epic language to make it vivid."

[7] This is a deliberately anodyne and, I hope, uncontroversial summary of what remains a hotly debated topic among Homerists. See the summary discussion in Robert Fowler, "The Homeric Question," in *The Cambridge Companion to Homer*, 220–232.

Table 6.1 The *Odyssey* by the book

Telemachus	Odysseus' journey	Odysseus' return	Order restored
1			
2			
3			
4			
	5		
	6		
	7		
	8		
	9		
	10		
	11		
	12		
	13		
		14	
15		15	
		16	
		17	
		18	
		19	
		20	
		21	
		22	
		23	
			24

as if the sequence of Odysseus' adventures in the course of his return from Troy *was* the poem, and the predominance of those adventures in ancient art might even encourage that perception. But the structure of the poem itself, as revealed here in Table 6.1 through the book numbers eventually imposed on the written text, tells us something else:

It is at once apparent that what we commonly call Odysseus' "odyssey" takes up just a little more than a third of the work as a whole (36 percent of its lines in the Greek text) and that the story is embedded in a larger context of homecoming, testing, and recognition – a larger narrative, not just a narrative frame – centered on events and characters in Ithaca that both open and close the story. Odysseus' arrangement of affairs on his return, where he confronts very material difficulties and dangers, is a still larger third of that whole (38 percent), and a secondary theme runs throughout as Telemachus learns what it means to be the son of Odysseus. The result is a vast cat's cradle of a narrative: pull any one of its threads (see the story from a different angle, emphasize a different character, etc.) and everything shifts as a new story emerges. And so it must as we move from epic to drama, which even at its most prolix cannot do all that epic does.

That is why, to take an easy example, when Giacomo Badoaro induced Monteverdi to write for the Venetian stage by offering him a libretto based on the *Odyssey*, he focused solely on the story of return in Books 13–23, and even that story was pruned significantly from five acts to three once Monteverdi began developing it into an opera. The final version of *Il ritorno d'Ulisse in patria*, which took Venice by storm in 1640, keeps the Phaeacians, turned to stone by a vengeful Neptune and thus deprived of their own return once they bring Ulisse to Ithaca, but not Badoaro's scene of Mercury escorting the suitors' ghosts to the underworld, an idea taken directly from the beginning of *Odyssey* 24.[8] When, two and a half centuries later, René Fauchois took up the same story, he also focused on events in Ithaca, but his elimination of Homeric possibilities is from the outset even more extensive: no gods, and thus no Phaeacians to bring his hero home, but no Telemachus either and no Laertes (now deceased), and, if not actually a different Penelope, certainly a different way to dramatize her situation.[9]

Fauchois' action opens with a chorus of servant women busily spinning as the suitors' raucous laughter is heard offstage. It is, of course, set up as an expository device since their comments serve to orient us to their mistress's dilemma, but their work, their complaints, and their daydreams are all deliberately anachronistic: these women sound much more like nineteenth-century seamstresses gossiping over their work than Homeric domestics, an indication from the outset that the story (or at least this perspective on the story) is not to be quite the familiar one. The suitors themselves then rush in, and only four scenes later, after Pénélope has repelled their increasingly bold and crude advances and she consents at last to finish the shroud she has been weaving for Laertes, does she extend

---

[8] The discrepancies between Badoaro's five-act libretto and the (anonymous) three-act score have occasionally cast doubt on the attribution to Monteverdi, but he frequently made significant editorial changes in his texts, and his authorship is now generally accepted. See Ellen Rosand, *Monteverdi's Last Operas: A Venetian Trilogy* (Berkeley: University of California Press, 2007), 3–9; and for the libretto's recasting of Homeric values, Michael Ewans, *Opera from the Greek: Studies in the Poetics of Appropriation* (Aldershot: Ashgate, 2007), 9–30. While film and television are naturally drawn to depiction of Odysseus' adventures, opera since Monteverdi has consistently focused on events at Ithaca. See the survey in Hall, *Return of Ulysses*, 60–71.

[9] In omitting Telemachus, Fauchois turns away from a longstanding French interest in this figure, which can be traced back to the 1699 didactic novel *Les aventures de Télémaque* by François de Salignac de la Mothe-Fénelon (see Hall, *Return of Ulysses*, 64–65).

hospitality to a mysterious beggar, and we find ourselves in more explicitly Homeric terrain.[10] Fauchois thus takes pains to put distance between his story and the larger Odyssean context and to signal the sincerity of his focus not on a story of return (as we find in Badoaro) but on the anguish of his title character.

Yet while the narrative arc of *Pénélope* and its emotional center are unquestionably Fauchois' creation, the text as performed owes a significant debt to his musical collaborator. Though Fauré had never written an opera, his interests in both Greek antiquity and musical theater were well established. He had already "restored" from ancient notation the music to a hymn from the second century BCE discovered by French excavators at Delphi (*Hymne à Apollon*, 1894), and he created an elaborate score, which included arias and choruses as well as incidental interludes, for *Prométhée* (1900), a spectacular outdoor tableau performed in the Roman arena at Béziers for individual voices, choirs, wind bands, strings, and harps that required several hundred performers.[11] In 1907, when the Wagnerian soprano Lucienne Bréval offered to put him in touch with Fauchois, who she said was at work on this Homeric verse drama, Fauré expressed interest, and a partnership was formed. The two apparently got on reasonably well, though at the outset all was not smooth sailing. Fauchois was destined to enjoy a long and successful career as a dramatist and actor, but he was then still quite young, with his ambition noticeably in advance of his experience. Like Monteverdi before him, Fauré found it necessary to trim frequently and sometimes even to rewrite what he found in the emerging libretto. One reason for this was simply to make Fauchois' occasionally wordy verses more musically tractable. As Fauré, ever the consummate technician, wrote to his wife in 1907:

---

[10] As already suggested by this prologue, the suitors will be more successful with the serving women (Act 1, Scene 5), a detail true to Homer (for example, *Od.* 20.6–13, 22.440–445) but which would offend the nineteenth-century sensibility of Camille Saint-Saëns, the work's dedicatee, who complained to Fauré after seeing the opera in Monte Carlo, "I don't like the way Fauchois has travestied the *Odyssey* by having the suitors fondle the servant-girls before Penelope's eyes! That is unthinkable." Gabriel Fauré, *Correspondance suivie de Lettres à Madame H.*, ed. Jean-Michel Nectoux (Paris: Fayard, 2015), 394. Badoaro's suitors are much more decorous (see Evans, *Opera from the Greek*, 19–21).

[11] The first two performances drew some 17,000 spectators. For the larger context of Fauré's Hellenism see Orledge, *Fauré*, 153–154; Jon Solomon, "The Reception of Ancient Greek Music in the Late Nineteenth Century," *International Journal of the Classical Tradition* 17 (2010), 497–525; James Sobaskie, "The Audacity of Pénélope: A Modern Reimagination of Homer's Heroine," in *Revisiting the Past, Recasting the Present: The Reception of Greek Antiquity in Music, 19th Century to the Present*, ed. Kataria Levidou and George Vlasto (Athens: Hellenic Music Centre, 2013), 70–92 (available for free download at https://hellenicmusiccentre.com, here 74–75).

The poem's author has given me too much text. He didn't consider that music draws out the verses tremendously, and that what one can read in two minutes takes at least three times as long when it's sung. I've thus been obliged to cut couplets or even groups of four or eight verses here and there and to see that the general sense loses none of its clarity. It's not always easy![12]

What began as Fauré's abridgment and realignment of words, however, perhaps inevitably led to the substitution of musical effects for verbal ones. So, for example, in the first act (Scene 4), Pénélope does not simply apostrophize her absent husband ("Viens! Viens! secours ma détresse!"), but does so to the sound of the "Ulysse" motive in the background, and one measure later the offstage voice of her approaching husband is heard.[13] Not long after, as she pulls apart the shroud she has been weaving (Scene 7), a chromatic figure by the flute within a sustained chord by the orchestra suggests the thread she is drawing out, a device singled out for praise by Saint-Saëns ("the cloth made visible by sound!").[14] These are quiet, subtle effects as the music guides our response to the words, but Fauré can also produce more overtly dramatic results, as is readily apparent by working back from the opera's great climax in the stringing of Ulysses' bow.

The bow as we see it in *Odyssey* 21 has multiple functions. It is on one level of plot what folklorists call a suitor test: the successful candidate will be the man who can string the bow and send an arrow through twelve axes in a line (*Od.* 19.572–581, cf. 21.74–78).[15] It is also a recognition

[12] Fauré to Marie Fauré-Fremiet, September 20, 1907, in *Gabriel Fauré: Lettres intimes*, ed. Philippe Fauré-Fremiet (Paris: La Colombe, 1951), 153. Fauré's well documented impatience with the libretto and his efforts to overcome its limitations are discussed in Orledge, *Gabriel Fauré*, 221–228 and Nectoux, *Gabriel Fauré*, 330–332. One result is that the "libretto" published by Heugel in 1913 as *Pénélope. Poème lyrique en trois actes. Musique de Gabriel Fauré* is for the most part Fauchois' original work. The text as actually set by Fauré exists in print only as part of the score and as an enclosure with the 1991 Erato CD. The libretto will be cited here using the pagination of the 1913 publication, with differences from the score-text noted when relevant.

[13] "A dramatic coincidence, yet it would seem he has been summoned by the very sound and power of her voice," remarked Sobaskie, "Audacity of Pénélope," 86–87, in a discussion well illustrated by annotated text and score. Steven Huebner, "Ulysses Revealed," in *Regarding Fauré*, ed. Tom Gordon (Amsterdam: Gordon and Breach, 1999), 220 notes that Ulysse's offstage cry ("Hola! ho! Hola! ho!") is itself essentially sound, "semantically amorphous at best." (Stephen Rumph has pointed out to me the similarity to Pelléas' entrance as he is drawn to Mélisande in the Tower Scene of Debussy's Act III.)

[14] His praise comes just after the complaint noted above, note 10. Other examples of such sound-play are discussed by Huebner "Ulysses Revealed" and Sobaskie, "Audacity of Pénélope."

[15] The folklorists' mainstay, Stith Thompson's *Motif-Index of Folk Literature*, Vol. 3 (Bloomington: Indiana University Press, 1956), defines an extensive set of such tests, H.310–359. The specific task Penelope sets for the suitors is not easily envisioned, though scholars persist in trying to do so. See the various attempts reviewed by Manuel

token, most explicitly and economically so for Fauchois (and Fauré) since they make action and revelation simultaneous as Ulysse lets his second arrow fly:[16]

Eurymache atteint est tombé. Pénélope s'est levée. Ulysse a dépouillé son déguise-ment et s'est redressé, terrible. Effroi des Prétendants.

PÉNÉLOPE: Ulysse! . . .

Eurymachus is struck and falls. Penelope rises up. Ulysses throws off his disguise and stands erect and menacing. The suitors are terrified.

PENELOPE: Ulysses! . . .

The situation in Homer is more complex, and not simply because Penelope is reluctant to draw the obvious conclusion from its result. As with the introduction of another recognition, Eurykleia's discovery of Odysseus' scar, the appearance of the bow is also marked by a digression – how Odysseus received it as a guest-gift from Iphitus in Lacedaemon (*Od.* 21.13–41) – which signals its importance to the story and foreshadows its role in punishing the suitors' offense to the norms of guest-friendship (*xenia*). It is not, however, only Odysseus whose identity becomes clear by means of this test. Telemachus also claims a chance to string the bow, and a curious thing then happens:

Three times he made it shudder, straining to bend it,
three times his power flagged – but his hopes ran high
he'd string his father's bow and shoot through every iron
and now, struggling with all his might for the fourth time,
he would have strung the bow, but Odysseus shook his head
and stopped him short despite his tensing zeal.

(*Od.* 21.125–129)

The test reveals Telemachus to be a worthy son, capable and also obedient, and thus fit to stand by his father's side in the climactic battle to come.[17]

Fernandez-Galiano in *A Commentary on Homer's Odyssey, Vol. 3. Books XVII–XXIV*, ed. Joseph Russo, Manuel Fernandez-Galiano, and Alfred Heubeck (Oxford: Clarendon, 1992), 131–147. Fauchois avoids the issue: nothing needs to be dramatized beyond the challenge of the bow.

[16] As is clear from their correspondence, the full stage direction, quoted here from the score and not from the published libretto (p. 75), reflects Fauré's idea of the action. Fauchois tended to note emotional effects but often left the details of stage business out of his original text.

[17] And also, presumably, a worthy successor, just as Iphitus was judged worthy to receive the bow from his father Eurytus (*Od.* 21.31–33).

That brings us to the bow's third function. It is in Homer a very material object. A weapon. Homer makes this clear when Odysseus at last gets his turn to string it:

> Now *he* held the bow
> in his own hands, turning it over, tip to tip,
> testing it, this way, that way ... fearing worms
> had bored through the weapon's horn with the master gone abroad ...

> once he'd handled the great bow and scanned every inch,
> then, like an expert singer skilled at lyre and song –
> who strains a string to a new peg with ease,
> making the pliant sheep-gut fast at either end –
> so with his virtuoso ease Odysseus strung his mighty bow.
> (*Od.* 21.393–395, 404–409)

That is the epic. The migration to opera brings a curious change to this bow. Both the thing itself and the task of stringing it are stylized, the bow often represented in productions of Monteverdi as a somewhat ungainly object, a prop designed to stymie the suitors and make them look ridiculous. Fauchois' suitors stand in awe of its size (Ctésippe: "Tu n'as pas regardé l'arc immense!" [You've never seen such a huge bow], p. 66) and weight, (Eurymaque: "Il est épais et lourd" [It is thick and heavy], p. 70), and the incidental music that attends their successive attempts to string it is at once suspenseful and potentially comic.[18] So unrealistic a weapon hardly matters in the two operas, where the number of suitors is reduced to three (Monteverdi) or five (Fauré), and they are thus not so very difficult to eliminate. Homer's Odysseus faced 108 suitors (*Od.* 16.250, 23.150), a fact which presented not just the tactical problem that makes sensible and realistic his caution in revealing himself to anyone at all, but leads to a pitched battle in the hall after he strings the bow, sends a first arrow through the axes, and then a second through the throat of the suitor Antinous. That sequence results in a furious rampage described with all the enthusiasm of an Iliadiac battle as Odysseus and his helpers slaughter in graphic detail all the suitors, their retainers, and those of his own household who had served them. Maidservants are then compelled to clean up the mess, after which they are themselves strung up by ropes in

---

[18] The Opéra national du Rhin (Strasbourg) production of 2015 represented the bow by an oversized metal bar. For the Vespertine Opera production in Seattle, from the same year, it was, rather prosaically, merely a bow. For the scene in *Il ritorno*, see Ewans, *Opera*, 26–28; and for variations in its staging, Marianne McDonald, "Mythical Musical Drama in Monteverdi," *Arion* 23 (2015), 149–181, esp. 172–176.

the courtyard and left to dangle like birds on a string (*Od.* 22.446–473). Small wonder the palace is then besieged by outraged townspeople grieving for the dead. Odysseus girds himself for what threatens to be a civil war, and chaos is averted only by a thunderclap and the appearance of Athena on the epic equivalent of the machine.

Reducing the number of suitors is not just dramatically convenient for the staging of the operas but makes possible what are in effect alternative endings. The Italian version also has a deeply problematic ending, though it is not the Homeric one. Its climax builds from a fundamental psychological insight: after twenty years of separation, the last ten under mounting pressure from the suitors and a growing tension between hopes and fears, how can Penelope possibly trust the mere evidence of her senses? How can she surrender at a stroke the wariness that has come to define her character? Badoaro (and Monteverdi) saw the problem clearly and built their final act around the need for Penelope to abandon her skepticism. This is affected less by Badoaro's somewhat mechanical expedient of Ulysses' ability to describe the coverlet on their marriage bed (not nearly as evocative a token as the secret of the Homeric bed itself, which was carved from a living tree and thus both literally and figuratively unmovable) as by Monteverdi's sequence of verbal and aural modulations that gradually overcome Penelope's resistance until she abandons recitative in her key for song in his.[19] In ending with this reunion they are, albeit unwittingly, reflecting the same impulse that led some of the greatest Homeric scholars of antiquity to identify the "true" end of the *Odyssey* not where the manuscripts end with Athena's imposed peace in Book 24, but back in Book 23 as Odysseus and Penelope at long last mount to their bed as husband and wife.[20]

Not so in the French version. As we have seen, Fauchois' Pénélope recognizes (and accepts) Ulysse as soon as he throws off his disguise, and notwithstanding the inevitable murder of suitors and retainers, the residents

---

[19] The progression is analyzed by Rosand, *Last Operas*, 288–294. See also Tim Carter, "'In Love's Harmonious Consort'? Penelope and the Interpretation of 'Il ritorno d'Ulisse in patria,'" *Cambridge Opera Journal* 5 (1993), 1–16, here 13–15.

[20] Two sets of ancient comments (scholia) record at *Od.* 23.296 that the Alexandrian scholars Aristophanes of Byzantium and Aristarchus placed the "end" (πέρας, Σ M, V, Vind. 133; τέλος, Σ H, M, Q) of the poem here, while a note by the twelfth-century commentator Eustathius makes it clear that discussion of the problem was well launched by his day. Whether these scholars meant by "true end" the actual finale, the emotional or thematic climax, or some significant compositional break is unclear. For the technicalities of the scholia, see Heubeck in *A Commentary on Homer's Odyssey*, 341–345; and for the compositional questions this testimony raises, John Miles Foley, *Homer's Traditional Art* (University Park, PA: Penn State, 1999), 157–167.

of Ithaca are at once overjoyed to find their king returned to them. The dramatic emphasis is determined not by the words but by the music: a quick shooting of the first arrow through the axes is followed by a more protracted and intense accompaniment as the second one aims at Eurymaque, and then by a long, celebratory unity of voices.[21] Order is restored, and everyone seems glad about it, including Fauré: "The opera finishes in a mood of serenity," he wrote his wife in 1912. "Everyone is happy and they sing, without shouting, 'Glory to Zeus.'"[22] This might seem on the face of it to be little more than a sop to what the great Fauré scholar Jean-Michel Nectoux called "psychological attitudes and bourgeois morality that belong to twentieth-century France."[23] Come to this joyous resolution from the violence and chicanery of the *Odyssey* or the psychological tension of *Il ritorno* and it can certainly seem contrived and even perfunctory, but a basis for presenting so upbeat an ending is actually established much earlier.

This opera handles the key questions – what does Penelope know and when does she know it? – differently from its predecessors, with the decisive moment coming not with some last test at the climax but in the second act, in a quite remarkable scene between Pénélope and the "beggar" Ulysse. The scene is, as often noted, not in Homer, but it is created from recognizably Homeric elements. The action takes place on a hill overlooking the sea, where Pénélope is accustomed to watch for Ulysse. Her questioning of the "beggar" beside her about his origin and arrival in Ithaca derives from *Odyssey* 19 (104ff.), but the setting, together with her reason for being there, recall (with gender roles reversed) a quite different moment in Book 5. There Odysseus, trapped on Calypso's island, is accustomed to sit each day on a promontory overlooking the sea and to pine for home:

[Calypso] found him there on the headland, sitting, still,
weeping, his eyes never dry, his sweet life flowing away
with the tears he wept for his foiled journey home . . .

But all his days he'd sit on the rocks and beaches,
wrenching his heart with sobs and groans and anguish,
gazing out over the barren sea through blinding tears.
                    (*Od.* 5.151–153, 156–158)

---

[21] I thank Carlo Caballero for pointing out to me the dramatic significance of the music: "the fact that Eurymachus is slain on stage is important for the dramaturgy, and Fauré clearly thought so, too, as he makes the glissando for this second arrow longer and denser than for the first arrow – it has extra will applied to it, the energy of vengeance" (personal communication).

[22] August 31, 1912, in Fauré-Fremiet, *Lettres intimes*, 207; quoted in Nectoux, *Gabriel Fauré*, 326.

[23] Nectoux, *A Musical Life*, 329.

Pénélope's longing here echoes Odysseus' longing there, her helplessness now echoes his helplessness then, but just as Odysseus in Book 5 leaves his post with hope when Calypso consents to his long-delayed departure, so there is something hopeful here, though even Fauré may not have recognized its full import. He was, we know, unhappy with this scene from early on in the collaboration, and by 1911 he had decided to rework it completely. The problem was simply put: "The situation," he wrote his wife, "is demanded by the theater, perhaps, but it's quite unbelievable – a wife sings to her husband and doesn't recognize him because he's wearing a false beard! And I have to force myself to feel conviction so that it comes through in her music."[24] The objection is not entirely fair, even here without Athena (or Badoaro's Minerva) to transform Ulysses' appearance: a wife may well fail to recognize a husband returned after twenty years of war and shipwreck, sending home nary a text nor a tweet in all that time. We might just as logically wonder why Pénélope fails to recognize a Ulysses theme playing in the background when she hears one. Yet the scene succeeds in making two important contributions to the credibility of the eventual resolution, as Fauré overcame his own initial objections and found the psychological truth beneath the theatrical artifice.

The first of these contributions comes by taking up Homer's intimation that Penelope, or at least some part of Penelope, *does* recognize her husband through his disguise.[25] A first hint of this came in Act One, Scene Three, when the "beggar's" offstage voice startles her with its familiarity, an effect emphasized by Fauchois, though muted when Fauré pruned the dialogue, and again in the following scene when Pénélope, although agreeing that neither the beggar's face nor age recalls her husband, breaks out: "Et cependant . . . ta voix . . . me rappelle elle-même | Quelque chose . . ." ("And yet . . . your very voice reminds me | Of something," p. 28), where Fauchois' original stage direction, missing from the performance script, has her staring intently at him (*fixant Ulysse avec attention*). This moment of suppressed inquiry comes just before Euryclée washes the beggar's feet and recognizes his scar, when, at the comparable moment in the *Odyssey*, Penelope, too, suddenly pulls back from the possibility of a sudden recognition:

[24] August 4, 1911 in Fauré-Fremiet, *Lettres intimes*, 196; quoted in Nectoux, *Gabriel Fauré*, 331.
[25] The possibility of an "early recognition" by Penelope is a recurring idea in Homeric scholarship. See most recently Steve Reece, "Penelope's 'Early Recognition' of Odysseus from a Neoanalytic and Oral Perspective," *College Literature* 38 (2011), 101–117, and for the ambiguities of her characterization within the epic tradition, Foley, *Homer's Traditional Art*, 27–31 and 142–157.

Up with you now, my good old Eurycleia,
come and wash your master's . . . equal in years.
Odysseus must have feet and hands like this by now.

(*Od.* 19.357–359)[26]

At the end of this scene in Fauchois' Act Two, the beggar's voice again takes Penelope to the threshold of recognition (p. 49):

PÉNÉLOPE: Oh! Ta voix, a l'instant, me rappelle ...

ULYSSE: Qui? ...

PÉNÉLOPE: Non!

Tu t'enorguellirais si je disais son nom

PENELOPE: Oh! your voice just now reminded me of ...

ODYSSEUS: Who? ...

PENELOPE: No! ...

You would become conceited if I spoke his name ...

Somehow, in some way, she knows. Her ability to foreshadow the suitors' end when she, like the Cassandra of Aeschylus' *Agamemnon*, envisions the great hall spattered with blood and gore – "Ah! Malheureux! . . . Je vois ces colonnes et ces murailles couvertes de sang et d'entrailles fumantes. . ." (Ah! Miserable ones! . . . I see these columns and these walls covered with blood and steaming entrails, p. 67) – will spring from this unconscious certainty.

The second move toward climax involves the bow itself. In proposing this test, Homer's Penelope seems resigned to the emergence of a successful suitor:

The hand that can string the bow with greatest ease,
that shoots an arrow clean through all twelve axes –

---

[26] Fagles' dots in line 358 represent a caesura in the original (νίψον σοῖο ἄνακτος | ὁμήλικα· καί που Ὀδυσσεύς), a strategic as well as metrical pause that betrays the thought Penelope is struggling to suppress.

he's the man I follow, forsaking this house
where I was once a bride . . .

(Od. 19.577–579, cf. 21.74–78)

Such ambivalence toward remarriage is a major source of tension throughout the *Odyssey* and a major interpretive crux. Fauchois' Pénélope is much
clearer in her intention:

Crois-tu que demain
Je mettrai ma main
Dans la main d'Eurymaque ou celle de Pisandre?
Je préfère aux enfers descendre . . .
Grâce au poison ou grâce au fer plus prompt
Je m'épargnerai le suprême affront . . .

Do you think that tomorrow
I will put my hand
In the hand of Eurymachus or that of Pisander?
I prefer to go down to Hell . . .
Either by poison or by steel, I will very quickly
Spare myself that ultimate insult . . .

(p. 47)

Talk of death and the suitors' cowardly expectations continues
for some ten more lines before the disguised Ulysse redirects the
conversation:

Ne m'as-tu pas, tantôt, toi, la nourrice
Montré le grand arc d'Ulysse
Aux murs suspendu?

Nurse, did you not just now show me
The great bow of Ulysses
Hanging on the wall?

This is another of the scenes Fauré cut to great effect, adding dramatic
point to the lines even before setting them to music. Talk of poison and
sword vanish in the final version, words are rearranged to more telling
effect, and the dialogue now moves directly to the central point of the
scene:

PÉNÉLOPE   Crois-tu que demain
             Je mettrai ma main
             Dans la main d'Eurymaque ou celle de Pisandre?
             Je préfère aux enfers descendre . . .

ULYSSE   Tantôt, aux murs suspendu,
              Ne m'as-tu pas, nourrice, montré l'arc d'Ulysse?

On learning the bow is intact, the beggar then offers his instruction.[27]

Ne sois donc qu'à celui d'entre les Prétendants
Qui tendra l'arc.
Pendant qu'ils se disputeront cette gloire impossible,
Ton époux peut encore revenir.

Then choose only the one from among the suitors who
Bends the bow.
While they quarrel over that impossible triumph
Your husband may come back.

The beggar's suggestion takes from Pénélope the initiative to impose tests
that consistently rests with her in Homer, and his commanding confidence
promises to relieve her of the moral dilemma of whether to accept one of
the suitors or remain faithful to her missing husband.[28] And, as we have
seen, her immediate recognition of Ulysse once he has strung the bow
eliminates those obstacles to acceptance that gave Monteverdi's version of
the story its psychological depth and emotional core. The result is a
streamlining of both the plot and of the psychology that motivates it.
Her fears readily yield to her hopes, making possible the serenity that
seems to have satisfied Fauré. But where does that leave the character of the
woman at the heart of the story?

Fauchois tried hard, perhaps too hard, to capture the emotional upheav-
als produced by Pénélope's difficulties, and time and again we see how
Fauré tightened the verse to intensify the drama of her situation. Discomfort with the result has nevertheless been registered since the beginning.
Saint-Saëns, in the audience for the first production in Monte Carlo, mixed
with his praise of the music a final complaint about the staging: "I don't see
the need to have Penelope always going around like a sleepwalker under
the pretext that she misses her husband. Penelope has an energetic character."[29] In 1913, Lucienne Bréval must clearly have played the title role in

---

[27] This is Fauré's significantly compressed version, which again cuts text, rearranges words, and
      reassigns lines to different speakers.
[28] The idea is not entirely without Homeric precedent. At *Od.* 24.167–169 the suitor
      Amphimedon, recalling these events for Agamemnon in Hades, attributes the test (contrary to
      the earlier narrative) to Odysseus.
[29] Camille Saint-Saëns to Fauré, March 12, 1913, in Fauré, *Correspondance*, 394. For the
      characterization of Pénélope as "dreamer and seer," see Huebner, "Ulysses Revealed."

that passive way, but it is not equally certain whether Saint-Saëns was contrasting what he saw with a memory of what he had once read in Homer or with something he heard in the music that had somehow gone unrealized in the production. Fauré, at any rate, was quite pleased with his two lead singers, Bréval and Charles Rousselière ("deux bons interprètes"), which suggests that a sleepwalking Pénélope did not trouble him. Notwithstanding the earlier pageantry of *Prométhée*, he generally resisted the enhancement of musical performance with gratuitous stage effects. In her gesture and stage business, rather more than in her singing, Pénélope clings to a middle register, and Fauré responded with some vehemence when his Monte Carlo producer, Raoul Gunsbourg, sought to turn the serene grandeur of the finale into something more dramatic.[30]

This *could* be taken as a virtue. Nectoux, who has done so much to restore interest in Fauré, certainly approves of the result:

in forgoing the *coup de théâtre* and the enticements of orchestral writing, both of which seemed to him too external, Fauré was blithely riding rough-shod over all the operatic conventions, the "old tricks." From the musical point of view one can only applaud this: *Pénélope* has the beauty of pure music . . . In fact *Pénélope* needs to be listened to as one listens to a string quartet or classical symphony, for the work is all music.[31]

The problem, at least for modern audiences, is that the work is *not* all music. It is opera, which means by definition that it is also expected to be theater. There is without question excitement in the music, but what does the audience see to correspond with what they hear? Two 2015 productions, which both met the work's musical challenges with acumen and skill, responded to this other, theatrical expectation in different ways.[32] As staged at Opéra national du Rhin (Strasbourg), and despite Fauchois' deliberate effort to distinguish his story from Homer's by strategic omissions and compressions, the *Odyssey*'s most obviously missing elements were thrust back into view: dancers re-enacted the trials of Odysseus' journey as Pénélope sat quietly with the beggar in the second act, and Telemachus was reintroduced to the action as a solo dancer.[33]

---

[30] So Fauré to his wife, February 24, 1913, writing of Gunsbourg: "His latest idea consists in modifying the end of *Pénélope* and replacing the peaceful finale with a lot of flash and noise." *Lettres intimes,* 215–216. The same letter notes his satisfaction with his two leads.

[31] Nectoux, *Gabriel Fauré: His Life through His Letters*, ed. Jean-Michel Nectoux, trans. J. A. Underwood (London: M. Boyars, 1984), 268–269.

[32] See note 18.

[33] And more: "There was water, a horse, the goddess Athena and all kinds of extras here and there" (blakesoperablog.blogspot.com/2016/02/gabriel-faure-penelope-strasbourg.html). Raoul

The Vespertine Opera Theater (Seattle) used a different strategy, though it was no less willing to indulge modern expectations over period aesthetics. In its version, the beggar's decrepitude was not a disguise. Ulysse was envisioned as a genuinely enfeebled war casualty, Pénélope's dependent as much as her rescuer. She then emerges both figuratively and literally as the stronger of the two.

This was clearly not Fauchois' original intention. His climax seeks to recall the original impact as Homer's Odysseus drops his disguise:

Now stripping back his rags Odysseus master of craft and battle
vaulted onto the great threshold, gripping his bow and quiver (*Od.* 21.1–2)

After striking Eurymaque with a second arrow, Ulysse, too, bounds up in full majesty, and in brandishing the sword Euryclée brings out from hiding he reasserts his dominance.[34] When Pénélope, Euryclée, and their attendants then all shout out together "Ulysse est de retour!" the return is both literal and figurative. Yet here again Fauré cut the text, and in doing so he shifted much of the drama from the words to the music. What we actually see (and hear) is then a Ulysse whose actions seem accompanied throughout by a certain hesitancy while Pénélope gains a corresponding dignity.[35] On that basis, one could say that the Seattle production simply brought a latent weakness in Ulysse to the foreground. Doing so, however, did mean that the subdued tone of the finale was heard not as Fauré's serenity but as a much more contemporary unease, and it raised a lingering question of

Gunsbourg, if not Fauré, would have understood. There was dance in the original production, too, but it was not intended to carry this narrative burden. See Carlo Caballero, "Dance and Lyric Reunited: Fauré's *Pénélope* and the Changing Role of Ballet in French *Opéra*," in *Bild und Bewegung im Musiktheater: Interdiziplinäre Studien im Umfeld der Grand Opéra/Image and Movement in Musical Theater: Interdisciplinary Studies around Grand Opera*, ed. Roman Brotbeck, Laura Moeckli, Anette Schaffer, and Stephanie Schroedter (Schliengen: Edition Argus, 2018), 51–64.

[34] Fauchois' original stage direction on p. 75 is unambiguous: "Ulysse, qui s'est redressé, terrible, et à qui Euryclée a passé le glaive qu'il avait caché sous le trône de Pénélope" (Ulysses, who has risen up, terrifyingly, and to whom Eurykleia has handed the sword that she had hidden beneath Penelope's throne.) In the final version, the sword and its symbolism are gone. See note 15.

[35] Thus Sobaskie characterized Pénélope as a strong and self-possessed modern woman, "whose virtue exceeds that of all other characters, including and especially her husband, whose doubt debilitates and diminishes him while enhancing and exalting her" ("The Audacity of Pénélope," 92). A debilitated, morally compromised Odysseus is well represented in twentieth-century drama, from Stanislaw Wyspanski, *The Return of Odysseus* (original 1917; translated into English by Howard S. Clarke, Bloomington: Indiana University Press, 1966) to Derek Walcott's stage version, *The Odyssey* (New York: Farrar Straus Giroux, 1993) and beyond. See the useful survey by Hall, *Return of Ulysses*, 181–184.

how, or to what extent, these two damaged people would ever be able to recover something of their former happiness.

All these interpretations, whether the work of librettists and composers on the page or of directors and conductors creating the look, sound, and action of specific productions, share one notable attribute, viz. their deliberate lack of fidelity to the tone and detail of the events at Ithaca as described in Book 22 of the *Odyssey*. We accept as a narrative necessity the fact of Odysseus' revenge, but we prefer to see as little of it as possible. The vicious slaughter of the suitors and their attendants, male and female alike, has thus spawned a long history of obfuscation and redirection.[36] The number of suitors is reduced, the carnage is muted or moved offstage, and emphasis shifts to the reunion of husband and wife, which, however problematic, is more congenial, more engaging, and ultimately more satisfying for modern audiences to contemplate. That is no fault and no surprise. The ability to support even radical shifts of interest and emphasis is central to the *Odyssey*'s greatness and to its enduring appeal. The poem that first gave us Proteus, the archetypal shape-shifter of antiquity (*Od.* 4. 384–480), is itself protean in form and meaning, always a challenge to artists and a source of fascination to audiences.

---

[36] Well observed by Hall, *Return of Ulysses*, 179–184.

7 | Orchestral Melody in *Pénélope*

Aspects of Wagner's Influence on Fauré

MATHIEU SCHNEIDER

In her "Étude comparée des langages harmoniques de Fauré et de Debussy," Françoise Gervais contends that "melody does not have an independent existence in Fauré's music. It is born of the harmony and remains inseparable from it."[1] Moreover, not a single chapter of this book, which has stood now for more than forty years as a musicological *summa* on Fauréan harmony, is dedicated to melody. Pages 73 and 74 discuss the interpenetration of harmony and melody, but with few examples, and the argument, judged against the quality and quantity of the analyses that surround it, seems very tenuous. It is no less astonishing that the majority of academic publications on Fauré's melody approach the question exclusively from the angle of genre, that is, in relation to the *mélodie* (French art song) with its peculiar issues of Fauré's rapport with poets, prosody, harmonic expressiveness, and even the role of rhythm. With the exception of some passages in Jankélévitch's work and Nectoux's monograph, the question of the role of melody as a horizontal line, in polyphony, and in the form and meaning of the musical work, has never been explored.[2] At least with regard to the eminently polyphonic and horizontal character of training at the École Niedermeyer, which formed the young Fauré, the question of melody seems significant.

It goes without saying that the study of melody in Fauré cannot be covered in a single essay. For that reason, I shall limit myself to the function of melody in the elaboration of musical form, and also give some consideration to its semantic role, in a single work, *Pénélope*. The choice is not random, for in opera, more than in instrumental genres, the question of melody is central. Melody nourishes the vocal writing, to be sure, but under the influence of Wagner's works, the orchestra also demands its say. Studies of *Pénélope* have never directly addressed this question; aside from

---

[1] Françoise Gervais, "Étude comparée des langages harmoniques de Fauré et de Debussy," *La revue musicale* 272 (1971), 73.

[2] See Vladimir Jankélévitch, *Gabriel Fauré: Ses mélodies, son esthétique* (Paris: Plon, 1938); and Jean-Michel Nectoux, *Gabriel Fauré: Les voix du clair-obscur*, second edition (Paris: Fayard, 2008).

Nectoux's remarks in an article on Fauré's theatrical aesthetic, scholars show more interest in the relationship with Debussy's *Pelléas et Mélisande* or in the treatment of classical antiquity.[3] While the subject is not exactly virgin territory, neither has it been favored by musicological inquiry. And for good reason: to view *Pénélope* from the vantage point of melody requires us to define the concept and array our analytical tools. And there's the rub, for musicology is much less well equipped to grasp a melody than to understand a succession of chords. This chapter thus falls into three parts. After reviewing the role played by melody in opera from the second half of the nineteenth century in relation to Wagner's idea of "orchestral melody," I shall evaluate the influence of that notion on Fauré's thought, before finally considering how, in practical terms, he used melody in *Pénélope* to construct its meaning and form. Since melody becomes a way of speaking "beyond" the text, it allows us to address the "ineffable" character of Fauré's music.

A New Way of Conceiving Melody: Wagner and Orchestral Melody

In the entry "Mélodie" in *Musiques: Une encyclopédie pour le xxie siècle*, Rossana Dalmonte offers three meanings for melody.[4] It may be:

(1) a succession of sounds;
(2) a theme; or
(3) a combination of the two meanings above; that is, the relation of different melodies, considered as successions of sounds, among themselves in polyphony.

This definition ultimately recaptures the concept of *melos* as laid out long ago by Plato, a concept at the crossroads of *harmonia* (superposition of sounds), *rhythmos* (scansion of time), and *logos* (relationship with text).[5]

This third meaning is almost an "anti-definition" of melody, as Dalmonte notes, because the musicologist apparently denies the existence of melody as a horizontal line in order to make it a real (or perhaps only

---

[3] See Nectoux, "Gabriel Fauré et l'esthétique de son œuvre théâtral," *Revue musicale de Suisse romande* 33, No. 2 (1980), 50–59.

[4] Rossana Dalmonte, "Mélodie," in *Musiques: Une encyclopédie pour le xxie siècle*, ed. Jean-Jacques Nattiez (Arles: Actes Sud; Paris: Cité de la Musique, 2004), Vol. 2: 67–88.

[5] Carl Dahlhaus and Lars Ulrich Abraham used the Platonic model as one point of departure in their theory of melody, *Melodielehre* (Köln: Musikverlag Hand Gerig, 1972).

virtual) point of intersection in musical form. From another perspective, this meaning raises the concept of melody to a formal, even ontological, level in the work (melody as the essence of the work) that, curiously, is not out of step with theories current in Fauré's own time. Indeed, it is around 1900 that the three senses of melody reunite: the linear series of sounds forms a "theme" (or more often a motive) that irrigates the music both vertically and horizontally and forms the link with the text. This might seem a tautology, but the rebirth of polyphony out of melody (one must use these terms to describe the phenomenon) is one property of music in Fauré's time. This rebirth came about through the development of the relationship between melody and harmony fomented and accompanied by Romanticism.

The outstanding French nineteenth-century treatise on melody is by Antoine Reicha (Paris, 1813), but his conclusions on the independence of melody from harmony and on the need to compose symmetrically structured melodies (along the lines of *galant* antecedent–consequent models) bear witness to a way of thinking that was strongly rooted in the eighteenth century.[6] Besides, nineteenth-century composers rarely cited Reicha's treatise. Fauré was no exception: Reicha's name never appears in his correspondence.

In contrast, from the start of the nineteenth century, philosophers set about restoring the value of melody. Rousseau had blazed a trail in his *Essai sur l'origine des langues* where he asserted, against Rameau, the claim that expression in music is borne by the melody.[7] A musical work can thus only be expressive by giving melody a more important role than harmony and by putting it in the service of the text and the meaning of the work. Disciples of Rameau, like Senancour, took up this theory in their turn,[8] and, indirectly, it would guide one of the key works of nineteenth-century French music theory, Berlioz's *Grand traité d'instrumentation et d'orchestration modernes* (Paris, 1844).[9] While this work is to all appearances a treatise on instruments and their technical capacities, it insists on two crucial points: the special expression of each instrument and the potential

---

[6] See Antoine Reicha, *Traité de mélodie, abstraction faite de ses rapports avec l'harmonie* (Paris: Chez l'auteur, 1814).

[7] See Jean-Jacques Rousseau, *Essai sur l'origine des langues* (Paris: Flammarion, 1993), 109–110.

[8] See more details in Mathieu Schneider, *L'utopie suisse dans la musique romantique* (Paris: Hermann, 2016), 29–34 (on Rousseau) and 77–92 (on Senancour).

[9] Hector Berlioz, *New Edition of the Complete Works, Vol. 24: Grand traité d'instrumentation et d'orchestration modernes*, ed. Peter Bloom (Kassel: Bärenreiter, 2003).

expressive role that the *individual* melody of each instrument can play in the polyphony.

During the same period in Germany, toward which the young Fauré had cast more than one sidelong glance, most notably in Schumann's direction, the idea of a new musical paradigm founded on the expressive primacy of melody had made inroads as well. It appears in Hegel, who saw in melody the governor of the "innerness of sounds" (*tönende Innerlichkeit*). If harmony is for Hegel the "law of necessity" (*Gesetz der Notwendigkeit*) that permits sounds to be organized in space and time, melody bears music's poetry, that is, the "soul's free resounding in the sphere of music" (*das freie Tönen der Seele im Felde der Musik*).[10] In the same period, Schumann would put Hegel's ideas into practice by giving melody the role of carrying the work, whether by processes of melodic ciphering (his "lettres dansantes" from *Carnaval*, Op. 9, come to mind), or, as in the *Humoreske*, Op. 20, by making the melody an "inner voice" (*innere Stimme*) that becomes the guiding thread of the work.

And so the path was prepared for Wagner, who in his writings and in his compositional practice laid the keystone of nineteenth-century melodic theory. Although his contemporaries may not have perceived his music as fundamentally melodic (they spoke more of his blustery orchestration or his leitmotivic "system"), his theoretical writings are saturated with melodic premises. For Wagner, new music must start with melody. In addition, in Wagner "melody" takes on a broader meaning than in Schumann: it determines the form, imparts meaning (of text and of music), but above all, it is unfurled vertically in the orchestra. Wagner explained this new element in his *Lettre sur la musique* (1861), written to Frédéric Villot on the eve of the premiere of *Tannhäuser* in Paris:

> The orchestra of a modern symphonist, on the contrary, brims with motives from the action through an intimate participation; for, on the one hand, as the harmonic foundation, the orchestra alone makes the precise expression of the melody possible, and on the other hand, it maintains, uninterrupted, the course of the melody itself. Thus the motives always make themselves understood to the heart with utterly irresistible energy . . . If we recognize this ideal form in the musical drama fulfilling conditions mentioned thus far, the orchestra is the marvelous instrument that alone can proffer this form.[11]

[10] See Georg Friedrich Hegel, *Werke, Vol. 15: Vorlesungen über die Ästhetik*, ed. Eva Moldenhauer (Frankfurt: Surhkamp, 2004), 129–132.

[11] Richard Wagner, *Une communication à mes amis, suivi de Lettre sur la musique* (Paris: Mercure de France, 1976), 224.

Wagner had already captured this idea theoretically in a concept articulated some ten years earlier, in *Opera and Drama*, the idea of "orchestral melody" (*Orchestermelodie*).[12] This concept may be summarized as follows. The dichotomy between melody and accompaniment that had dominated opera from the time of Monteverdi yields to a symphonic-vocal polyphony that knits voice and orchestra together into one complex tissue. Within this context, melody is no longer the principal line that the listener hears emerging over the orchestra but the fundamental line that underlies the musical composition, and which, like the inner voice of Schumann's *Humoreske*, is not always discernible. According to Wagner, it must therefore be fertilized by "the melody of verse" (that is, the intrinsic music of the poetic text) in order to give birth to a thematic-melodic complex, which then emerges in the orchestra. Orchestral melody is the presentiment (and foundation) of a dramatic gesture that, nourished by poetry, gives birth to a music that together with the voice conveys what Wagner called "reminiscence," that is, the physical and acoustic trace of this music. Orchestral melody is at the same time the poietic principle of music (the Kantian *Einbildungskraft*) and its realization in the orchestra – in other words, a music in which the distinction between voice and orchestra vanishes in favor of a unique and fully meaningful polyphonic complex (see Figure 7.1).

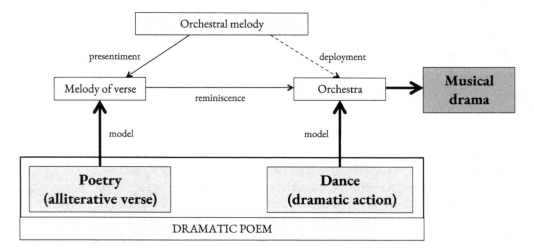

Figure 7.1 Diagram of the poietic principle in Richard Wagner, *Oper und Drama* (1851).

---

[12] Richard Wagner, *Œuvres en prose, Vol. 2: Opéra et drame*, ed. and trans. J. G. Prod'homme (Paris: Delagrave, 1907–24), 194–198.

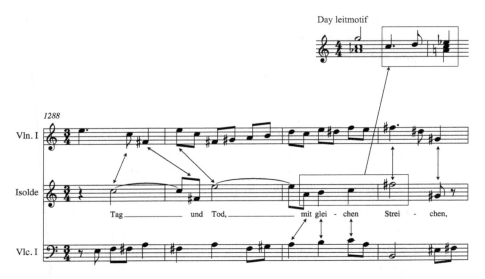

Example 7.1 Application of orchestral melody in Wagner, *Tristan und Isolde*, mm. 1288–1291

How is this realized concretely within a work? It is not hard to find palpable examples of this orchestral melody in Wagner's work, as Thomas Grey has demonstrated.[13] I should like to review an example here that will clarify my argument, which comes from the Act 2 duet of *Tristan und Isolde* (see Example 7.1). In this example, the principal melody is in the orchestra, or more precisely, in the string choir. Isolde could easily have taken up the melody, as if she were carried away by it. That would have been the normal way of composing an *arioso* in Wagner's age. What is striking in this extract, however, is the relative poverty of melody in Isolde's part. The vocal part is less expressive than the orchestra and, indeed, seems incoherent with its large intervals. A closer look reveals that Isolde actually doubles the orchestra but that she only takes snippets of the melody. The notes she chooses form other leitmotives, among them the Day motive. Now, at this precise moment in the drama, Brangäne has just warned Isolde that daybreak is near and that she and Tristan risk discovery after their night of love. The orchestral music suggests this risk to Isolde, which she in turn communicates in a felt but not outwardly intelligible way to Tristan.

In this extract, the form rests entirely on a melodic idea in the orchestra, which through a skillful marriage with the "verse melody," that is, the text

---

[13] Thomas S. Grey, *Wagner's Musical Prose: Texts and Contexts* (Cambridge: Cambridge University Press, 1995).

and dramatic situation, constructs a symphonic-vocal complex that under-scores, in counterpoint with the lulling melody of the orchestra, the urgency of daybreak.

This example eloquently realizes what Wagner, ever mindful of Hegel, theorized in his writings:

Now that we have given the melody of spoken verse what it could express to us, and that we have given it that quality as a medium of such melody as is apt to it, the activity in which it only, serenely, expressed what its nature endowed it to express, we must define a capacity for language in the orchestra, and this is its ability to affirm the inexpressible.[14]

In other words, Wagner's musical dramas are a tipping point in the history of opera: it is no longer harmony that supports vocal expression, and it is no longer the voice which is the principal melody; rather, it is the orchestra that guides the music, nourishes the voice and, interacting with it, produces the deep meaning of the work.

Fauré's Theoretical Stance

How is Fauré's music situated in relation to these models (Schumannian and Wagnerian) of melodic deployment? We unfortunately lack any the-oretical writing from him that could inform us on this question; we have only his music and letters. But in *Pénélope*, Fauré clearly worked differ-ently. Nectoux quite rightly emphasizes that Fauré, "like Wagner, subor-dinated the voice to the symphonic tapestry."[15] Might it not be too bold to suggest that Fauré, who knew Wagner's music well without ever having been its ardent champion, was inspired by the methods of the master of Bayreuth in his opera? Many signs lead us to think so.

To begin with, we may read in a letter to his wife dated August 16, 1907, while he was composing the first act of *Pénélope*:

The Maids are going to say who these Suitors are; what they have just done; the resistance Penelope, sad Penelope, has shown them; the inclinations the Suitors are arousing in these easy maidens, and so on. Now, all this has to be intelligible to the listener's ear, the dialogue has to be clear and, depending on which character is under discussion, the music needs to indicate *who* is being discussed. There you have it, that's the Wagnerian system: but there's none better.[16]

---

[14] Wagner, *Opéra et drame*, 194.   [15] Nectoux, *Gabriel Fauré*, 209.
[16] Gabriel Fauré, *Lettres intimes*, ed. Philippe Fauré-Fremiet (Paris: La Colombe, 1951), 144.

The "but" at the start of that last phrase has a touch of regret about it. Nonetheless, Fauré knew he was using leitmotives. But he particularly knew he was using them for a good reason: so that the orchestra could help the listener find his way in the drama; that is, so that the orchestra also becomes an actor in the drama. But here his adoption of the Wagnerian system is not superficial anymore: it implies the orchestra's capacity to *say* as much as the voice. This "saying" can explicitly indicate factual matters (for example, showing who is being discussed), but it can also evoke an ambience that enhances the context of the drama. Fauré said as much himself concerning the Maids working at their spindles and distaffs in Act 1:

It's not what they're saying that matters; it's the atmosphere, it's the slackness of their action shaded by reverie. Thus, it falls to the orchestral parts [*symphonie*] to comment on all that, and words should intervene and be integrated into an uninterrupted musical flow.[17]

The importance accorded to the orchestra betrays the latent influence of Wagner. We recall that Fauré himself avowed, in a letter to his wife written from Bayreuth in 1896:

I'm filled to the brim with this *Ring* cycle, it haunts me day and night! I do not think these works are clear exemplars or that it would be possible to imitate them. But boons and lessons still emerge from them in a general sort of way. They seep into you like water into sand.[18]

One senses this "water seeping into sand" all through Act 2 of *Pénélope*: the bassoon melody echoing the English horn at the beginning, the scene with the shepherd and Penelope waiting as she looks out to sea, built on chromatic motives – these are elements derived directly from *Tristan* and afforded by Fauchois' libretto. As for the orchestration, Debussy did not hesitate to compare it to that of *Parsifal*, and not without reason: there is an identical complement of brass (four horns, three trumpets, three trombones, and a tuba) and the same predilection for low woodwind timbre (bass clarinet, contrabassoon).[19]

Nevertheless, we must not conclude from these various arguments, picked out here and there, that Fauré was a Wagnerian. His stance toward the inventor of the music drama was much more nuanced. Though he made the pilgrimage to Bayreuth, he was never fond of *Tristan* but rather

---

[17] August 12, 1907, in ibid., 142.   [18] August 8, 1896, in ibid., 17.

[19] See Nectoux, *Gabriel Fauré*, 337.

declared himself ready to kneel before *Die Meistersinger* and the *Ring*.[20] This remark may seem surprising, for *Pénélope* might be understood, if not exactly as an homage to *Tristan*, at least as a reverberation of it: at Penelope's first entrance, there is an explicit reference to the "Tristan chord," on the same pitches and in the same voicing, and the pastoral scene at the beginning of Act 2 is a barely disguised allusion to the "alte Weise" of *Tristan's* third act.

As Carlo Caballero rightly emphasizes, one of the characteristics of Fauré's aesthetic attitude was "originality."[21] In the present context, this would mean the will to affirm a personal thought and style within a paradigm that takes up both French opera and Wagnerian music drama. Fauré knew how to remain himself even as he gathered from contemporaries and predecessors what could best serve his intentions.

Moreover, Fauré's conception of melody and form, which is indebted both to nineteenth-century traditions (Beethoven, Schumann, Saint-Saëns) and the Franckist school, led him to develop an approach to musical form that included building entire sections on unceasing motivic development. While such developmental features have little place in the work of Wagner, who changes the physiognomy of his leitmotives rather little, they are common coin in the French school. With Fauré, motives are repeated over and over, always slightly varied, so much so that they could mold themselves to the dramatic context even better than Wagner's. The composer of *Pénélope*, moreover, was clear on that point in another letter to his wife:

And when I say I am *testing* this theme, here's what that means: I look for all the combinations to which I might be able to bend this theme [that of the Suitors] depending on the circumstances. For example, one of the Maids says, speaking of one of the Suitors, "Antinous is handsome." Then my theme has to spread its tail – like a peacock.

I also look to see whether this theme could be combined with that of Penelope. I seek all the means of modifying it, of drawing different effects from it, whether taken as a whole or broken into pieces ... In short, it's as if I am making *index cards* that will serve me as I have the work underway, or if you like, as if I'm making *studies*, as one would for a painting.[22]

Finally, in the realm of prosody, many have sought to compare Fauré to Debussy, in whose hands the text takes on such striking relief. Fauré seems

[20] Gabriel Fauré, *Correspondance*, ed. Jean-Michel Nectoux (Paris: Flammarion, 1980), 72.
[21] Carlo Caballero, *Fauré and French Musical Aesthetics* (Cambridge: Cambridge University Press, 2001), 77.
[22] Letter of August 16, 1907, cited in note 16.

less limpid in his declamation; it is less "natural" and does not always follow the accents of spoken French or of versification. The mezzo-soprano Claire Croiza summed up Fauré's prosody admirably when she said, "Debussy is rhythmically faithful to the text; Fauré takes a walk in the forest with his poet in order to lead him. His declamation is impossible outside of the realm of song."[23] The reason for this is simple, and Fauré was aware of it: "It would be wrong to think that the poetic form doesn't matter: the musical form completes it felicitously, that's all. The essential thing is to understand one's poet, to feel with him or her."[24] In other words, music is not a double of the text: music should capture the text's atmosphere and, by prosodic lags, by the melodic line and the orchestral accompaniment, should show us what is hidden in the "forest" Claire Croiza spoke of. Perhaps in doing so it allows us to approach the ineffable.

And so, we see that there truly is no dogma in Fauré's art. Neither Wagnerian nor Franckist, he was both at the same time, or simply himself. In any event, the following reflections on his aesthetics clearly emerge:

(1) In opera, the gravitational attraction of Wagner is undeniable, notably in the relation between voice and orchestra and the use of leitmotives;
(2) Fauré, true to the French tradition, seeks in his own way to exploit variations of his motivic ideas as much as possible;
(3) Fauré's prosody does not retrace the poetic rhythm, but seeks an independent state apt to suggest ideas (or "moods," "atmospheres") in counterpoint to those of the text.

Orchestral Melody in *Pénélope*

We have postponed until now a fundamental move for understanding the role of melody in *Pénélope*, analysis of the score itself. One could almost flip open a page at random to find a good example of Wagner's concept of orchestral melody, so much does this opera seem to raise it to an absolute formal principle. Nevertheless, it is more evident in some scenes than others. This is the case in the second scene of Act 2, which follows the duet between Eumaeus and the Shepherd.

Not only does the symphony orchestra structure the scene here – and thus the orchestral melody, which drives the form – but this orchestral melody, originally a theoretical principle in Wagner, is embodied in a "melody" in the basic sense of the word, that is, in a horizontal line that

---

[23] Quoted in Nectoux, *Gabriel Fauré*, 359.   [24] Ibid.

Example 7.2 Trumpet theme (A) and chorale (B), *Pénélope*, Act 2, Scene 2.
Piano-vocal score, Paris: Heugel, 1913, 126

is easily perceived and clearly identifiable. Indeed, Fauré begins the scene with a highly expressive theme (A) in the trumpet, doubled by the first violins but without harmonic accompaniment; this effect prolongs the overall pastoral atmosphere (see Example 7.2). The trumpet clearly functions to add solemnity to the entrance of Penelope and Ulysses, whom she still does not recognize. The rest of the orchestra answers with a kind of chorale (B), whose top line is actually just a prolongation of the chromatic inflection of theme A and whose harmony wavers between A minor and A major owing to the mobility of the note C (now sharp, now natural), which echoes the G/G♯ equivocation in theme A. The chorale begins and ends on I^6 of A major, a classical framing device for the beginning of a recitative, which also constitutes the harmonic space within which

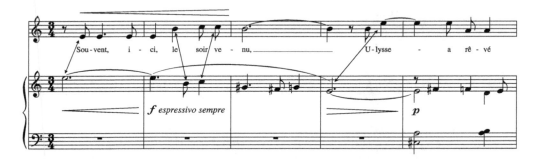

Example 7.3 Melodic intersections between Penelope and the orchestra, *Pénélope*, Act 2, Scene 2.
Piano-vocal score, 126–127

Penelope's first phrase unfolds ("C'est sur ce banc, devant cette colonne"). Then the melodic line, still unaccompanied, falls by step, its chromaticism taking support from the pitches of theme A.

This passage is constructed entirely from the trumpet melody (A). First, it occupies the acoustic space by itself at the beginning; second, the tail end with its chromatic instability (G♯/G) gives birth to the chromatic theme of the chorale; third, the melody also suggests the harmonic ambivalence between C♯ and C, which renders the harmony unstable (now major, now minor); and fourth, it forms the supporting points for the second part of the vocal line ("Qu'au souvenir des temps heureux"). What is more, this melody, following the very principles that Fauré took from Wagner, is *orchestral*: instrumental at the outset, unfolded in the orchestra's chorale, it ends by infecting the voice. Moreover, even when the vocal line becomes harmonic (singing across the A-major chord), it merely produces a horizontal projection of what we heard in the orchestra. The orchestra is thus indubitably the source of the musical form. The orchestra comes first, the voice second.

The rest of the scene only confirms this analysis. Theme A returns, and this time Penelope joins her voice to the sounds of the trumpet, in which she finds, as in a tracery, the supporting pitches of her own song (see Example 7.3). Then the chorale (B) comes back and, once again, the voice seems to seek its own articulation in the chorale. In this scene, as in the earlier passage from Wagner's *Tristan*, the vocal melody comes from the orchestra; it is like a twin, or more precisely, to borrow a term from science, an emergence.

The primacy of the orchestra also appears in many other parts of the score, even if it does not always maintain the same rapport with the voice

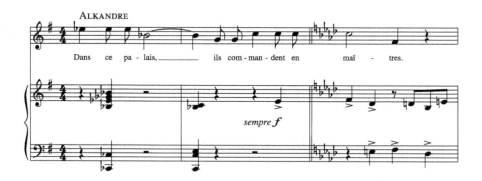

Example 7.4 The orchestra's melody in Cleone's arioso, *Pénélope*, Act 1, Scene 1.
Piano-vocal score, 22

(in many places Fauré preserves the principle of accompanied melody).
Nevertheless, the ear is continually captivated by the motives played by the
orchestra, which are often more striking than the voice because of their
more melodious and expressive character. Let us consider Cleone's arioso
from Act 1 (see Example 7.4). The *Allegro* section is clearly dominated by

the *marcato* motive in the orchestra. The orchestra has, in virtually Schoenbergian terms, the "principal voice" (*Hauptstimme*), whose weight is only reinforced by the fugato at the beginning of the section. Curiously, the voice does not take up the orchestral motive: here we have something different from the previous example of correspondence, even if inverted, between the voice and orchestra, but instead a sort of independence that leaves the voice *outside* of the orchestra. The *marcato* clearly suggests virility, especially since it sounds in the low register and with a martial tone. The fugato, for its part, multiplies this virile quality, as indeed the libretto here explicitly implies in referring to those "who command as masters," that is, the suitors of Penelope.

Here, the orchestra translates the power, virility, and unrestrained immoral behavior of the suitors – they who have impudently usurped Ulysses' position. The text also suggests their progress toward a sort of orgy: they command as masters, they party, they drink, they raid the herds for feasting. And if the voice suggests this growing tension by rising half-steps from C to E♭ on "ils le boiront jusqu'à la dernière goutte" ("they'll drink every last drop of it"), what enables the musical translation of the poetic hyperbole is again the increasing polyphonic density in the orchestra accomplished by the fugato and the separation of high and low registers. Although the voice is not left wholly outside the expressive dimension, everything happens as if Fauré decided to relieve the voice of dramatic expression in order to give it the freedom to declaim the text.

A Prosody Paradoxically Strengthened

The strengthening of the orchestra through what we might call a Fauréan appropriation of Wagner's "orchestral melody" brings with it a certain retreat of the voice. This retreat is mostly formal, in the sense that singing no longer organizes musical time. At times, as in the last example, the orchestral priority can even lead to an absence of singularity in the vocal line, which renders it almost bland, or blank, in comparison to the melodic vitality of the orchestra. This might lead one to think that the voice, and by extension the text it bears, loses importance. Yet the exact opposite occurs: in minimizing the melodic quality of the vocal part, Fauré favors the text.

In the previous two examples, one is struck by the repetition of pitches. In Italian *bel canto* melody (in Bellini or Verdi, for example), vocal style demands a melodic line that moves and avoids as much as possible the *recto tono*, except perhaps in recitatives. Repeated notes are frequent in

Example 7.5 Cleone's melody, *Pénélope*, Act 1, Scene 1.
Piano-vocal score, 22

Example 7.6 Servants' dialogue (Lydia), *Pénélope*, Act I, Scene 1
Piano-vocal score, 26–27

Fauré, in recitative-like sections as well as in ariosos. These repetitions make any interval that much more marked and expressive when it occurs. This alternation of *recto tono* and large intervals is a typical prosodic strategy of Fauré's. We find a fine example in Cleone's arioso in the same scene we examined above.

Examining metric alignment in the setting of the verse, "Et chaque jour, c'est un festin," we will notice that the musical phrase is constructed so that the two strong accents fall on "jour" and "-tin," points where the hemistich is articulated in this verse (see Example 7.5). The overall dactylic rhythm does not change this accentuation: it weakens "-que" in relation to "cha-" (in accordance with linguistic practice) and, curiously, "fes-" in relation to the indefinite article "un." But Fauré's prosody plays more with pitch than rhythm. And it is there that the repeated notes play a role: if the syllables of "chaque" are on the same C♯ and if, for this reason, it is the rhythm that gives "cha-" a greater stress than "-que," then the ascent from G to A on "fes-" can be heard as emphasizing the first syllable of "festin," and, therefore, as underlining the word. By making the voice rise on "fes-," Fauré created a registral accent, a device found everywhere in his music.

The importance of repeated notes is even more obvious when they follow neither the metrical accent nor the rhythm and generate a registral accent by themselves. Such is the case in Lydia's reply a bit later in the same scene: "N'avons-nous pas en nous, toutes, notre mystère?" (Do we not have within us, all, our mystery?) (see Example 7.6). At the beginning of the phrase, the repeated notes occur on the weak beats. On "notre mystère," by contrast, we witness a moment of magic in Fauréan prosody: the voice rises a fourth on the weakest beat of the measure ("mys-"). The departure from the principle of repeating notes on the weak beat, and the sudden leap up a fourth, throw this "mystère" into particular relief, yet without betraying the linguistic rhythm, which puts an accent on the second syllable ("-tè-"). Fauré could have repeated another F for "mys-"; that choice would have been metrically correct, but it would have robbed this "mystère" of all its mystery and power.

Fauré cannot grant the text all its poetry without releasing it from its melodic obligation. By entrusting the latter to the orchestra, which comments on the text, he allows what is happening on stage to be heard; indeed, he explains to us what one has not (yet) understood. Doing so frees him to choose a vocal melody that best showcases the text and also allows him to imply ideas "beyond the text." We can now better understand why Claire Croiza compared Fauré's music to a "forest": the orchestra, the text, and the voice each unfold a meaning, interrelated to each other yet, at the same time, in a complex interdependence.

From the Infinite to the Ineffable

In refusing a systematic coupling of voice and orchestra, Fauré frees up an intermediate space allowing a layer of "the not said" to take form. In Wagner, this happens through the use of leitmotives. Fauré's way of composing does not suggest a Wagnerian infinitude, for his use of leitmotives is much less systematic. Fauré's practice leaves room, however, for what Jankélévitch rightly calls "the ineffable" – that is, a plasticity of text that Fauré seeks at any cost (he who hated texts that were too "strong") and that music will offset. Let us return to Act 2, Scene 2.

Theme A is a strong compositional gesture. While it prolongs the previous scene, it breaks the musical discourse with its timbre, its lack of accompaniment, and, above all, the character – noble, proud, and affirmative – of its melody. In terms of the drama, the arrival of theme A coincides with the entrance of the queen, Penelope. Now, from the letters Fauré wrote his wife at the start of September 1907, we know that he had already reflected on how to mark Penelope's entrance in Act 1.[25] In the first act, the composer used an orchestral interlude with a march-like character; in

---

[25] Letters from September 2, 5, 7, and 15, 1907, in *Lettres intimes*, 150–152.

the second act, the approach is different and maybe even more striking, for the solo theme emerges suddenly, isolated, from the orchestral texture. What explains such a powerful melodic gesture? At this moment, Penelope is not alone: Ulysses is with her, but Penelope does not yet know that he is her husband.

Fauré rejected leitmotives in the narrow sense defined by his epoch. If he had proceeded in the conventional way, he would have sounded Ulysses' motive at the start of the scene, or reprised theme A exactly when Penelope pronounced his name. But he did nothing of the sort, for Ulysse's motive does not appear in the first part of the scene, nor does theme A have any relation to the music Fauré associated with Ulysses in Act 1. The meaning, therefore, lies in the evocative power of this theme, which suggests the arrival of a powerful person (trumpet, solo writing: we think it is Penelope, but in reality it is Ulysses) and in its capacity to nurture Penelope's discourse, as indicated earlier. It is the character of this melody and the free space it builds between voice and orchestra that allow this meaning to emerge.

The Fauréan ineffable is therefore not the Wagnerian infinite. In Fauré's music there is not an immediate, univocal bond between text (suggesting an idea or personage) and music; rather, this bond is in a constant state of construction in the in-between (or "in-bethreen") of text, vocal line, and orchestra. The orchestra evokes the meaning of the text first, so that the voice is free to carve out the meaning of individual words and let the deeper meaning flow from the free play between the meaning of text set to music and that of words translated in the orchestra. Act 1, Scene 2 furnished our evidence, but one could analyze many other parts of the opera and arrive at the same conclusion. Fauré's form is thus more "fragmentary" or "piecemeal" than Wagner's: there are only a few motives and they return repeatedly across the work. The compositional strategy is redefined with every scene or dramatic unit, starting from a significant motive which, through the play of orchestral and vocal developments – as Wagnerian as Franckian in manner – engenders its own explicit and implicit discourse.

Conclusion

From this chapter on the role of melody in excerpts from *Pénélope*, we may draw the following conclusions:

(1) The opera is based on strong melodic gestures that structure the form;
(2) These gestures are very often carried by the orchestra;
(3) The melodic dominance of orchestra over the voice stems from Wagner;
(4) These melodies, nevertheless, do not constitute leitmotives, but are more often used locally;
(5) The vocal melody is thus relieved of expressive functions that would compel word-painting;
(6) And, consequently, the vocal melody may be used to play with the prosody of the text and its versification to reveal their "ineffability."

These conclusions cannot be generalized to Fauré's entire dramatic and vocal œuvre since the relationship between the voice and accompaniment in his *mélodies* is sometimes very different and does not always follow the procedures described here.[26] It seems at any rate to have been the medium of opera, where Wagner's leitmotivic practice had already taken hold with Chabrier's *Gwendoline*, Chausson's *Le roi Arthus*, and, above all, Debussy's *Pelléas et Mélisande*, which led Fauré to reconsider, more thoroughly than in other genres, the roles of voice and accompaniment. Neither truly Wagnerian nor truly Franckian, Fauré found his way with *Pénélope*, this opera too long forgotten by the public. We certainly find proof here of his "sincerity" and "originality."

Translation by Carlo Caballero and Stephen Rumph

---

[26] This is especially true of Fauré's last three cycles, which were written after *Pénélope*. Nevertheless, in the *Cinq mélodies "de Venise," La bonne chanson*, and *La chanson d'Ève* the piano part separates itself from the vocal line and achieves a motivic autonomy.

8 | Fauré the Practical Interpreter

Any consideration of Fauré as performer is inextricably bound up with how he edited and marked up his scores for performance. A central concern of this chapter is, therefore, how we may read through his notation, its quirks and its variants, to sense Fauré the performer. Most immediately, can doing so shed light on works that have long been neglected or regarded as problematic? The issue needs confronting if Fauré is not to remain peripheral in the repertoire except for a few works, mostly earlier ones. I, too, found many of Fauré's later works initially impenetrable, until rehearsing and performing them made sense of each one – provided their narratives are coherently articulated and paced in performance. It often involved interaction with critical editing, through reciprocal processes of source discoveries, on the one hand, and practical experiment with extant readings on the other, particularly when these revealed ambiguities.[1] For all its inevitable subjectivity, such practical exploration is indispensable in any attempt to recreate historically documented musical results (as explored below), especially when the published scores in themselves do not easily yield those results.

---

[1] This chapter's discussion relates to initiatives in the following critical editions of Fauré, edited by Roy Howat, which provide details of manuscript sources mentioned in this chapter: Hamelle-Leduc HA 9690 (1er Quintette op. 89 [Paris, 2006]) and Peters Editions EP 7430 (*Dolly*, Op. 56 [1995]), 7487 (*Sonata No.1 for Violin and Piano, Op. 13* [1998]), 7514 (*Anthology for Flute and Piano* [1999]), 7515 (*Anthology for Violin and Piano*; [1999]), 7526 (*Pavane*, Op. 50, arr. flute, 2 voices & piano [1999]), 7601 (*8 Pièces brèves*, Op. 84 [2003]), 7659 (*13 Nocturnes* [2006]), 7956 (*Thème et variations*, Op. 73 [2009]), 71904 (*13 Barcarolles* [2011]), 11385 (*45 Vocalises*, ed. with Emily Kilpatrick [2013]) and 711391–3 (*Complete Songs*, ed. with Emily Kilpatrick, Vols. 1–4 [2014–20]). Illustration in performance of various relevant issues can be viewed at www.youtube .com/watch?v=IcH8BQAdJPI&feature=youtu.be (presentation with Royal Academy of Music graduate students at the Oxford Lieder Festival, October 19, 2015) and heard on four CD albums: Gabriel Fauré, *Complete Works for Violin and Piano*, Alban Beikircher with Roy Howat, BMG/Arte Nova Classics 74321 92763 2 or SBM377242 (2004); *Belle Époque: A Portrait of Gabriel Fauré* (piano solos and duets), Roy Howat with Emily Kilpatrick, ABC Classics, 476 3423 (2009); Gabriel Fauré, *Songs for Bass Voice and Piano*, Jared Schwartz with Roy Howat, Toccata Classics TOCC 0268 (2015); and Gabriel Fauré, *The Complete Verlaine Settings*, Tony Boutté (tenor) with Roy Howat and Emily Kilpatrick, Edition Peters Sounds EPS 004 (2017).

A basic element that leaps from the pages of any Fauré biography is his lifelong activity as performer of his music. Only the premieres of his solo piano works were consistently passed to concert pianists, a matter easily attributable to public profiling and a sensible wish to put the music into the hands of pianists. (Fauré subsequently performed them often, mostly at less formal gatherings or soirées.)[2] For his chamber music and songs, whose piano parts are often at least as demanding as his solo pieces, Fauré was at the keyboard for virtually every premiere and for many ensuing performances. Only after 1916 did impaired hearing prompt him to hand off chamber music premieres, mostly to Alfred Cortot, although as late as 1919 he accompanied Madeleine Grey in *La chanson d'Ève* and rehearsed her thoroughly in his *Mirages*.[3] His fullest explanation can be read in a letter of September 25, 1906 to his wife:

I'm accepting [an invitation to perform my First Quintet] with the Capet Quartet … It's best for a while if I agree to play it myself. It's the best way of getting the work into the brains even of the performers. Capet, who's fine in Beethoven, didn't understand the Quintet when he played it at the Salle Érard.[4]

That particular work and letter raise queries to which we shall return. Given Fauré's personal diffidence in some respects, his constant presence onstage conveys a determination to have his music heard in optimum condition. He evidently had no personal doubts about his pianistic ability, in which matter he is never known to have deferred to virtuosi.

How do these documented attitudes and habits chime with established perception of Fauré? A persistent thread is summed up by a question I hear repeatedly: "Isn't Fauré's *Pavane* supposed to be a sad or tragic piece?" (We shall return to that question.) Another persistent trope is that of regarding understatement as inherently essential to Fauré performance. I recall once hearing refined sighs of audience admiration in a major recital hall after Fauré's Third Nocturne was played in a whisper throughout, somewhat under its tempo marking. It was handled with finesse, but Fauré marked the opening of the piece *mf*, and its ensuing dynamics range mostly

---

[2] The composer's younger son Philippe noted the virility his father brought on such occasions to pieces like the Fourth Barcarolle and Sixth Nocturne (and his measured tempo in the often rushed Second Impromptu); see Philippe Fauré-Fremiet, *Gabriel Fauré, nouvelle édition* (Paris: Albin Michel, 1957), 75–76, and Jean-Michel Nectoux, "Entretien avec Emmanuel Fauré-Fremiet, propos recueillis par Jean-Michel Nectoux, les 14 janvier et 11 février 1971," *Bulletin de l'Association des amis de Gabriel Fauré* 9 (January 1972), 13.

[3] Robert Lortat took the piano for the 1921 premiere of the Second Quintet, and Magdeleine Panzéra-Baillot for that of *L'horizon chimérique* in 1922.

[4] Gabriel Fauré, *Lettres intimes*, ed. Philippe Fauré-Fremiet (Paris: Grasset, 1951), 133.

between *p* and several *forte* passages; of its 110 measures, only one
thirteen-measure passage is marked *pp*. A Welte reproducing piano roll
of the piece that Fauré recorded in 1912 normally plays back (given good
replay equipment) pretty well on his tempo marking of ♩ = 80 (accompanying his heading "Andante con moto"), and with a generous range of
dynamics.[5]

Accounts and discussion of Fauré's piano playing appear in various
sources and surveys.[6] Constantly at the fore is his reported insistence on
directness of expression, with strong support from the bass, and natural
forward motion. Both his sons related their father's horror of sentimental
lingering or any swooning effects, including his embarrassment at any
show of audience emotionality – a state Fauré was wont to dispel by
clownish gestures like putting his feet on the keys.[7] It is unfortunate that
no recordings exist of Fauré playing chamber music or with singers. All we
have are five Welte reproducing piano rolls recorded in 1912, plus fifteen
Hupfeld rolls from 1908 with less interpretative encoding.[8] Allowing for an
unavoidable degree of mechanical approximation, they all convey an
essential directness and simplicity of line.[9] Rhythmic fluctuations tend to
be large-scale – for example, gradually increasing the tempo into the
middle of the First Barcarolle – or focus on specific gestures, one of which
we shall consider presently.

What Fauré reciprocally expected in performance can sometimes be
extrapolated from variants or apparent oddities in his musical notation.
A recent study notes unconventional word underlay in several early songs,
to a degree that has variously attracted criticism or defense from special-
ists.[10] A prime example (in every sense) is the first vocal entry in his

---

[5] See note 8 below.

[6] A variety of recollections and summaries can be found in Fauré-Fremiet, *Gabriel Fauré*, 76 and
156–162; Marguerite Long, *Au piano avec Gabriel Fauré* (Paris: Julliard, 1963), 103 and
105–106; Nectoux, "Entretien avec Emmanuel Fauré-Fremiet," 12–18; J. Barrie Jones, "Fauré's
Performance Practice," *Tempo* 151 (new series, December 1984), 32–35; Nectoux, *Gabriel
Fauré: A Musical Life*, trans. Roger Nichols (Cambridge: Cambridge University Press, 1991),
43–48; and Roy Howat, *The Art of French Piano Music: Debussy, Ravel, Fauré, Chabrier* (New
Haven: Yale University Press, 2009), 321–323.

[7] Nectoux, "Entretien avec Emmanuel Fauré-Fremiet," 17–18.

[8] For a full list and details see Howat, *The Art of French Piano Music*, 338 (Appendix 3).

[9] For detailed technical discussion of multiple mechanical issues, including Fauré's Welte roll of
the First Barcarolle, see Roy Howat, "Between and Beyond the Perforations in Debussy's
Welte Rolls," in *Claude Debussy: seine Klavieraufnahmen*, ed. Tihomir Popović (Franz Steiner
Verlag, forthcoming).

[10] Roy Howat and Emily Kilpatrick, "Editorial Challenges in the Early Songs of Gabriel Fauré',
Notes 68, No. 2 (December 2011), 239–283, quoting contrasted opinions on Fauré's

Example 8.1 Fauré, "Le papillon et la fleur," mm. 10–13

surviving output, at measure 10 of "Le papillon et la fleur," composed probably when Fauré was fifteen or sixteen. The main reading in Example 8.1 shows the first published version from 1869; the auxiliary staff shows how it was amended for the 1879 publication of the first collection of *Vingt mélodies*.

It would be easy to assume that the purpose of Fauré's amendment was to shift the weak end-syllable of "pau-vre" away from the half-measure stress. Why then do subsequent reprints of the *Vingt mélodies* from 1887 revert to the original reading – clearly a deliberate decision, as it involved amending the printing plate? In fact, the 1879 revision merely shunts the issue to the next measure, which again has a weak syllable on the half-measure – as also in measures 14 and 15, and through most of the song.

Could the young Fauré really have been so stubbornly heedless? A clue to his whole output emerges if we let that vocal line run according to its syllabic rhythm, independent of the piano's 6/8 vamping: starting with "La *pau*-vre *fleur* di-*sait* au *pa*-pil-*lon*" (the "long" or end syllables italicized here), 3/4 hemiola patterns result across measures 10–12, 14–16, 18–20, and 22–24. (M. 23 can work in either 3/4 or 6/8, given its syllabic fluidity.) Fauré's contrastingly clear 6/8 vocal rhythm in measures 13, 17, 21, and 25 then neatly sets off the poem's coquettish pairing of alexandrines with trisyllabic lines. The main payoff comes in the third strophe (m. 30, from "Mais hélas") where the poem's inflections run with the piano's 6/8, setting the stage for the contradicting exclamation in measure 38 – "Mais *non*, tu

syllabification by Mimi Daitz ("Les manuscrits et les premières éditions des mélodies de Fauré: Étude préliminaire," *Études fauréennes* 20–21 (1983–4), 21), and Pierre Fortassier ("Rythme verbal et rythme musical: À propos de la prosodie de Gabriel Fauré," in *Mélanges d'histoire et d'esthétique musicales, offerts à Paul-Marie Masson*, Vol. 1 (Paris: Richard-Massé, 1955), 30.

vas trop *loin* parmi des *fleurs* sans *nom*-bre" – to punch itself out in emphatic hemiolas against the piano, a pattern that then largely holds through the rest of the song.

A simpler explanation for the variant vocal entry of 1879 in Example 8.1 homes in on Fauré the practical interpreter. The offbeat version of that entry is notoriously tricky – it takes skill not to come in late – and Fauré's on-beat variant simply offers a safer foothold, even if he later abandoned it, doubtless because of its structural cost (and banality). Equally revealing of Fauré at the piano is the song's opening in its original manuscript key of D♭: under the hand, it runs uncannily close to Chopin's Waltz in D♭, Op. 64 No. 2 – a piece that similarly features right-hand 3/2 hemiola patterns over the left hand's 3/4. Try overlaying Hugo's poem on measure 5 onwards of Chopin's Waltz, starting like Fauré with "La" on the second beat: the underlined syllables coincide with Chopin's right thumb g's, the others with the c″s, "céleste" marking the top of the run at measure 9. It is tempting to wonder if Fauré did something of the sort in a moment of creative schoolboy frivolity.

Fauré's output is pervaded by that sort of rhythmic play: the same pattern recurs (for example) at the opening vocal entry of the song "Notre amour" (Op. 23 No. 2), and in the central part of his First Barcarolle (the right hand from m. 37 marking 3/4 time over the left hand's 6/8).[11] Given the school literature prizes that he won, and his apparent lifelong ability to spout verse practically on the spot, we can safely conclude that what happens in "Le papillon et la fleur" is not the result of negligence.[12] Fauré's underlay there suggests a dialogue between creative daring and practical interpretation, relying on the singer's intelligence (or, at worst, blithe indifference to the piano) to *dire le texte* appropriately. It also vividly bears out the advice of Fauré's mezzo-soprano colleague Claire Croiza, for

---

[11] For numerous related examples of metrical juxtapositions and alternations pervading Fauré's Barcarolles and other works, see p. iv of the preface to the 2011 London Peters edition of Fauré's *Barcarolles*, ed. Roy Howat (EP 71904), and Howat, *The Art of French Piano Music*, 141, 275–278.

[12] The school literature prizes are listed in Nectoux, *Gabriel Fauré, A Musical Life*, 9. A collection of correspondence in rhyming couplets between Fauré and Dukas is now in the Irving Gilmore Library, Yale University. Philippe Fauré-Fremiet devotes a page specifically to Fauré's careful respect for the poetic meter and rhythm of "Le papillon et la fleur," solving defects of underlay in various earlier settings of the poem; he also quotes some of his father's casual rhymes, including an alexandrine couplet worthy of the Surrealists, "Je regardais passer l'omnibus sur le pont, | Avec cet air pensif que les omnibus ont" (Fauré-Fremiet, *Gabriel Fauré*, 39–40, 54–55). We can probably assume, too, that the text of Fauré's cantata *Le ruisseau*, Op. 22, is by Fauré himself (the score identifies no author, as would otherwise be legally obligatory, and a few phrases in the text echo poems Fauré had already set).

singers first to learn to speak the poem of any Fauré song before fitting the music around it.[13]

Equally remarkable is how quirkily Fauré often plants weak words like "le" on a first beat, a habit that has implications for pacing. "Le jour qui luit est le meilleur" in "Lydia" (*c.* 1870) is a classic case, each "le" avoiding a banal textbook upbeat position, leaving instead an undercurrent of rhythmic counterpoint against the piano (the vocal first beats should obviously not be accented, and a flowing, speech-like tempo is of the essence).[14] "Seule!" of 1871 presents a more declamatory example, with "Le vent du soir" launching measure 11. In "Le papillon et la fleur," even the on-beat version of "La" in Example 1 (the short-lived 1879 revision) conveys Fauré's stubborn refusal to be so ordinary as to place it on an upbeat. This constant aversion to the obvious, besides marking him out as the composer he was, illustrates Fauré as a "practical interpreter" who would let the rhythmic and textural counterpoints in his songs make their own effect, the vocal line often not directly supported by what the piano does. (The almost autonomous piano part of his song "Clair de lune" makes this particularly clear, the singer effectively delivering the vocal line across it.)

If Example 8.1 showed Fauré ultimately sticking with the boldness of his original concept in "Le papillon et la fleur," some ensuing songs show moments of bold underlay toned down in later sources, prompting obvious queries. As I noted in an earlier study, this especially involves "S'il est un charmant gazon" (published as "Rêve d'amour") and "Seule!" where the revised underlay suggests fireproofing against misaccentuation in the course of hemiolas or other metric play.[15] It also, however, leaves a scent

---

[13] Claire Croiza, *The Singer as Interpreter: Claire Croiza's Master Classes*, ed. and trans. Betty Bannerman (London: Gollancz, 1989), 80.

[14] Note Fauré's comparative placing of the subsequent "Un" (m. 20) on an upbeat (vocally essential) but of the ensuing "Une," "Les," "Je" and "Que" all on first beats, as well as "Et" in measure 5 – plus (for good measure, so to speak) "Sor-tent" straddling the bar line into measure 27, sidestepping the obvious on every occasion.

[15] For comparative examples, see Howat and Kilpatrick, "Editorial challenges in the early songs of Gabriel Fauré" and Vol. 1 of the Peters complete edition of Fauré songs. In "S'il est un charmant gazon," the revisions, variously made between 1875 and 1890, shift "-te" (of "toute"), "-gne" (of "digne") and "-ve" (of "rêve") away from the first beat in measures 14, 44 and 58, respectively, at the expense of losing a hemiola across measures 13–14 and of slacker rhythm across 57–60; in measures 43–44 his 1890 revision fireproofs the hemiola at the cost of parking "di-" (of "digne") for two beats on a high top note. At measures 45–46, Fauré's 1875 revision does improve underlay by introducing a hemiola, tied over the bar line as an obvious safety measure. His 1890 revision of "Seule!" shifts "-te" of "Sainte" away from beat 1 in measure 30, at the expense of losing his original bold attack into "Ton dôme blanc" at measure 29, beat 1. Tellingly, he avoided making the same revision a strophe earlier (to move "-te" of "conte" off m. 12, beat 1): it would equivalently have entailed moving "Le" away from beat 1 in measure 11!

of compromise, the original reading arguably providing the freshest or most cogent diction, provided the metric play is recognized. That Fauré eventually opted for safety in these cases, but not in "Le papillon et la fleur," suggests that the taut underlay of "Le papillon" allowed no space for maneuver; to change the underlay, he would have had to recompose the song.

Some instrumental works show bold gestures at a more fundamental level that did not make it to print, arguably impinging on how Fauré is widely perceived as well as performed. In the third movement of his Violin Sonata, Op. 13, the autograph score used for the 1877 premiere shows expressive hemiola "sighs" across the 3/4 meter as the scherzo part of the movement winds down, as shown in Example 8.2. The final reprise of the passage in measures 311–316 slightly varies that again (as shown in the Example). Should the gesture seem unfamiliar, it is because the Breitkopf & Härtel first edition of 1877 ironed it out in favor of three-note violin slurs across each measure (extending piano slurs by one beat to match in mm. 107 and 313). Before we explore why or how, a few more examples will broaden the context.

Example 8.3a shows an equally bold autograph reading in measures 9 and 10 of the Fifth Barcarolle (first printed in the 2011 London Peters edition), with a right-hand octave A♮ in each measure against left-hand A♭; the 1895 first edition, engraved from that manuscript, diluted that to A♭ for both hands each time. The autograph reading can be defended as compositionally essential, not only for its polyphonic sense, but in terms of the repetition of the figure in measures 11 (right-hand D♮s in Example 8.3a) and 52–53 (see Example 8.3b, left hand), and in providing a vital antecedent for the later clash of A♯ against A♮ at measure 112. Nor is there any shortage of historical precedents, from well before J. S. Bach

Example 8.2 Fauré, Violin Sonata in A Major, Op. 13, iii, mm. 105–110

Example 8.3 Fauré, Fifth Barcarolle, Op. 66
a. Mm. 9–11, with accidentals as in Fauré's autograph
b. Mm. 52–53 (all sources)

Example 8.4 Chopin, Nocturne, Op. 62 No. 2, m. 52

onwards. Measure 52 of Chopin's Nocturne in E Major, Op. 62 No. 2, presents a particularly close example (see Example 8.4).

"Le pas espagnol" from the *Dolly* suite, Op. 56, shows a similar case at measure 63, a treble $g''\flat$ against an uninflected g in the tenor line, a polyphonically correct and pleasing false relation which the 1897 Hamelle edition neutralized (by carrying the right-hand flat over to the tenor g). Finally, Example 8.5 shows measure 26 of Fauré's "Vocalise-Étude" of 1907, the main vocal staff giving Fauré's autograph reading and the auxiliary staff the version published from that autograph.

All these original readings are doubly remarkable for the sharpened focus they bring to the whole piece around them, as against the published readings' blander portrayal of Fauré as a composer. So who or what engendered the printed dilutions? There is a strong case for attributing

Example 8.5 Fauré, "Vocalise-Étude," 1907, m. 26

them to well-intentioned engravers or house editors (whom I still sometimes see making similar interventions).[16] The Op. 13 Sonata was published in Leipzig by Breitkopf & Härtel, whose monumental project at the
time was the Mozart Gesamtausgabe, throughout which Breitkopf's editors
saw fit to rephrase Mozart, adding long legato slurs in place of Mozart's
shorter gestural ones, or even where he left none. They would hardly have
hesitated a moment to do the same with a young French unknown, at what
might have seemed a moment of Gallic giddiness unbecoming of a
sonata.[17] The Fifth Barcarolle and *Dolly* were both engraved by the Leipzig
firm Röder, who communicated with Hamelle in German and assumed
matchingly Germanic concepts of modal and harmonic regularity. (The
Fifth Barcarolle shows additional source evidence that the printed reading
must have been the engraver's initiative.)[18] Example 8.5 is most telling for
the autograph's refreshing avoidance of the obvious at the optimal
moment: its printed reading, with nothing musical to commend or justify
it, can only suggest engraver inattention or misguidedness.

Why did Fauré make no known attempts to redress these apparent
corruptions? His modest personal demeanor could at worst take the form
of a musical deference that tolerated external tampering. As late as 1923, he
let the violin part of his *Andante*, Op. 75 be rebowed by Édouard Nadaud,

---

[16] When I first proposed adding a cautionary ♮ to the tenor line g at measure 63 of "Le pas
espagnol" for the Peters edition of *Dolly* (EP 7430), a house editor resisted determinedly,
arguing in favor of the Hamelle reading and relenting only when shown similar false
relations in Mozart (some of which, ironically, the 1870s Breitkopf Mozart *Gesamtausgabe* had
modally neutered).

[17] A 2012 Henle edition of the sonata (HN 980, ed. Fabian Kolb) follows the Breitkopf
phrasing without even mentioning the autograph variant; we might infer that its editor's
assumption of correctitude in 2012 Munich was still that of 1876 Leipzig.

[18] See the critical commentary in EP 71904.

considerably to its detriment,[19] and his letters around the publication of the Sonata, Op. 13 in 1876–7 convey evident overawe at being taken on by Germany's high seat of musical *Wichtigkeit*. He might just have accepted such dilutions as a sort of editorial consensus from on high, perhaps even as a protective bumper bar against critical hostility. A prime explanation, though, may lie in Fauré the practical interpreter envisaging how such bold moments might or might not fare in the hands of unknown amateurs.

We may still wonder how Fauré played those passages after publication. A frequent trait among composers may have come (literally) into play, of viewing published works more distantly, the mind compositionally focused on newer works in progress.[20] Fauré's two piano roll recordings of his Third Nocturne offer a dose of everyday reality: the 1908 Hupfeld roll takes measure 66 straight off the printed page, omitting to rectify an obviously missing flat in the first edition (for the left hand's upper gs); the 1912 Welte roll remedies it. If Fauré's fingers in 1908 followed the page before his ear could intervene (in a piece he had composed twenty-five years earlier), in 1912 he had perhaps just practiced it more.[21]

In an appraisal of Fauré's playing as heard through his Welte rolls, J. Barrie Jones observes that "the difference between Fauré and so many of his contemporaries was his ability to 'change gear' more smoothly than most."[22] This is quietly but dramatically illustrated by the First Nocturne where Fauré, in the course of preparing a re-edition of his early Nocturnes published in 1924, deleted the first edition's indication "Un poco più mosso ma non tanto" at measure 21, starting the piece's long central section. If, as seems probable, his deletion was a reaction to hearing pianists suddenly hare off there at double speed,[23] it unfortunately left the whole Nocturne readable – in all reprints from 1924 onwards – at the opening Lento ♩ = 52. By 1950 Fauré's son Philippe

[19] Nadaud's fingerings and rephrasing, added for the 1923 Paris Conservatoire exams, were incorporated in Hamelle reprints, Fauré having apparently forgotten how carefully he had matched the violin line's phrasing to bowing for the piece's publication in 1897; see the commentary in EP 7515.

[20] See for example Louis Aguettant's account of fruitlessly trying to winkle an explanation from Fauré of the intricate thematic links running through *La bonne chanson*, in "Rencontres avec Gabriel Fauré," ed. Jean-Michel Nectoux, *Études fauréennes* 19 (1982), 5–6.

[21] Hupfeld roll 53082, Welte roll 2775. Although the note could feasibly have been altered on either roll by in-house editors, in practice neither Hupfeld nor Welte appear to have attended to such details in this repertoire, leaving many passing fluffs in Fauré's rolls uncorrected.

[22] Jones, "Fauré's Performance Practice," 33.

[23] On a Welte roll (7075, issued in 1925), Magdeleine Brard (who knew Fauré) does exactly that, after having slowed to a halt at the end of measure 20.

was wondering why so many pianists dragged that passage out in a way his father had never intended.[24]

Jones also observes more specifically that Fauré's Welte roll of the First Barcarolle shows him lingering over the middle of measure 17 before regaining tempo through the last three sixteenth notes, a gesture repeated in the identical measures 19, 87, and 89.[25] The first edition notates the gesture with a *rit.* indication in the second half of each of these measures, which again Fauré deleted for the re-edition eventually published in 1926. If his deletion was prompted by hearing pianists botch the gesture (probably by making a rallentando to the bar line), his deletion unfortunately occludes an expressive gesture crucial to the piece's opening section and reprise.[26] Reportedly, Nadia Boulanger once asked Fauré, late in his life, why he sometimes did not make his intentions clearer on the page, to which his reply was that *les bons interprètes* understand without having to be told, whereas inept ones never will, regardless of what is marked.[27]

The role of tempo and flow in musical expression and perceived structure is fundamental here. A memoir by the violinist Hélène Jourdan-Morhange illustrates Fauré the practical interpreter with two wry anecdotes:

I had the joy of playing all his chamber music with [Fauré]. It would be difficult for me to describe his special wishes, in the way that I could with Ravel. Just one directive stands out, and very strongly so: play in time without slowing, without even taking time to "prepare" those voluptuous harmonies that the slightest hesitation might underline for the audience's ears ... [As] a pianist he was formidable: he permitted no liberties and his supple playing was more redolent of a brilliant improvisation than of fixed architecture ... One day, accompanying me at one of the "Five o'clock" performances at *Le Figaro* in the rue Drouot, he found himself obliged also to play for the lady singing his songs. Poor singer! Accustomed to stretching out pauses and languishing at the ends of phrases, she was horrified to be dragged along by the piano on a road without undulations ... the motorway of the future! Infuriated by this dreamy interpreter, Fauré ended by leaving the piano at a run, seized his hat and disappeared into the street without even returning to bow to the audience alongside the mortified singer.

For Fauré, completely kind as he was, could be terribly direct with those who struck him as snobbish – most usually fashionable ladies. Well known is his reply

---

[24] Fauré-Fremiet, *Gabriel Fauré*, 158.   [25] Jones, "Fauré's Performance Practice," 34.

[26] For more discussion of these and some related passages see Howat, *The Art of French Piano Music*, 267–268 and the commentaries to Peters editions EP 7569 and 71904.

[27] Reported in conversation by the late John Streets.

Example 8.6 Fauré, "S'il est un charmant gazon," piano ending, mm. 73–76, as in the 1864 autograph

to an elegant society lady who told him, in a tone of affected disenchantment, "*Ah, cher Maître*, I can no longer bear Wagner" ... "Rest assured, Madam," said he affably, "that isn't of the slightest importance."[28]

Claire Croiza similarly emphasized the "forward-movement, a [sense of] *allant*" characterizing his music, one that must not be "deformed" by slowing, particularly in a diminuendo or at the end of a song. "I am certainly among the interpreters of Fauré who adopt the fastest tempi," she added, "and yet the composer himself often found I did not go fast enough."[29]

We may read what she meant from an early autograph of Fauré's Hugo setting "S'il est un charmant gazon," dated May 5, 1864, eleven years before the song was published. Headed "Animé" rather than the edition's "Allegretto," the early manuscript shows essentially the same song but with a more aerated piano texture and a snappier ending (see Example 8.6). Why does the song's published version end instead with a relatively pedestrian rerun of its opening eight-measure ritornello? Had Fauré just forgotten the original reading, years after giving away his early fair copy?[30] Or did he deem it too flippant for the public (and critics), despite how neatly it encapsulates the caprice of Hugo's poem? An immediate practical issue, though, is that it falls flat if taken under tempo. ($\quarternote$ = *c*. 152 suggests itself for Example 8.6; the whole song is practicable at or fairly near that.) Ironically, the published version, by making "safe" allowance for more staid performance, soon became defined by it (a matter the Peters complete edition addresses by printing both the 1864 and 1875 versions).

---

[28] Hélène Jourdan-Morhange, *Mes amis musiciens* (Paris: Les éditeurs français réunis, 1955), 22–23.

[29] Croiza, *The Singer as Interpreter*, 79–80 and 92 (original in Hélène Abraham (ed.), *Un art de l'interprétation: Claire Croiza; les cahiers d'une auditrice, 1924-39* (Paris: Office de centralisation d'ouvrages, 1954), 199 and 212.

[30] Early manuscripts survive for "Le papillon et la fleur" and "Mai" that omit their piano postlude: see commentary to the complete Peters edition (EP 711391), pp. 132, 134.

Croiza's remarks on tempos bear on how Fauré may have played four other songs, two famous, two relatively neglected. An early autograph of "Mai" conveys a strong hint of Fauré the practical interpreter in his quietly startling placing of *A tempo* (after a brief *rall.*) at the quarter-note upbeat to measures 27 and 60 – instead of after the ensuing bar line, as in the song's published sources – in each instance propelling the song through a comma and line break in Hugo's poem. Anyone who has heard a singer park for a leisurely breath on these bar lines can understand why. The marking also implies a lively tempo supporting the freshness of Hugo's poem along with the propulsive impetus of Fauré's anapestic ♪ ♪ ♩ rhythm for the opening words "Puisque Mai." At too lazy a tempo, that rhythm loses purpose.

The same rhythmic propulsion ♪ ♪ ♩ launches an ardent suitor's address to Lydia in the eponymous song, and calls into question the hymn-like solemnity persistently meted out to this paean of earthly love – a poem that eagerly lists Lydia's multiple attractions before pleading to "die" in their delights (obviously in the madrigal sense).[31] At issue, perhaps, is a literalistic misreading of the poem's final "mourir toujours" (after "l'éternelle tombe" a few lines earlier). The complete Peters edition also raises the query of whether the song's c time signature is a corruption of ¢. (No manuscript survives, but two other Fauré songs from the same time, "Seule!" and "L'Absent," show ¢ in their original sources corrupted in later prints to c.) To grasp what such *Falschgewicht* does to "Lydia" (and to its tempo-linked syllabification), I can only suggest imagining (or trying to imagine) the similarly textured opening of Beethoven's "Waldstein" Sonata around ♩ = 80. (The words "Lydia, sur tes roses joues" fit uncannily well across mm. 3–4 of the sonata, which even provides a requisite Lydian fourth in m. 2.) If that seems patently absurd, no less so is "Lydia" at the ♩ = 52 heard on some commercial recordings (and by some famous singers).[32]

An added hazard there is the tempo heading Andante, which Fauré often uses literally as *allant*, necessarily so in his 1870s Baudelaire settings "La rançon" and "Chant d'automne," in each of which one pivotal moment defines a minimum tempo for the song. In "Chant d'automne" this comes with the transition into the coda ("Lento ma non troppo" from m. 57, in 9/8), where the sixteenth note takes over exactly from the preceding eighth note (the piano thus continuing the preceding pattern but now under voice hemiolas, a combination we have noted before). To enable that, measure

---

[31] As Claire Croiza diplomatically puts it, "The 'mourir toujours,' of course, really means 'vivre, aimer toujours'" (Bannerman, *The Singer as Interpreter*, 82).

[32] Even Fauré's protégé Charles Panzéra recorded "Lydia" at a stolid ♩ = 72, with a surprising speckling of misreadings from Magdeleine Panzéra-Baillot at the piano.

1 of the song has to be launched at a lively clip, one that then makes sense of the poem and brings the entire song to vocal and dramatic life.

In "La Rançon," the key moment is Baudelaire's enjambment across the poem's last two lines, "Dont les formes et les couleurs | Gagnent le suffrage des Anges," which is respected in a manuscript reading of the song across measures 59–63 (shown as an *ossia* option in the Peters critical edition). The attendant risk is of syllabic "grounding" if the passage is under tempo, because of how the three syllables "Ga-gnent le" are necessarily stretched across three successive first beats in 3/4 meter. When the song was published Fauré played safer, delaying the final line's entry by a measure and fitting "Ga-gnent le" across four beats instead of the manuscript's eight – but losing the continuity of enjambment. That failsafe, besides compromising the poetic sense, triggers the very danger it seeks to avert by occluding the song's main pointer to tempo.[33] If we could somehow hear Fauré play these songs, these would be key moments to observe.

However practical an interpreter he was *in situ*, Fauré himself admitted to moments of vagueness in defining tempos on paper.[34] The long-printed metronome markings for the song "Nell" and the Allegretto section of the Sixth Nocturne are so implausibly slow as to be widely ignored in practice.[35] They bear on less known instances (flagged in the Peters critical editions) in the *Pièces brèves*, Op. 84,[36] and the songs "Notre amour" and "Chanson d'amour" (from Opp. 23 and 27), two songs that exude a strong whiff of Cherubino, setting off the nimble syllabic patter of Armand Silvestre's amorous rhymes.[37] The implications extend to Fauré's ensuing

---

[33] For comparative analysis of Fauré's three Baudelaire settings (possibly first envisaged as a set, an option enabled in the complete Peters edition), see Roy Howat and Emily Kilpatrick, "Le wagnérisme de Fauré: *Pénélope* (1913) et les mélodies," in *Le wagnérisme dans tous ses états, 1913–2013*, ed. Cécile Leblanc et Danièle Pistone (Paris: Presses Sorbonne Nouvelle, 2016), 25–38.

[34] Fauré to Marguerite Baugnies, July 1888, *Correspondance, suivie de Lettres à Madame H.*, ed. Jean-Michel Nectoux (Paris: Fayard, 2015), 146. The Peters editions listed above note variant tempo headings for specific pieces ranging from Allegro moderato to Quasi adagio.

[35] The printed $\quarternote = 66$ for "Nell" and $\quarternote = 76$ for the Nocturne's Allegretto section (the latter marking introduced in the 1924 revised edition) both suggest misprints for 96 (see commentaries in EP 11391 and 7659). A few similarly misprinted metronome markings in other Fauré works are resolved by manuscripts (see note 36 immediately below), but none survives for "Nell" or the 1924 revision of the Nocturne. For "Nell" Pierre Bernac conservatively suggests $\quarternote = 76$ (*The Interpretation of French Song* [London: Gollancz, 1970], 112), though Percy Grainger (a Fauré devotee) marked his published solo piano transcription of "Nell" at a much bolder $\quarternote = 116$, a tempo almost equaled in recordings of the song by recent performers, including Ian Bostridge with Julius Drake, Dame Kiri Te Kanawa with Roger Vignoles, and Barbara Hendricks with Michel Dalberto.

[36] The *Pièces brèves* instances, involving some 72 markings that suggest errors for 92, are the more confusing because of the precipitous $\quarternote = 96$ long printed for the first piece, a simple misprint for $\quarternote = 69$.

[37] The Cherubino element is supported by Silvestre's subtitle for those poems, "Vers pour être chantés."

Silvestre setting, the *Madrigal*, Op. 35 for mixed voices. Composed for the wedding of his friend André Messager, it embodies the mischievous prank (for nuptials) of setting a poem about love's travails to the theme of Bach's cantata *Aus tiefer Not schrei' ich zu dir*, a cheeky blend that ill warrants any solemnity in performance.[38]

For gravity we may look instead to Fauré's last Verlaine setting, "Prison" of 1894, with its sobering final line, "Dis, qu'as-tu fait, toi que voilà, | De ta jeunesse?" ("Say, what have you done, you there, | With your youth?"). At Fauré's indication ♩ = 60, the song's relentless succession of quarter-note chords literally ticks away the seconds – a rare if not unique case of a programmatic metronome indication.[39] A widespread tendency to perform the song more ponderously, presumably in pursuit of *Tiefernst*, prompts a closer look at its tempo heading, Quasi adagio (one that Fauré used more often than Adagio). Literally, it signifies "almost at ease" – synonymously readable here as "not quite at ease" for a song that is anything but at ease in its text and its merciless rhythmic straitjacket.

Some habits are based on entrenched misconceptions. In the 1970s, the conductor Sir Adrian Boult endeavored to counter the funereal performances he repeatedly heard of Fauré's *Pavane*, Op. 50. Noting that the piece's sung text is a deliberately frivolous parody, Boult recalled having heard, in his youth, Fauré play the piece on several occasions, "no slower than ♩ = 100!"[40]

Yvonne Lefébure in turn recalled Fauré lamenting that "for his taste [his] slower tempos – including the theme of the Variations – were always taken too slow."[41] That specific reference highlights an evident disaster of notation in the *Thème et variations*, Op. 73, which has long put pianists off the work (as I know from many conversations): editions since 1910 have indicated ♩ = 50 through the *Thème* and Variation 1, in place of the ♩ = 66 or 69 printed in the two original editions of 1897.[42]

---

[38] The Bach allusion, first noted by Charles Kœchlin, is amplified in Nectoux, *Gabriel Fauré: A Musical Life*, 108.

[39] In practice, that connotation can still communicate itself a notch or two under Fauré's marking (as acoustics or vocal timbre may necessitate).

[40] Letters from Boult to Robert Orledge (dated September 18, 1975) and to *The Musical Times* (printed in the June 1976 issue), quoted in the various Peters editions of the *Pavane* (EP 7383, 7514, 7526). The orchestral score's ♩ = 88 allows for the greater weight of orchestra, though I have heard the piece work well with orchestra and chorus around ♩ = 96, notably in a 1971 recording conducted by Antonio de Almeida (ORTF 995 012).

[41] Yvette Carbou, *La Leçon de musique d'Yvonne Lefébure* (Paris: Van de Velde, 1995), 123.

[42] The 1897 London Metzler edition heads the *Thème* Allegro molto moderato ♩ = 69, the 1897 Hamelle edition Andante moderato ♩ = 66, with L'istesso tempo for Variation 1; the

Example 8.7 Fauré, *Thème et variations*, Op. 73, transition from Variation 1 into Variation 2, mm. 12–13

The original tempos are crucial to the neatly overlapped transition from Variation 1 into Variation 2 (see Example 8.7), gently notching up the quarter note across the double bar. Possibly an error for 60, the later 50 marking results instead in what can be heard from most recordings: a slowing through the first measure of Example 8.7 to a pause on the F♯ (of all places) before Variation 2 spurts off at double speed, shredding the continuity and unbalancing the whole work. Both of Fauré's sons singled out the *Thème et variations* as a piece Fauré was wont to play at soirées or gatherings:[43] it is impossible to imagine him (of all people, in such surroundings) plodding at ♩ = 50 through the repetitions that make up the twenty measures of the thème and twelve measures of Variation 1.

Supported as they are by Fauré's reported remarks, these two works provide context for some later works that often cause perplexity, notably the Ninth, Tenth, and Twelfth Nocturnes, which show opening printed metronome markings unsustainably slow beyond (or even within) the first measure or two.[44] What is involved structurally is clear from measures 26–33 of the Ninth Nocturne, where small-scale sequential repetitions

1910 instead opens with a catch-all Quasi adagio, adding ♩ = 50 for both the thème and Variation 1. For more discussion of tempo and articulation through the work, see the Peters edition (EP 7956) and Howat, *The Art of French Piano Music*, 273–274.

[43] Fauré-Fremiet, *Gabriel Fauré*, 75; Nectoux, "Entretien avec Emmanuel Fauré-Fremiet," 13.

[44] Possible explanations for various suspect metronome indications by Fauré over the 1900s include the severe headaches and dizziness to which he was prone, plus a possible eyesight issue (see Howat, *The Art of French Piano Music*, 270).

across each pair of measures need to be heard as increments within a larger four + four-measure sequence that builds to the tonal goal at measure 34; otherwise the goal disappears over the horizon and the continuity collapses. It is salutary to imagine whether the ever-alert Fauré would have played these pieces as dramatic narratives, or just as four-or-more-minute blocks of introspective rumination. In that regard, I have noted elsewhere a succession of suspiciously slow markings from the early 1900s that has contributed to an entrenched ethos of "slow" Fauré that often extends to playing well below his nimble but highly effective metronome markings in works like *La bonne chanson*.[45]

Some performers have been more proactive about the oddly staid ♩ = 80 for the Allegro commodo finale of Fauré's Cello Sonata, Op. 109. A few recordings take it nearer ♩ = 126, making a massive difference of perceived character.[46] The issue emerges amusingly from a 1962 Erato recording by Paul Tortelier with Jean Hubeau, mostly taken around ♩ = 100 but with Tortelier audibly moving the tempo on whenever he can before Hubeau pulls it back again!

A revealing anecdote in that context comes from the pianist Éric Heidsieck, a lifelong Fauré devotee, who rerecorded Fauré's cello sonatas with Tortelier in 1974. As Heidsieck recalled, Tortelier warned him in advance that he could not make sense of the First Sonata's finale, which he considered "un morceau raté [a dud piece]."[47] In response, Heidsieck illustrated at the piano to Tortelier how he envisaged the movement, relative to the exuberant liveliness he sensed in works like Fauré's *Fantaisie*, Op. 111 for piano and orchestra. Tortelier listened attentively, then excused himself briefly to practice and rebow his part. They then recorded it at the buoyant ♩ = 126–132 audible from their disc.[48] At a 1975 launch concert for the disc (as recalled by Heidsieck), Tortelier announced to the audience that he and Heidsieck would play the two sonatas in reverse order (instead of the programmed chronological order) "so that we can end with the First Sonata, whose finale is so marvelous."

That issue most radically affects all three movements of Fauré's First Piano Quintet, Op. 89, a work revered in some quarters as exceptionally

---

[45] See my earlier discussions of Fauré tempo ethos in "Gabriel Fauré: Editions, Musical Anatomy, Performance," *Piano* 14, No. 2 (March–April 2006), 27–35, and *The Art of French Piano Music*, 263–278 (Chapter 18, "A Fresh Look at Gabriel Fauré").

[46] Steven Isserlis and Pascal Devoyon, on BMG 09026 68049 2 (1995), take it around 120; cellist Neil Heyde and I perform it around 126.

[47] Recounted to the author in conversation in 2005 by Heidsieck (a disciple of Alfred Cortot who premiered that sonata in 1917 with Gérard Hekking, later the teacher of Tortelier).

[48] La Voix de son Maître LP 5630/1 (1975), also His Master's Voice ASD 3153.

serene – effectively, two movements of slow string melodies plus a sedate finale, all enveloped by leisurely piano figurations – but which has suffered such neglect since Fauré's death that by 1974 it had gone out of print, having been widely regarded as (at worst) dreary, or "une œuvre ratée" (verdicts I've heard often enough from fellow musicians).

Research for a new Hamelle–Leduc edition issued in 2006 linked the work's perceived slowness directly to metronome indications printed in just the score (not parts) of the 1907 Schirmer first edition, starting with ♩ = 69 for the first movement. Without these indications all three movements are readable quite differently, particularly via the bowing and fingering marked by the Ysaÿe and Capet quartets on the surviving manuscript string parts used for the Quintet's first four performances in 1906, with Fauré at the piano.[49] Any string player can quickly sense the tempos underlying such markings; the equivalent goes for a few strategic fingerings Fauré left on the piano part.

Experiment and workshops on that basis with string-playing colleagues instantly took the first movement up to a minimum ♩ = 100, and the other two movements proportionately, turning the entire work into something of comparable vigor to the two Piano Quartets. (A composer colleague opined that it was "like seeing someone wake from a coma.") The essential issue can be seen in Example 8.8, showing the two instruments that play in measures 1–5: that of whether Fauré's tempo headings are to be read against the opening piano figurations or against the slower-paced string lines and harmonic rhythm. My suspicion was (and still is) that the Schirmer metronome markings were added in New York just before printing (possibly by Charles Martin Loeffler, who was acting as intermediary between Fauré and Schirmer).[50] By proof stage the tempo headings would already have been duplicated immediately above the piano figurations (unlike in the autograph score, now lost, which would show them only above Violin 1), leaving them visually easy to miscorrelate against the piano part.

As it is, two reviews of the Quintet's 1906 Paris premiere (where it was reported as being rapturously received) labeled its first movement an "Allegro," and Fauré's original marking Allegro molto moderato (as shown

---

[49] Should such extrapolation appear subjective, we may observe that it lies at the basis of sciences such as archaeology.

[50] Whether Loeffler actively participated in preparing the Quintet for publication is not documented, though Fauré—as was his lifelong wont with colleagues—is likely to have entrusted him or Schirmer's editors with late-stage editing, given communication times across the Atlantic. In 1918 Loeffler freely edited Fauré's First Violin Sonata (Op. 13) for an edition by the Boston Music Company (a Schirmer affiliate), inter alia changing all its metronome indications (see commentary in Peters Edition EP 7487).

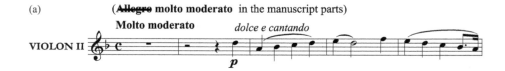

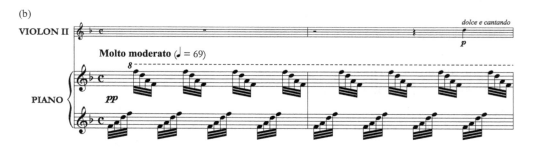

Example 8.8 Opening measures of Fauré, Piano Quintet in D Minor, Op. 89
a. As seen by the second violinist in the manuscript and Schirmer parts
b. As seen by the pianist, who sets the tempo

in Example 8.8a) exactly matches his tempo heading for the very vigorous first movement in each of his two Piano Quartets (and perceivably for the same reason: the string players have to allow for a very busy piano part). Fauré's deletion in the Quintet of the word "Allegro," shortly before the work went to print, was easily explained by experiment: most violinists invited to play Example 8.8a tend to set off around ♩ = 132 or higher. Fauré, in no need of self-instruction at the piano, would have been aiming his indications at keeping the string players in reasonable check – particularly given his comment about exactly that in the letter quoted near the start of this chapter. For the Prague-based Panocha Quartet, with whom I first performed the Quintet in its entirety, the resulting reappraisal "made the work worth playing," prompting audience enthusiasm that as often as not included encoring the finale.[51]

On the other side, this prompted shock (the difference is certainly startling) from some devotees long accustomed to regarding the Quintet as a specially serene or meditative work (an issue revealing of Fauré reception generally). The new Hamelle edition accordingly summarized the evidence, leaving decisions to performers, and the work now appears,

[51] Fauré biographer Jessica Duchen wrote of the 2005 London performance: "It was FAST. Very fast. But fabulous: out came the Fauréan élan so often missing from interpretations that decide it should be as esoteric as esoteric can be. The last movement worked for me for the first time ever. The performance really moved. In every way." (https://jessicamusic.blogspot .com/2005, posting of November 25, accessed October 3, 2018).

rather like the *Pavane* and the finale of the First Cello Sonata, to be leading a double existence.

It may seem improbable that the humble "Berceuse" from *Dolly* could partly explain the First Quintet, but here is how it might. Consider how the "Berceuse" is habitually heard, at the "Listen with Mother" tempo of $\bullet = c.$ 60 (despite Fauré's Allegretto heading). Note by contrast the 1897 English Metzler edition, which shows Fauré's marking $\bullet = 92$ for the piece, an indication absent from the usual Hamelle edition. Then try Fauré's pedaling, marked in all sources across just the first beat of each measure. Around $\bullet = 92$ that pedaling suffices; slow it down and the second beat immediately needs pedal (as is done almost universally). We may safely deduce that Fauré set his pedaling with $\bullet = c.$ 92 in mind; the parallel with the Quintet lies in inferring tempo through the viability of performing markings. (That nimble tempo for the "Berceuse" requires light finger work in the seconda part, but is viable and above all makes sense of the piece's middle section, reminding us that the infant is meant to be lulled to sleep, not bored into a stupor). That piece, too, will doubtless lead a double life in terms of tempo and perceived mood.

The "ineffable" label was first applied to Fauré in print by Vladimir Jankélévitch, with connotations related to the latter's professional field of philosophy. The problem arises if the word is misconstrued as a gauze over incomprehension, the music perceived as agreeably perfumed but meandering or evocative of undefined mystery. No reminiscence of Fauré as composer, performer, administrator, or colleague paints his aims as ever being so woolly; the consistent tenor that does come across is an often startling directness in Fauré's verbal and musical communication, a total absence of snobbery or pretension, and a constant current of wit near the surface.

That last quality merits addressing in a composer whose music rarely resorts to overt burlesque. A few musicians even see no humor at all in Fauré's music, despite all its perceptible compositional playfulness at deeper levels than just passing moments like the *Dolly* suite's fleeting allusions to the lullaby "Do do l'enfant do" and Fauré's own Violin Sonata in A Major.[52]

---

[52] Pianist Paul Crossley is quoted as saying specifically of the solo music, "I don't find any humour. Not at all. Not a bit ... And I'd go further. Apart from the Sixth Barcarolle, I find absolutely no lightness in the music. It's very, very serious indeed [with] no hint of that real Gallic charm. It's all immensely earnest." ("At the Piano with Fauré: A Conversational Symposium" [with various pianists, compiled by Jeremy Siepmann], *Piano* 14, No. 2 (March/April 2006), 17.

It should not surprise us from a composer whose son underlined his father's lifelong "taste for humorous verse and jokes, pranks and parody, even in music," and who, even at the Église de la Madeleine, might lace an organ improvisation with a popular song or mischievously swerve into a distant key at the moment of handing over to his co-organist.[53] If that native sense of mischief – what Hélène Jourdan-Morhange called his "esprit de gavroche" [street-urchin wit] – shows in the occasional banana skin like a C♯ tied to a D♭ in a sight-reading test piece (treacherously placed just after a vertiginous downward leap), it's equally there in a fugue concocted from six repeated E's (the third of the *Pièces brèves*); in the way his progressions habitually move a step faster than we expect (try sight-reading almost any of his songs, or guessing what is immediately over the page); in the musical wit with which he treats poetic texts, from the quicksilver of Silvestre to the - tight-packed syllabic and rhythmic virtuosity of Verlaine; in his way of letting some vocal lines scrape almost insolently against their accompaniments; in his loop-the-loop progressions that fly off in a cape of sharps only to reappear in flats (or without them); and in constant rhythmic play about where and when sounding strong beats do or don't coincide with bar lines.[54]

That last element can be attributed in equal measure (as it were) to the cross-rhythms of Fauré's meridional folk heritage, and to the plasticity of the language he spent his life setting, its poetry defined by strict rules of line and rhyme but with freedom of rhythm within, and the rules themselves ever open to subversive elements like enjambment. The spoken-French tendency to aim for the final syllable of a phrase also explains much about why slowing phrase endings literally introduces a foreign accent to Fauré's music. The compromises he sometimes evidently accepted suggest that Fauré the teacher and educator would, at worst, rather hear an amateur do rough justice under tempo than have it just botched.

That said, enough is on record to convey a clear idea of why Fauré performed so persistently, and in large part how. For a musical public often

[53]   Fauré-Fremiet, *Gabriel Fauré*, 54: "Toute sa vie Gabriel Fauré a eu le goût du vers humoristique, de la blague et de la parodie, même musicale."

[54]   Jourdan-Morhange, *Mes amis musiciens* (Paris: Les éditeurs français réunis, 1955), 24. The enharmonic spelling comes in measure 21 of the 1903 violin *Morceau de lecture*, published in Peters Edition EP 7515. Relatively little explored, his individual manner of text-painting includes musical allusions such as the fleeting blend of *Das Rheingold* and *Tristan* that aptly underpins the climax of "Les berceaux" at measures 19–20 (a steelier version of *Souvenirs de Bayreuth*).

discouraged by terms like "mysterious" or "ineffable," or by funereal renderings of "Lydia," the *Pavane*, the First Quintet, or some of the *Nocturnes*, we can pierce the haze as performers and scholars (if we dare) in the manner that Boulez deemed necessary with Debussy a few decades ago.[55] The fact that it no longer seems so necessary with Debussy should encourage us to persevere. In Stephen Rumph's words, "Perhaps then Fauré can escape the gilded cage of ineffability to which his devotees have too long consigned him."[56]

---

[55] Marianne Wheeldon, in *Debussy's Legacy and the Construction of Reputation* (New York: Oxford University Press, 2017), demonstrates in detail how much Debussy's posthumous reputation owes to sustained effort by a group of determined supporters influential in the musical press. Fauré had little comparable promotion: his main press supporter, Pierre Lalo, was a dullard beside the likes of Debussy's Louis Laloy.

[56] Stephen Rumph, "Fauré and the Effable: Theatricality, Reflection, and Semiosis in the mélodies," *Journal of the American Musicological Society* 68, No. 3 (Fall 2015), 553.

9 | Fauré, Orientalism, and *Le voile du bonheur*

CARLO CABALLERO AND LESLEE SMUCKER

It is no surprise that Fauré has never been associated with orientalism or exotic musics. Aside from a few paragraphs by Sylvain Caron, no one has ventured to write a study of Fauré and orientalism.[1] Indeed, it almost seems as if the composer himself ordained this dissociation for his own legacy. His final two song cycles, *Mirages*, Op. 113, and *L'horizon chimérique*, Op. 118, bring the point home. The titles of both works evoke faraway geographies. But the first song of *Mirages*, "Cygne sur l'eau," works in the opposite direction: the itinerary reaches inward. The poet's charge to the dreaming swan, a metaphor for her thoughts, ends with a retreat from the allure of distant places:

Then I said, "Turn back, beautiful chimerical swan,
from this slow voyage toward restless destinies;
no Chinese miracle, no strange America
will welcome you to secure harbors;

the balmy gulfs, the immortal isles
await you, black swan, with dangerous reefs;
stay on the lakes mirroring unerring
these clouds, these flowers, these stars, and these eyes."

The poem recoils from exotic temptations. In contrast, "Danseuse," the last song in this same cycle, bathes nakedly in the distant, imaginary space of ancient Greece, to which Fauré returned lovingly and often. No one could deny Fauré's affinity for Greek Antiquity, which the composer himself openly avowed,[2] but music historians generally set the European classical world apart from the "real" Orient. We will return to this characteristic difference in Fauré's œuvre: the affection for Mediterranean Antiquity in the context of greater wariness toward other exoticisms. Several scholars have seen *Mirages* (1919) as an oblique tribute to Debussy, who died the

---

[1] Sylvain Caron, "Mélodie et orientalisme: De l'évocation du merveilleux aux séductions de l'avant-garde," *Revue musicale OICRM* 3, No. 1 (February 2016), 93–114.

[2] François Crucy, "Les grandes figures contemporaines: Gabriel Fauré" (interview), *Le petit parisien*, April 8, 1922.

year before.[3] Be that as it may, the cycle also inscribes Fauré's difference from Debussy – in the way it turns its face away from China and America in the first song and embraces the ancient Hellenic world in the fourth song.[4] As for Fauré's next (and last) book of songs, *L'horizon chimérique*, one searches in vain for exotic shores. The alluring "horizons" of the title remain unspecified, bounded only by the abstract opposition of land and sea. It is the desire to travel, or to remain on land, or to feel the rhythm of the open sea that these songs hymn, not any specific geography.[5] The voyage, once again, is metaphysical.

Fauré's Orient

In his superb little book *Orientalism,* Ziauddin Sardar frames the West's imagination of the East succinctly: "The Orient, the land to the east of the West, is a realm of stories. Its actuality has always been encapsulated in forms of storytelling as fact, fiction and fable. It invites the imagination."[6] The existing literature about Fauré seems to support received wisdom that he was uninterested in the imagination of distant cultures or musical exoticism. Even when confronted with the twenty-eight-page autograph manuscript of Fauré's exquisite music for Georges Clemenceau's play *Le voile du bonheur* (1901) – the unpublished work which stands at the center of our argument – the experts demur. Robert Orledge dryly noted, "This score is best considered as a curious excursion into the fashionable

---

[3] Roy Howat proposed that "Reflets dans l'eau," the third song in *Mirages*, was possibly an homage to Debussy (*Debussy in Proportion: A Musical Analysis* [Cambridge: Cambridge University Press, 1983], 192–193). Katherine Bergeron and Carlo Caballero advanced this idea somewhat further with consideration of the cycle as a whole; see Bergeron, *Voice Lessons: French Mélodie in the Belle Epoque* (Oxford and New York: Oxford University Press, 2010), 334–336; and Caballero, "Vowel Sirens," *Journal of the Royal Musical Association* 138, No. 1 (2013), 214–215.

[4] Katherine Bergeron (*Voice Lessons*, 323) suggests that Renée de Brimont's line, "Nul miracle chinois, nulle étrange Amérique," was meant as an allusion to the Chinese Magician and the Little American Girl, two characters in *Parade*, a Ballets Russes production that had premiered a year before (May 1917) with music by Satie.

[5] This emphasis on sentiment over geography is also true of Jean de La Ville de Mirmont's book of fourteen poems. A single reference to the Antilles in the book happens to occur in "Je me suis embarqué," a poem Fauré set to music, but the composer omitted the entire strophe.

[6] Ziauddin Sardar, *Orientalism* (Buckingham [United Kingdom] and Philadelphia: Open University Press, 1999), 1. We find Sardar's book far more penetrating and trenchant than Edward Said's earlier book of the same title (Sardar's critique of Said on pp. 65–76 should be required reading). Said's monograph was a watershed but unfortunately continues to overshadow Sardar's later contribution.

fin-de-siècle world of *chinoiserie*."[7] Jean-Michel Nectoux suggests that "in contrast to Saint-Saëns, Debussy, or Ravel, Fauré surely lent no more than an amused ear to the unusual timbres of non-European musics presented by the World's Fairs in Paris, and without his creative process being affected in the least by them."[8] *Le voile du bonheur* still remains unpublished and (so far as we can determine) was never performed between 1930 and 2014.[9] Its dismissal by the two most prominent scholars writing during the revival of Fauré research during the 1980s arguably muted further inquiry into a score then only available to researchers in manuscript.[10] This casual silence kept a comfortable distance between Fauré and most of his contemporaries on the matter of orientalism. As Nectoux already begins to remind us, Debussy was far from the only composer whose interest in the music of the Far East stood in contrast to Fauré's seeming indifference. We must also reckon with Fauré's teacher, Saint-Saëns, perhaps the most prolific orientalist composer of all. Students of Fauré's such as Messager, Ravel, and Schmitt, and for that matter contemporaries, such as Bizet, Massenet, Delibes, Roussel – indeed practically every French composer of the late nineteenth century, had a hand in musical orientalism. Fauré's exclusion from this activity was rather extraordinary to have passed so long unquestioned.

Our call for some revision on this topic should not be equated with a direct critique of Nectoux or Orledge. Both scholars paid close attention to Fauré's aesthetic legacy and his extant pronouncements. They did exactly what most musicologists and historians properly do: attend to the testimony of the artist under scrutiny. Let us consider two examples of such testimony. While Fauré was thinking about composing an opera based on Pushkin's *Mazeppa* in 1885, he learned that Chaikovsky had already

---

[7] Robert Orledge, *Gabriel Fauré*, revised edition (London: Eulenburg Books, 1983), 132.

[8] Jean-Michel Nectoux, *Gabriel Fauré: Les voix du clair-obscur*, second edition (Paris: Fayard, 2008), 208. This translation and all the following ones are ours unless otherwise attributed.

[9] In January 1930, the Théâtre de la Renaissance revived Clemenceau's play, probably as a tribute to the great politician who died the year before, and according to the title page of the script in *La petite illustration* 461 (January 4, 1930), Fauré's music was again used for this late production. This was the same theater where the premiere took place in 1901. Breaking the reign of silence at the opposite end of our two dates was a beautiful performance by members of the Orchestre de Paris under the sponsorship of the Musée Guimet, published on March 11, 2014 (https://youtu.be/0gWgC5YA2e4), apparently as part of the exhibition "Clemenceau: Le tigre et l'Asie." Strangely, this performance makes no mention of Gabriel Fauré in title or description; his authorship remains "under the radar" even in the age of YouTube.

[10] The manuscript (Paris, Bibliothèque nationale de France, Dépt. de la Musique, MS 17786) was made freely available on line by Gallica (https://gallica.bnf.fr/ark:/12148/btv1b55007812f) in April 2014, greatly expanding access to it.

written an opera on the same topic. This caused Fauré to reflect on the specially nineteenth-century question of "local color" in a contrarian, almost modernist way:

I don't think there's any reason for a French composer to renounce setting the same subject after him, as he is such an essentially Russian artist. Not that I myself have any pretention of turning *Mazeppa* into an essentially French opera: I will even admit to you that in general I cannot have any truck with such subtleties in dealing with this art called music, whose primary quality is to be a universal language, or rather the language of a country so far above all others that it lowers itself when it translates the feelings or traits of character proper to any particular nation.[11]

It is apposite to remember that *Mazeppa*, an Eastern European tale, lay in the realm of the Orient for Romantic writers. If it is difficult for us to think of Ukraine as the Orient, *Les Orientales*, the most famous book of French poems devoted to Eastern fantasy, serves as a reminder. In it, Victor Hugo devoted a famous poem to the legend of Mazeppa. Fauré's *Mazeppa* never came to fruition, and so we can only imagine what the composer had in mind. Eight years on, Fauré again had occasion to comment on local color. He was coming to grips with writing incidental music for Molière's *Le bourgeois gentilhomme*. He composed three pieces and probably would have completed the commission if the Éden-Théâtre had not gone bankrupt in March 1893, while Fauré was still working on the score. A letter he wrote to Marcel Girette includes a significant comment on exoticism, and Fauré's confession gives support to Nectoux's and Orledge's positions: "I really don't have a knack for comedy, and I'm scared of the *Turkish Ceremony* … I have a problem with turbanized music!"[12]

Yet we may be permitted to see these private confidences about *Mazeppa* and *Le bourgeois gentilhomme* in a different light from Fauré's earlier biographers. These scruples do not prove that Fauré was uninterested in the Orient. Rather, they suggest that he was troubled by trite, conventional, or parodic musical representations of foreign cultures (e.g., "turbanized music"). Fauré seems to have wanted to do something

[11] See Jean-Michel Nectoux, *Gabriel Fauré: A Musical Life* (Cambridge and New York: Cambridge University Press, 1991), 137, translation by Roger Nichols modified by the authors from the French original in Gabriel Fauré, *Correspondance, suivie de Lettres à Madame H.*, ed. Jean-Michel Nectoux (Paris: Fayard, 2015), 122.
[12] Jean-Michel Nectoux, *Gabriel Fauré: Les voix du clair-obscur*, 207. Nectoux does not include this letter in the *Correspondance*.

different, to write music that, while not necessarily devoid of exotic indices, focused on human interests in a spirit of inclusion rather than exotic distancing. *Le voile du bonheur* is perhaps too strange a score to show us what Fauré's balance of universalism and particularism could have looked like in *Mazeppa*, but at least it gives us more insight into his aesthetic direction than the lost or unfinished scores. Fauré's reference to "turbanized music" also shows his awareness of a significant and perhaps dubious artifice. This implicit critique is more developed in the letter on *Mazeppa*, when he goes on to compare Brahms' "exploitation of Hungarian themes" (presumably in the *Hungarian Dances*) to "a pretty costume."[13] This skepticism reminds us of Sardar's fundamental critique of orientalism: "While Orientalism is real, it is still, nevertheless, an artificial construction. It is entirely distinct and unattached to the East as understood within and by the East ... Orientalism will always impede understanding between the East and the West."[14]

As a Southerner in northern France, Fauré might have donned a costume of his own. Contemporary reactions to his origins and appearance remind us that the composer felt the disturbances and pleasures of being observed as an exotic figure, however subtly. His situation was different from that of Ravel and Debussy partly because his music did not conspicuously raise questions about the relationship of persona to territory. Ravel, with his Basque roots, could rely on heritage to ally his art with the Iberian Orient, which he did proudly and publicly. Debussy conjured his orientalism through wide-ranging imaginative genius rather than origins (his were purely Île-de-France) or travel (annoying to Debussy). Fauré, the Ariégeois from southernmost France, could have claimed an autochthonous Pyrenean or Provençal genius for his art if he had wished. Déodat de Séverac would later do just that, evoking his native Languedoc in music. Fauré did not noticeably extend his physical charisma or his Southern origins into his music, but public observation imposed this identity upon him. His childhood in Ariège mattered. Fauré made his career in Paris, and for the Parisians and other northerners, an exotic image of the South sprang from the medieval history of Gaul, which we may briefly recall here.[15] Following the conquest of Occitan by the Omayyads, an Islamic

---

[13] Fauré, *Correspondance*, 123.   [14] Sardar, *Orientalism*, vii–viii.

[15] One of the few scholars of orientalism to mention this perspective on southern France is Jonathan D. Little, *Literary Sources of Nineteenth-Century Musical Orientalism* (Lewiston, NY: Edwin Mellen Press, 2011), 26–27. This press has a dubious reputation, but Little's book has serious value.

caliphate could have continued to advance into the central and northern marches of Gaul if not for Charles Martel, the Battle of Tours, and other reversals of the Omayyad conquest. Although the Muslims were driven out of the southern French regions, these lands would remain "a realm apart" and, like adjacent Spain, touched by some vague Saracen fancy in Parisian minds. Fauré's rolled Rs, olive complexion, and seductive, feline gaze played into a social persona he turned to his advantage. Nectoux records his nicknames in the 1870s: "the cat," "the odalisk" (the latter significantly orientalist).[16] Fauré cut an exotic figure in Parisian salons – just exotic enough to be intriguing, however, not disruptive. Nectoux writes, "His hair was thick and black, but began to go grey in his forties, when it made striking contrast with his olive complexion and with the dreamy, almost oriental expression in his dark, gold-flecked eyes."[17] We will only appreciate the relative understatement of Nectoux's imagery once we return to the far more extravagant language of contemporary testimony. In 1888, in the first essay devoted exclusively to Fauré as a composer, Hugues Imbert wrote:

Gabriel Fauré is of medium height, but strongly built. His face is striking and tan, a man from the *Midi* through and through; his eyes, with their indefinable expression, have a velvet glow, slightly veiled, but flashing at times. In these eyes there is something of the incandescent mirror of the South, of the very special reflection of the Ouled-Naïl of Algeria.[18]

Imagination of the "South" clearly had ample geographical reach in 1888. Colette admiringly described Fauré around 1904 as "a swarthy emir" with a "silver mane."[19] His student Charles Kœchlin noted, "Fauré's build resembled that of a peaceful Arab merchant."[20] Another student, Émile Vuillermoz, invoked "his swarthy complexion like that of an Arab nobleman."[21] The first time Vuillermoz saw him in person, he was "won over and charmed ... Framed by a beautiful head of prematurely silver hair, the color of this Ariégeois was somewhat amber, like an Indian sultan."[22] These testimonies could be multiplied. Odd as it seems, in his physical presence, Fauré reminded contemporaries of a man out of some

[16] Nectoux, *Gabriel Fauré: Les voix du clair-obscur*, 66.
[17] Nectoux, *Gabriel Fauré: A Musical Life*, 32.
[18] Hugues Imbert, *Profils de musiciens* (Paris: Librairie Fischbacher et Librairie Sagot, 1888), 78.
[19] Colette, "Un Salon de musique en 1900," in *Maurice Ravel par quelques-uns de ses familiers* (Paris: Éditions du Tambourinaire, 1939), 119.
[20] Charles Kœchlin, *Gabriel Fauré*, trans. Leslie Orrey (London: D. Dobson, 1946), 21.
[21] Émile Vuillermoz, *Gabriel Fauré*, trans. Kenneth Schapin (Philadelphia: Chilton, 1969), 2.
[22] Ibid., 16.

vague Orient, and, as we see in the astonishing quotations above, it extended from North Africa to the Levant to India. Such loose cultural extensions may disturb readers today, but they prompt reflection on an aspect of cultural orientalism that touched Fauré in person.

Besides his music for Clemenceau's pseudo-Chinese morality play (as it turned out, this was the last incidental music Fauré ever wrote), there is much more to say about his predilections for similar projects. Fauré kept returning to distant cultures as settings for his theatrical works. Let us size up their geographies. *Caligula* is set in a romanticized imperial Rome. *Shylock*, a version of Shakespeare's *Merchant of Venice*, is set in sixteenth-century Venice. *La Passion*, of which only one movement seems to have been composed, would be set in first-century Jerusalem. *Le bourgeois gentilhomme*, with a primary plot in seventeenth-century Paris, has an important Turkish or Ottoman intervention whose satirical, parodic function troubled Fauré. *Pelléas et Mélisande* takes place in the imaginary but vaguely medieval realm of "Allemonde." *Prométhée* and *Pénélope* are both taken from ancient Greek literature. While Prometheus' tribulations are set in the Caucasus Mountains, Odysseus returns in disguise to the Aegean island of Ithaca where Penelope awaits him. *Le voile du bonheur* is set in Peking, an imperial China of no specific century. Finally, *Masques et bergamasques* situates a handful of characters from the *commedia dell'arte* in a Watteauesque neverland. Not a single one of Fauré's theatrical projects is set in the modern world.[23]

If we examine Fauré's entire œuvre for oriental themes (we again take that term in its broadest, nineteenth-century, Hugolian sense), we discover a sub-catalogue that is larger than we might expect (see Table 9.1). Were we to draw up a similar table for Ravel's music, of course it would be longer and, more importantly, occupy a larger proportion of Ravel's comparatively slim catalogue of works. Fauré was not only less drawn to oriental themes than Ravel; his creative response to such themes was generally less elaborate. Table 9.1 nonetheless gives us pause for its geographical range and variety of media. Our redaction, by the way, is narrower than we might have made it. We do not include a song like "Les matelots" merely because it mentions the Sunda Islands and India, just as we omit "Cygne sur l'eau," the first song of *Mirages*, which names China and America in the negative.

---

[23] Fauré's earliest operatic project, *Barnabé* (c. 1879, of which a sextet is extant in manuscript) is set in France, but the century cannot be determined from Fauré's summary of the plot (*Correspondance*, 94–95). Like many *opéras-comiques* with similar plot devices and *libertinage*, it was probably meant to take place in the eighteenth century.

Table 9.1 A glimpse of Fauré's Orient

Composition (poet)	Genre	Year	Geography	Notes
Super flumina Babylonis	motet (psalm)	1863	Babylon, Euphrates River	exotic chromatic "melismas" in middle section; Aeolian mode elsewhere
"Seule!" (Gautier)	song	1871	Istanbul	references to terebinth tree, Hagia Sophia, Hellespont; drawn from a series of poems evoking the Ottoman Empire (this poem falls between "Ghazel" and "Sultan Mahmoud")
Les djinns (Hugo)	chorus	*c.* 1875	Arabia, Muslim world	Jinn are supernatural creatures of Arabian folklore, depicted by Victor Hugo in *Les Orientales*. Central prayer to the Prophet ("Prophète, si ta main me sauve . . .")
"Les roses d'Ispahan" (Leconte de Lisle)	song	1884	Persia	Ispahan (Iran) is the setting; Mosul (Iraq) also mentioned
La vocation de Bouddha (Samain)	opera	1892	India	unfinished project, also called *La tentation de Bouddha*
Valse-Caprice No. 3	piano solo	1893	Spain	*jota* episode, mm. 343–390
"Le pas espagnol" (from *Dolly*)	piano duet	1896	Spain	*espagnolade*
"Le parfum impérissable" (Leconte de Lisle)	song	1897	India	"the rose of Lahor," "the burning sand"
Le voile du bonheur (Clemenceau)	incidental music	1901	China	allegorical play by Georges Clemenceau set in Peking
Preludes, Op. 109: No. 1 and No. 2	piano solo	1910	Spain	composed a few months after Albéniz's death, possibly in homage to him; middle section of No. 1 and all of No. 2 have Spanish elements: guitar evocations and Phrygian mode
"Jardin nocturne" (from *Mirages* by Renée de Brimont)	song	1919	Tunisia or Algeria	drawn from a group of Brimont's poems (beginning with "Chapelet Musulman") evoking Algiers, Biskra, Kairouan, and Tunis. In this poem only the "noirs orangers" and "palmes invisibles" betray an exotic locale

Note. Two other operatic projects might be included in this table: *Mazeppa* (1885, discussed above and set in Ukraine) and *Lizarda* (1881, whose name sounds Portuguese but whose locale is unknown). Music has not survived for either project, and although we know from a press announcement that *Lizarda* would have been an opera in three acts on a text by Armand Silvestre for the Opéra-Comique, we have been unable to determine anything more about Silvestre's text.

We recognize a difference between passing mention and evocative response. More debatably, perhaps, this table leaves out the worlds of the ancient Mediterranean: Greece, Rome, and most of the Levant; that is, pagan antiquity and the biblical world. A work like *Le jardin clos* would be especially representative of this omitted zone of Fauré's music, as it seems to bridge the pagan and the biblical. Several of its poems trope the Song of Songs, whose *hortus conclusus* gives the work its title and resonates with that uniquely sensual book of the Old Testament. But sometimes the songs of *Le jardin clos* conjure up a ubiquitous eros-drenched world that might as well be Crete or Alexandria as Judea (e.g., "In the Nymphaeum"). Perhaps the geographical scope of *Le jardin clos* and *La chanson d'Ève* is best defined as belonging to climates where one can grow jasmine.

And yet that botanical gambit once again ties the Mediterranean world to the Middle East, India, and the Far East (jasmine grows in all these places): the continuities of Oriental geography remain undeniable. The reason we draw the lines as we do – which is the reason we include in Table 9.1 the Ispahan of "Les roses d'Ispahan" but not the Jerusalem of the Requiem, the China of *Le voile du bonheur* but not the Ithaca of *Pénélope* – is that the heritage of the Bible is the heritage of Christianity, and therefore "west of the East" (to extend Sardar's elegant terminology). Similarly situated are the heritages of Greece and Rome. France embraced the cultural legacy of Greek antiquity as the ancestor of its own classical arts and Rome as its political ancestor in republic and empire. In short, the vectors of Mediterranean Antiquity (Greece, Rome, the maritime Levant) point westward, toward French assimilation; whereas in contemporaneous European conceptions other foreign cultures were exoticized, marked by difference rather than identity.[24] To be even clearer, we could reduce the distinction to gross political terms: the French placed their mark on Saigon by colonial imposition (eastward), whereas they adopted Athens as a forebear by submissive reception (westward).

East of the West, West of the East

The contrarian steps forward: one may easily challenge this configuration of Orient and Occident, and the counterarguments are relevant to Fauré's

---

[24] We might have omitted *Super flumina* from Table 9.1. Its text, after all, is a Biblical psalm. But the evocation of Babylon (a point of exile far to the east) seemed to elicit an exoticizing response from Fauré's pen, and so it may be justified for inclusion in the composer's imaginary Orient.

music. Despite the powerful continuities of classicism, the worlds of ancient Greece and Rome, like other distant cultures, could be exoticized by French composers and repeatedly, extravagantly were, especially in the realm of theatrical dance music. The three most overtly exotic-sounding pieces Fauré ever wrote all, excepting *Le voile du bonheur*, evoked ancient Greece: the two dance scenes from *Pénélope* (in Act 1 and Act 3) and "Danseuse," the last song of *Mirages*. A fourth example, the "Air de danse" from *Caligula*, set in ancient Rome, may sound less overtly exotic to the ear but falls into the same category. All of these are either music for dancing or music evoking dance. Ballet, as a theatrical medium inviting sensual fantasy and coloristic exoticism, was a hotbed of orientalism during Fauré's lifetime. Greek and Roman ballet *divertissements* were as welcome on French stages as ones from any other fantasy land, particularly if they provided a historical pretext for decorative states of drapery and undrapery. In *Pénélope*, Fauré's two dance scenes reveal their exoticism through melodic style and orchestration. The dance melody in Act 1 is rhythmically evasive, full of wide leaps, and played by a very "Greek" solo flute against the delicate accompaniment of harp, pizzicato strings, triangle, and tambourine. The mode wavers between Aeolian, Dorian, Phrygian, and minor. In contrast, the dance number in Act 3 conjures up a chromatic genus (of Fauré's own invention) within the tight span of a perfect fifth. The half-step inflections contrast with the more diatonic dance in Act 1 and make it sound even more archaic and exotic.[25] The orchestration of the dance in Act 3 is also parallel to Act 1 in conception, though here Fauré assigns the melody to the striking combination of flute and bassoon in unison, accompanied by antique cymbal, harp, and pizzicato strings. In both dances, we infer the implication of neo-Grecian choreography from the combination of woodwind melodies, plucked strings, and percussion – surrogates for aulos, lyre, and sistrum (or cymbal).

Plots set in ancient Greece or Rome elicited similar exoticizing music from many French opera composers before Fauré. Massenet's *Thaïs* (1894), Saint-Saëns' *Les barbares* (1901), and Erlanger's *Aphrodite* (1906) all come to mind. Likewise, in Fauré's song "Danseuse" (*Mirages*, 1919) the

---

[25] Yet, curiously, both dances take E as a tonic. Is it a coincidence that all the analytical examples of Greek tetrachords on the first pages of Théodore Reinach's *La musique grecque* (Paris: Payot, 1926) likewise use E as their tonic (pp. 10–12, 15)? Fauré had collaborated with Reinach, providing various harmonic redactions of the *Hymne à Apollon* (138 BCE) discovered by French archaeologists. The chromatic scale Fauré invented for his dance scene in Act 3 of *Pénélope* (E–F♯–G–G♯–A, with a lower neighbor D♮) does not correspond to the pitches Reinach gives for the Greek genus (E–F–F♯–A) but has a tonic E and a central half step in common with it.

contrast between the bare simplicity of the first part of the song (with its diatonic modalities, sharp dotted rhythms, and reciting tone) and the otherworldly incursion of a chromatic genus at the return to the opening music at measure 43, leaves an unforgettable impression, at once mechanical and melting. Norman Suckling deemed this song "one of the most vertiginous things ever written."[26] Yet it too has a heritage. Gounod's "À une jeune Grecque" (possibly composed as early as 1862, but published posthumously in 1895) sets a text by Sappho and provides key premises for Fauré's "Danseuse." Both songs take D-Aeolian as their starting point and use the Phrygian mode and non-functional chromaticism as a contrasting element.

At least nine of Fauré's works, among them his three longest compositions, were inspired by Greek and Roman Antiquity.[27] And yet the exotic dances of *Pénélope* were an exception to his musical approach; elsewhere his music associated with Antiquity is indistinguishable from his other music. We can understand this seemingly inconsistent approach to evocative material by recalling the history of a changing topos: eighteenth-century (and earlier) classicizing approaches to the Greco-Roman world versus nineteenth-century exoticism. Jonathan D. Little writes, "Whenever nineteenth-century authors, painters or musicians looked to ancient or modern Greece for inspiration, they made their Greece a much more 'exotic' place than it had been during the neoclassical eighteenth century. Having previously been regarded as a country and civilization more akin, in all but climate, to the West than to the East, Greece subsequently became the repository of all sorts of 'Oriental' traits."[28] *Against* this orientalizing tendency, Fauré's Greece – in *Prométhée, La naissance de Vénus*, or even "La rose" – answers to eighteenth-century classical ideals rather than to exotic (romantic) ones. In other words, Fauré's Greece and Rome are proxies for France and part of its ineradicable classical bias.[29]

---

[26] Norman Suckling, *Fauré* (London: J. M. Dent, 1951), 86. Bergeron, *Voice Lessons*, 327–336, offers a remarkable reading of "Danseuse."

[27] Those three big works are *La naissance de Vénus, Prométhée*, and *Pénélope*. The other seven are *Caligula*, "Lydia," "La rose," *Le jardin clos, Mirages*, and Fauré's two settings of the Delphic hymn to Apollo ("Hymne à Apollon"). On this last, see Samuel Dorf, *Performing Antiquity: Ancient Greek Music and Dance from Paris to Delphi, 1890–1930* (New York: Oxford University Press, 2019), 21–46.

[28] Jonathan D. Little, "Sources of Nineteenth-Century Musical Orientalism; or, From 'Oriental' Inspiration to Exotic Orchestration" (Ph.D. dissertation, Monash University, 1994), 256.

[29] Sardar points out that the advent of Islam strengthened the tendency of Christendom (only later called "the West") to define itself through the legacy of Greece and Rome, "to demonstrate the Otherness of the Orient, its separation from the Western birth and discrete identity of

Perhaps here he betrays his identity as a "man of the *Midi*," a Southerner, who does not see the Mediterranean south as "other." In any event, we cannot reconcile this contradiction. In Faurés time Greece, Rome, and the biblical world lay suspended between exotic removal and native assimilation.

The pervasive treatment of the Iberian Peninsula, especially Spain, as a domain of the Orient is likely to puzzle modern readers. Spain, after all, is one of the westernmost countries of Europe! It was the sustained Islamic and Arabic influences in Spain that had given it a special position, as our comments on the history of southern France already suggested. In the Middle Ages, Spain had been a key center for the revival of Greek and Roman learning through the cultivation and scribal activity of Arabic scholars, who had further advanced the state of knowledge in their own scholastic and scientific traditions. Here was a moment when the East rescued the West in spite of itself. Victor Hugo fixated upon Spain in the preface to *Les Orientales* as the place where the Gothic and the Orient met. In an elaborate paragraph, he conjured up a Spanish city with both a Gothic cathedral and an Islamic mosque as an emblem for his artistic vision exalting the medieval and the Oriental against the classical and Western.[30] Thus Spain was not just an outlying Orient, but one which functioned to unify the Romantic idealization of both the medieval and the exotic. As Table 9.1 suggests, Fauré (like Berlioz, Lalo, Chabrier, Ravel, and so many other composers) occasionally yielded to this other Orient, all the more readily for its proximity to the Pyrenean provinces where he grew up. Faurés deep friendship with Isaac Albéniz, whose music he loved, sustained this interest in Spanish styles.

Among creative artists in France, Victor Hugo had more influence on the French Oriental imaginary than anyone else. In the generation of poets who followed Hugo, Théophile Gautier and Leconte de Lisle prominently took up the torch of orientalism. Settings of these three poets account for seventeen of the forty-eight songs Fauré wrote before 1891, more than a third. Yet only a few have Oriental vectors. *Les Djinns,* Op. 12, for mixed

Western self-consciousness" (*Orientalism*, 16–17). Sardar thus seems to suggest that the emergence of Islam eventually resulted in a "de-Orientalization" of those ancient Mediterranean cultures that the West wished to recruit to its own spiritual destiny. This point is helpful in understanding the ways in which ancient Greece, for example, may appear in one historical evocation as Western, even proto-French, and in another as drenched in oriental fantasy.

[30] Victor Hugo, "Préface" (1829) in *Odes et Ballades; Les Orientales*, ed. Jean Gaudon (Paris: Garnier-Flammarion, 1968), 320–322.

chorus and orchestra (or piano) sets one of the most famous poems in *Les Orientales*; it is a tour de force of Hugolian verse-craft. Hugo depicts the gradual approach of the jinn (winged demons), their arrival, and the return to silence by increasing the syllabic length of the verses in each strophe from two to ten syllables and then reversing the process. Fauré seized on this poetic form with the dynamic equivalents in music: crescendo and decrescendo, density of musical texture, and (in the outermost verses only) speed of textual delivery. The music is characteristic in that the underlying tempo ($\rfloor$ = 138) is nonetheless unaltered from first measure to last. Fauré sets up a structural palindrome at measure 97 (when the verse returns to four-syllable lines and the music likewise rewinds) and in this way marks the descending arch of the poetic structure without adhering to a palindromic scheme throughout. Although the excitement and elegance of Fauré's composition shows how much inspiration he drew from Hugo's fantasy, the musical style has nothing specifically Arabic or Islamic about it. One can only remark that the male choral prayer to Muhammad at the center of the piece ("Prophète, si ta main me sauve"), with its solemn trombones, is a lot more stirring than the motets Fauré was then composing for the Catholic Church. Perhaps the theatricality of Hugo's poem gave his ecumenical spirit a breath of freedom, but in the end all the "orientalism" of this choral work resides in Hugo's text and tale.

Considering the poems he chose from their work, Fauré was perhaps more at ease with the quieter orientalism of Gautier ("Seule!") and Leconte de Lisle ("Les roses d'Ispahan," "Le parfum impérissable"). Fauré took the poem he called "Seule!" from a sequence of lyrics by Gautier that evoke the Ottoman Empire. The composer changed Gautier's narrator from male ("seul") to female ("seule"), and he probably did so for reasons of genre. As Stephen Rumph pointed out to us, the text evokes the theme of the European woman imprisoned by distant foreigners. Although the poem does not mention imprisonment explicitly, the original position of the poem between "Ghazel" and "Sultan Mahmoud" in Gautier's *Poésies nouvelles* confirms Rumph's interpretation. Berlioz's song "La captive" (Hugo, *Les Orientales* again) and Lalo's "Esclave" (Gautier again) are examples of songs on the same theme. Although the verses of "Seule!" evoke the Hagia Sophia, Hellespont, and the terebinth tree, Fauré responds with an austere song, devoid of Middle Eastern musical coloring.[31] A tolling octave

---

[31] Contrast it, for example, with Bizet's setting of Victor Hugo's "Adieux de l'hôtesse arabe" (1866), which is tricked out in all the "Turkish" or Middle Eastern topics then available to French composers.

in the right hand of the piano evokes the monotony and loneliness of imprisonment, while a rising three-note motive in the bass heightens emotional tension. These musical means are abstract and would be just as suitable for a penitential motet as for Gautier's oriental scene.

Of Fauré's songs on Eastern themes, only "Les roses d'Ispahan" (1884) approaches the style of languid orientalism plied by his contemporaries. Leconte de Lisle's first two verses associate the cities of Ispahan and Mosul with roses and jasmine respectively. The opening refrain in the piano turns on *mi–fa–sol* in the treble, blissfully circling, while harmonic ninths, sevenths, elevenths, and added sixths are formed by the minimal, purely diatonic motion of the alto line. We might say that, in this song, at last, Fauré seems to have discovered his duty to indolence in depicting the "timeless East" by unleashing his own predilections for harmonic opulence. In contrast to such a reading, the Canadian scholar Sylvain Caron has viewed the song in a less obvious way. He singles out Fauré's setting of Leconte de Lisle as innovative for its deliberate abstraction from local color and conventions (presumably comparing it to earlier songs by French composers such as Delibes and Bizet). To Caron, this geographical distancing seems worth praising:

In the end, the nostalgia emanating from "Les roses d'Ispahan" does not come from lost love but rather an ideal, unattainable universe formed of beauty and sensuality that the real world cannot contain. In this respect, Fauré acknowledges traditional representations of the Orient but holds the Orient at a distance, deliberately situating it beyond our world in a self-referencing prospect [*une perspective d'autoréférentialité*].[32]

Caron's analysis seems to confirm what we have already surmised about the lack of local color in *Les Djinns* and "Seule!" – that Fauré's indifference to exoticism simply proves he was as good as his word in the letter concerning *Mazeppa*: that the only "race" in these landscapes is the human race, that his interest lay in what is "universal" to human experience, not "the feelings or traits of character proper to any particular nation." Caron, however, takes his observations a step further. He adopts "Les roses d'Ispahan" as the first in a series of studies of what he calls "avant-garde" approaches to orientalism.

Caron's placement of Fauré in a line of innovation that other scholars might have chosen to begin with Debussy, or even Messiaen, is refreshing.

---

[32] Caron, "Mélodie et orientalisme," 100.

But his reading may go too far in protecting this nineteenth-century song from old-fashioned Parnassian fantasies about the East. Caron stresses the otherworldly abstraction and self-referentiality of "Les roses d'Ispahan," yet a different listener might find that such attributions of "ineffability" ignore the flavorful, superficial details Fauré meant his audience to savor in 1884. We have already spoken of the indolent opulence of the opening refrain, and we might add that the opening vocal melody is pentatonic until the second syllable of "jasmins" (pentatonicism is another reliable signifier of the Orient, as are the syncopated ostinato rhythm in the left hand and the tonic pedal point). The question of exotic flavor really comes to a head in measures 52–59, the end of the third strophe (see Example 9.1). Most of the passage is built on a pedal point on the local tonic, E. While this stasis serves as a bridge before the modulation back to D major, it also provides an opportunity for harmonic indirection. After three measures in minor mode, Fauré shifts to Phrygian, with a prominent F♮ dissonance over the E in the bass (mm. 55–57). The parallel 6/3 chords anchored on the Phrygian F in the right hand of the piano are extrinsic to the surrounding minor tonality, and both this parallelism and the half-step dissonances (E–F, B–C) place the music in an "oriental" territory that later compositions by Debussy and Ravel would more specifically token as "Spanish." The most outrageous passage occurs in measures 57 to 59, when the bass finally moves. Here half-step dissonances occur on the downbeats and also within each measure: the alto descends F–E–D against E–E♯–F♯ in the bass, and the first two measures both have horizontal cross-relations (G♯–G and E–F). The accumulation of all these half-steps creates an extravagant harmonic transition.[33] It might be Persia, it might be Spain, but it is still a deliberate evocation of an exotically flavored music, meant to be noticed. We would suggest that this song is less abstracted from orientalism than Caron submits. The surface harmony of the song, whether soft or harsh, invites us to enjoy a direct relationship to the exotic atmosphere of the poem. The craftsmanship is original, but the impulse is conventional.

---

[33] Famous examples of half-step clashing in *espagnolades* include Ravel's "Alborada del gracioso" (1904–05) and Debussy's preludes "La sérénade interrompue" and "La Puerta del Vino" (1910–13). Fauré himself exploited such half-step clashes not only in the brief passage from "Les roses d'Ispahan" but also quite exuberantly in the *jota* episode of his Third Valse-Caprice (mm. 343–389), published in 1893.

Example 9.1 Fauré, "Les roses d'Ispahan," mm. 52–60

Sylvain Caron's broader historiography of the French *mélodie* argues for a gradual shift from exotic evocation (Fauré, Debussy) to abstract structural innovation (Ravel, Delage) across the turn of the century. To some degree, the contrasts he draws out correspond to what we will call first-degree and second-degree orientalism in the last part of this paper. While one may slice the territory as Caron does, we find his historiography too teleological, ultimately driven by myths of structural purity dear to academic discourse about "modernism."[34] We would argue for a less chronologically presumptive approach to orientalism in music. In other words, we would avoid a historiography that presumes nineteenth-century composers shallowly worked a trite field of sentimental fantasy, and later "modernist" experimenters overturned or extended this field merely (somehow) by taking timbre as a primary structural feature. In the presence of orientalist

---

[34] See especially Caron, "Mélodie et orientalisme," 97. In particular, we are suspicious of any history that treats "self-referential music" ("musique . . . surtout autoréférentielle," ibid., 98) as a real phenomenon. Although Caron seeks to trace an account of progressive Western sensitivity, his structuralist arch of progress describes the opposite – a process of self-absorption, annexation, and effacement of the other in favor of Western formalist priorities.

materials, within different stylistic premises, later composers are capable of banal evocation, and earlier ones capable of surprising structural abstraction.

Fauré seems to be one of those who preferred abstraction of materials, or their internal transformation, to extrinsic evocation. If, following Caron, we find this to be a valid assertion about most of his early "orientalizing" compositions, it is perhaps even more true of *Le voile de bonheur*. However, the tendency to detach traces of reality or anecdote from easily identifiable sources does not make Fauré a more "advanced" composer than his contemporaries who chose the route of more concrete evocations. He is no more advanced than the Debussy of *Ibéria*, no less advanced than the too frequently disdained Delibes of *Lakmé* or "Les filles de Cadix." Fauré's tendency to dream in tones, to lose his imagistic point of departure in enigmatic contrapuntal eddies, is simply a mark of his personal way of making art.

Within the quandary of our initial inquiry, we are faced with a composer whose physical appearance sometimes made his contemporaries think of an expansive "exotic South" but whose music did not – except by its mysterious seductiveness or in a few exceptional pieces. So perhaps this chapter should, like the black swan in *Mirages*, turn back, cling to the shores of the Mediterranean to reassure readers that Fauré's only deeply felt Orient was that of European antiquity. A rich essay could hew to that geographical limit, but the present chapter attempts to scope out the outer edges of Fauré's Orient, a space in which fewer compositions unfolded to fruition, but which were not unknown to his mind and which have a definable position in his artistic journeys.

Finally, there are hidden oriental obliquities in Fauré's work, exotic locations sensed but unspecified. Robert Orledge was the one who first noticed the geography behind the "invisible palms" and "black orange trees" of "Jardin nocturne," the third song from *Mirages*.[35] Its dreamscape is North African, drawn from a group of poems that evoke Algiers, Biskra, Kairouan, and Tunis in Renée de Brimont's *Mirages*, a book of poetry that Fauré's friend Gabriel Hanotaux gave him. One may also speculate on the specific imagery of other songs. The eighth song of *La chanson d'Ève*, "Dans un parfum de roses blanches," seems to invite us into an exquisite *japonerie*. The tonally unanchored, dreamy evanescence of Fauré's music snakes ever downward on a chromatic motive until it lands on a diatonic

---

[35] Robert Orledge, "A Voyage of Discovery into Fauré's Song Cycle *Mirages*," in *Regarding Fauré*, ed. Tom Gordon (Amsterdam: Gordon and Breach, 1999), 367, note 18.

plagal cycle under the final sentence, "Dans le silence il tombe des pétales" ("In the silence petals are falling"). The poem's opening image of Eve in dwelling in a "perfume of white roses," the final image of petals falling silently – all this under the spell of Fauré's harmony – could belong to a *haiku* or a print by Hasui. But this is fancy. For all Fauré tells us, we might as well imagine *La chanson d'Ève* being set in Lugano or Annecy as in Kyoto or Ispahan. We could make a less oblique proposal about the whole of *La chanson d'Ève*: all of its songs could be included in Fauré's Orient, for it is set in the Garden of Eden – east of Eden, and how far east? If the idea of "Dans un parfum de roses blanches" transporting us to Japan is too much to believe, Fauré takes us at least as far as India in the final song, "O mort, poussière d'étoiles," with its powerful evocation of death as the Hindu *nirvana*.[36]

Le voile du bonheur (The Veil of Happiness)

In one of the first performances of Fauré's incidental music to the play *Le voile du bonheur* from 1901, Fauré wrote to Marguerite Hasselmans asking her to go to the hall to see whether she could hear the ensemble. Fauré complained that the author, Georges Clemenceau, and director, Firmin Gémier, had put the ensemble in a "treacherous hole" – referring to the pit of the Théâtre de la Renaissance – making it impossible for the music to be heard in the hall.[37] This letter turns out to be clairvoyant. Fauré's music for Clemenceau's play *Le voile du bonheur* retreated into silence: unpublished and barely heard of since.[38] This obscurity, as we suggested above, partly explains why Fauré's response to orientalism has remained outside public or scholarly purview.

Georges Clemenceau's one-act play was written in 1901 in the style of a Chinese fable. The main character, Tchang-I, is blind. When he secretly restores his own sight with the use of powerful drops supplied by a healer,

---

[36] Carlo Caballero, *Fauré and French Musical Aesthetics* (Cambridge: Cambridge University Press, 2001), 214–217.

[37] Fauré, *Correspondance*, 587. Fauré wrote Mme. Hasselmans from Garches and told her he had heard reports of the inaudibility of the music; he had not experienced a live performance for himself.

[38] Nectoux, *Gabriel Fauré: Les voix du clair-obscur*, 209 notes that Fauré signed a contract for publication of the work with Hamelle on September 15, 1902, which is how it came to be assigned the opus number 88. But publication never occurred.

he finds that reality is far different from what he imagined. Unable to cope with this reality or even confront his family and servants with their misdeeds, he chooses to return to blindness.

Clemenceau, a statesman and journalist best known for his involvement in the Dreyfus Affair and for his leadership at the end of World War I, spent significant time traveling and collecting artifacts from the East. Indeed, his fame as a political leader is such that his interest in the cultures of India and the Far East, deeper than Fauré's, has received relatively little attention. It is difficult for us to convey the depth of Clemenceau's respect for Chinese cosmology, or the sympathy he developed for Chinese traditions when he visited the country in person. One must read the sprawling, late philosophical volumes he wrote in his retirement, *Au soir de la pensée* (1927, translated as *In the Evening of My Thought*) to take the measure of his enthusiasm. He repeatedly laments the militant outcomes of Christianity compared with, in India and China, "a general tolerance unknown to our narrow sympathies."[39] He prefers the social conduct of the Chinese temple to that of the Christian church.[40] He elaborately praises the pilgrimages of Faxian and Xuan-Zang to India:

> In comparison, the lofty propaganda of Saint Paul among the Gentiles was mere sport. Undertaken from a motive exactly opposite to that which animated the Christian apostle, the mission of the two Chinese pilgrims was not to spread their own beliefs, but to be sure they had them in their pure form ... Their plan had such moral elevation that nothing in the history of religion can, I believe, be compared with it ... I salute them in passing, too happy if I can make a few people appreciate the beauty of their example.[41]

Clemenceau not only traveled to the Far East but also admired Asian *objets d'art* and amassed an astonishing collection of some 3,500 Japanese ceramic incense boxes (*kōgō*), miniature artworks in many forms stylistically marked by their period and region of fabrication.[42] In public life, as is well known, he opposed French colonial expansion. He condemned territorial annexations founded on European motives of "civilization" as covert racial

[39] Georges Clemenceau, *In the Evening of My Thought*, Vol. 1, trans. Charles Miner Thompson and John Heard, Jr. (Boston and New York: Houghton Mifflin, 1929), 421.
[40] Ibid., 414, 418, note 2.   [41] Ibid., 419–420.
[42] Five hundred and sixty-six *kōgō* from Clemenceau's collection were exhibited and catalogued in 1978; see *Shugyoku no kōgō ten: satogaeri shita Kuremansō korekushon*, shusai Montoriōru Bijutsukan, Asahi Shinbunsha [*Exhibition of Kogo: Japanese Ceramic Incense Boxes from the George [sic] Clemenceau Collection*, organized by The Montreal Museum of Fine Arts and the Asahi Shimbun] (Tokyo: Asahi Shimbun, 1978), 4.

aggressions and betrayals of the principles of the French Revolution.[43] In contrast to Fauré's diffuse interest, Clemenceau's knowledge of China was extensive. In spite of all this, we shall maintain, in the fourth section of this essay, that *Le voile du bonheur* is not really a play about China or Chinese traditions at all.

As we see in many manuscripts of incidental music, Fauré notates one or two lines of dialogue at the top of each scene to indicate how the music should be coordinated with the action. The music provides short interludes and transitions between scenes. Fauré also sometimes embeds music in the scenes themselves, as when Tchang-I plays his lute or companions raise their glasses in a toast. Fauré's small interludes are effective in the play, but also work alone as unusual, epigrammatic concert music. The instrumentation is extremely striking: flute, clarinet, violin, viola, cello, harp, tubaphone, and gong. In addition, a solo trumpet is used to announce a messenger in Scenes 8 and 9. This chamber ensemble has no parallel in any of Fauré's other works, and the Chinese setting of Clemenceau's play inspired Fauré to compose music whose stasis and minimalism are also unique in his œuvre (see Example 9.2). The work is built from a series of pentatonic melodies that pass gently from one instrument to another against a backdrop of ostinato patterns.[44] The effect is one of trance-like circularity.

Fauré's cultivation of a Zen-like paucity in *Le voile du bonheur*, along with its unusual orchestration, permits us to understand why Nectoux attributed the orchestration to another hand.[45] However, the state of the manuscript (indubitably autograph, as Nectoux acknowledges) and the musical content of the work allow us to assert that the composition and orchestration are Fauré's. Nectoux suggested dubious circumstances around the work in his authoritative biography of Fauré. He hypothesizes that *Le voile du bonheur* was orchestrated by Émile Vuillermoz, Fauré's pupil. But even in the biography that Vuillermoz himself wrote in the last year of his life (1960), he never claimed to have done anything more than

---

[43] For an especially cogent essay on this topic, see Charles-Robert Ageron, "Clemenceau et la question coloniale," in *Clemenceau et la justice* (Paris: Publications de la Sorbonne, 1983), 69–84.

[44] We have come to the conclusion that all the melodies in the work are original with Fauré; there seems to be no borrowed material.

[45] Nectoux, *Gabriel Fauré: Les voix du clair-obscur*, 209. This is a unique assertion. Orledge's discussion of the work (*Gabriel Fauré*, 131–132) raises no questions around Fauré's orchestration. Orledge's back matter also explicitly lists *Le voile du bonheur* among the scores that Fauré orchestrated, as opposed to those he farmed out (270).

Example 9.2 *Le voile du bonheur*, Scene 3, No. 1, mm. 17–33

conduct the small ensemble at the premiere.[46] Nectoux acknowledges this fact but finds that Fauré's envoi, "To my collaborator on *Le voile du bonheur*," on a copy of Vuillermoz's book *Musiques d'aujourd'hui* (to which Fauré wrote the preface in 1923), proves that *Le voile* was not entirely Fauré's work.[47] More generally, Nectoux expresses surprise at the presence of Eastern influences in a work by Fauré. As we read earlier, Nectoux acknowledges that Fauré almost certainly heard exotic music at the World's Fairs in Paris but assures us that, unlike Saint-Saëns, Debussy, or Ravel, Fauré would have lent it only "an amused ear." Did Nectoux first presume that *Le voile du bonheur* was not an authentic work by Fauré, or did he first presume that Fauré was uninterested in Eastern musics, and therefore that *Le voile du bonheur* must have been a joint effort?

When Fauré delegated an orchestration project, he did so to save time under the pressure of a deadline, and such orchestrations survive in a hand other than Fauré's. Given his consistent habits and extant manuscripts, we cannot find any reason why Fauré would have written out a copy of such a short, simple score in his own hand if he had not orchestrated the piece himself. In other words, if Nectoux's hypothesis were true, we would have a score in the hand of Vuillermoz, not the complete autograph score that survives – and survives with Fauré's own working revisions. Besides these objections, we note that the pitch content of the score is so slender (see Example 9.2, for example) that it is difficult to imagine a more primitive version (a "short score" of some type) that did not already specify different instrumental timbres.

In October 1901, Fauré wrote Marguerite Hasselmans that he would have to leave Garches to attend a rehearsal at the Théâtre de la Renaissance in the presence of Clemenceau and the actors. He added, "The minuscule but difficult bit of labor on this score for the Renaissance [Theater] is finally complete and has been sent off to the copyist."[48] This glimpse into

---

[46] Vuillermoz, *Gabriel Fauré*, 23. In a much earlier text, not cited by Nectoux, Vuillermoz describes *Le voile du bonheur* in greater detail, yet is even more modest in describing his own role ("le hasard m'avait fait témoin"); see his chapter "Gabriel Fauré" in *Histoire du théâtre lyrique en France*, Vol. 3 (Paris: Radio-Paris, 1939), 95.

[47] We find the composer's envoi unremarkable. It is entirely consonant with his characteristic graciousness toward professional colleagues; Fauré, who was away from Paris for the premiere of the work, would have remembered Vuillermoz's willingness to direct the little orchestra with gratitude. This signed exemplar of *Musiques d'aujourd'hui* is not extant but was described to Nectoux by a third party, Bernard Gavoty (1908–81), whose oral testimony about the orchestration (supposedly from Vuillermoz) Nectoux also mentions. See Nectoux, *Gabriel Fauré*, 209.

[48] Fauré, *Correspondance*, 585.

the creative process implies the completion of an autograph manuscript (*minuscule mais difficile*) from which instrumental parts and a scribal copy of the score would be produced for use in the theater. In fact, the autograph bears pencil marks in another hand, marks of a type that will be familiar to students of manuscripts in this period as the planning ("casting-off") a copyist makes for a manual copy of the score.[49]

Comparing *Le voile du bonheur* to a chronologically proximate manuscript of Fauré's with a similar number of parts – *La bonne chanson*, which he arranged for voice, piano, and string quintet in 1898 – we can observe not only the same hand but also Fauré's unique way of cancelling staves and systems. These artistic crisscrossing squiggles and lines appear in Fauré's other manuscripts, but the similarity we can observe between *La bonne chanson* and *Le voile du bonheur* is especially striking (see Figures 9.1 (a) and 9.1(b)). Moreover, it is apparent (especially in passages scraped away with a razor) that Fauré was making compositional decisions in the fair copy of the full score of *Le voile*. These late-stage changes are further evidence of his responsibility for the orchestration of the work.

Perhaps Jean-Michel Nectoux was too eager to protect Fauré's reputation as a composer of "pure music." One might characterize Fauré's incidental music for Clemenceau's play as an instance of what Ralph Locke calls "transcultural composing."[50] This can never be a "pure" process. *Le voile du bonheur* shows a composer influenced by Eastern culture, however transiently, and his fascination and inspiration are born out of an almost idle curiosity, nothing like the heavy hand of imperial correction. With *Le voile* in his œuvre, Fauré stands closer to Debussy, Roussel, Ravel, and Delage as a French composer stimulated by Eastern – in this case specifically Chinese – culture. Vuillermoz, who conducted Fauré's ensemble in 1901, recalled the score many years later, in 1939:

Only someone who did not know anything about Fauré would think him capable of respecting for even a moment the facile conventions that operettas and music halls had established for "Chinese music." With rare discretion and delicacy, he

---

[49] See the circled numbers in light pencil on MS 17786, which indicate the pages the scribe planned for his copy, and the uncircled "2"s, which indicate the second systems on those pages. If ever found, the scribal copy of the score would have twenty-nine pages, only one more than Fauré's filled autograph pages. A manual copy of a score generally occupies close to the same number of pages of the original, whereas an engraver's copy takes fewer pages than the original, and engravers use a more complex system of marking. Fauré generally had a second copy of a score made so that he could retain one for himself and for use in rehearsals.

[50] Ralph Locke, *Musical Exoticism: Images and Reflections* (Cambridge: Cambridge University Press, 2009), Chapter 9, 214–275.

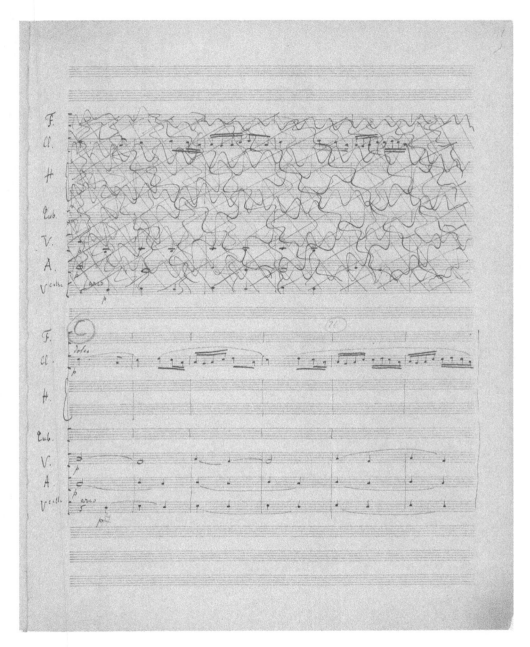

Figure 9.1(a) Fauré, *Le voile du bonheur* (Paris BnF Musique, MS 17786), 15.
Courtesy of the Bibliothèque nationale de France

Figure 9.1(b) Fauré, *La bonne chanson*, Op. 61 (Paris BnF Musique, MS 22409), 63.
Courtesy of the Bibliothèque nationale de France

enveloped his Far Eastern characters in gentle, suggestive timbres. Like the serenity of Confucius's philosophy, this music hovered like a perfume.[51]

Is *Le voile du bonheur* an example of "submerged exoticism" or of "transcultural composing"? Ralph Locke uses both terms (of his own devising) with deliberate flexibility in his book *Musical Exoticism*. Either term is suggestive and perhaps heuristic, but we shall leave those terms aside to argue, in the last section of this chapter, that *Le voile du bonheur* is an example of what we will call "second-degree orientalism," following Patrick Vauday's analysis of Western visual arts whose forms have been decentered by Eastern traditions. In any case, it is clear that *Le voile du bonheur* directly challenges the status Locke grants Debussy's "Pagodes," published in 1903, two years after Fauré's work: "The radical modernity of Debussy's 'Pagodes' is that it uses 'black-note' pentatonicism more consistently in both melody and accompaniment than did any previous piece."[52] *Le voile du bonheur* was unknown to Locke. "Pagodes" has many merits, including harmonic complexity, but *Le voile du bonheur* is the earlier and more extensively pentatonic piece.

Eastern religious thought and culture had been on Fauré's mind as early as 1892, when he contemplated an opera on the theme of "The Vocation of Buddha," but Fauré found the libretto by Albert Samain unworkable.[53] *Le voile du bonheur* perhaps rekindled ideas about the opera that he had contemplated nine years earlier. The timing of the cultural exhibits at the World's Fairs (*Expositions universelles*) of 1889 and 1900 offers the possibility that they influenced Fauré's potential Buddha opera in 1892 as well as *Le voile du bonheur* in 1901. Both fairs hosted various musical and theatrical ensembles from around the world. The World's Fair of 1889 has been more closely studied by musicologists because it was the first to feature the Javanese gamelan and Vietnamese theatrical troupe that so fascinated Debussy.[54] We must now wonder, was there Chinese music at either Fair? The official report from 1900 tells us that China did not accept the invitation to exhibit in 1889.[55] For the Fair in 1900, however, China

---

[51] Vuillermoz, "Gabriel Fauré," 96.   [52] Locke, *Musical Exoticism*, 234.

[53] Caballero, *Fauré and French Musical Aesthetics*, 174–175; Georges Jean-Aubry, "Gabriel Fauré, Paul Verlaine et Albert Samain, ou Les Tribulations de 'Bouddha': Lettres inédites," in *Le Centenaire de Gabriel Fauré (1845–1945)* (Paris: Éditions de La revue musicale, 1945), 39–58.

[54] See Anik Devriès, "Les musiques d'Extrême-orient à l'Exposition universelle de 1889," *Cahiers Debussy* 1 (new series) (1977), 24–37; and Annegret Fauser, *Musical Encounters at the 1889 Paris World's Fair* (Rochester: University of Rochester Press, 2005).

[55] *Paris Exposition 1900: Guide pratique du visiteur de Paris et de l'exposition* (Paris: Hachette, 1900), 351: "En 1889, la Chine avait refusé de prendre part à l'Exposition." However, maps of

had a prominent pavilion and teahouse built next to the Trocadéro. In 1900, all of the musical exhibitions were housed in or around the Trocadéro. Among the many foreign musics clustered there, Chinese musicians played in an attraction called "Le Théâtre chinois au Trocadéro." Whether this theater was in the Trocadéro itself or (more likely) in the Chinese pavilion, tearoom, or surrounding gardens, it included musicians, singers, actors, and acrobats and was advertised repeatedly in Judith Gautier's series of six pamphlets, *Les musiques bizarres à l'Exposition de 1900*. Gautier, a sinologist and elder daughter of the poet Théophile Gautier, devoted one of these six booklets specifically to *La musique chinoise*. After an introductory essay by Gautier, the pamphlet contains three pieces transcribed for voice and piano by her friend Louis Bénédictus; Gautier indicates that these specific pieces were performed in the "Théâtre chinois."[56]

Fauré would have traversed the exotic soundscape of the Trocadéro gardens repeatedly, because he attended the rehearsals and eventual performance of his own Requiem Mass in the great hall of the Trocadéro on July 12, 1900, one of the official events of the Fair. What foreign music he stopped to listen to, and what he thought of it, we do not know. In 1889 as in 1900, Fauré would have had the opportunity to hear Javanese and Indochinese music. In 1900, besides the new appearance of a Chinese ensemble, the charismatic dancer Sadayakko brought attention to Japanese music as never before. We would not argue that the orchestration of *Le voile* stems from a specific combination that Fauré seized upon in these Eastern ensembles, only a general impression of delicacy, repetitiveness,

the 1889 exhibition plainly show a "Pavillon chinois" along the edge of the fairgrounds parallel to the Avenue de Suffren. Was it thus listed as part of hopeful planning, or was it actually mounted (perhaps by the French government for public interest)? Why, moreover, does Louis Bénédictus include a "marche chinoise" entitled "Les ordres du général" in *Les musiques bizarres de l'Exposition* (Paris: G. Hartmann, 1889)? We see no sign of Chinese musicians in other documents concerning 1889, but there is a great deal of inconsistency in the abundant historical records.

[56] See Judith Gautier, *Les musiques bizarres à l'Exposition de 1900: La musique chinoise* (Paris: Enoch, 1900). Other than pentatonicism, none of these pieces shows a specific melodic relationship to the music of *Le voile du bonheur*. We bring up the presence of Chinese music only to establish potential exposure and awareness by Western musicians at the Fair in 1900. The advertising for the performances read in full: "Le Théâtre chinois | au Trocadéro | Musiciennes et chanteuses chinoises | Comédiens et jongleurs célèbres à Pékin." Although Julien Tiersot claimed there were no Chinese musicians at the World's Fair in 1900, he seems to have been mistaken; see his "Ethnographie musicale: Notes prises à l'Exposition universelle de 1900: Musique chinoise et indo-chinoise," *Le Ménestrel* 67, No. 2 (January 13, 1901), 12.

and the use of a small number of solo string and wind instruments in combination with metal percussion. There was really no other model for the orchestration of *Le voile du bonheur*. Fauré might have been present at the single, rather exclusive performance of Debussy's incidental music for Pierre Louÿs' *Chansons de Bilitis* at *Le Journal* in February 1901: a quintet for two harps, two flutes, and celesta. This work has some parallels with Fauré's in its intimacy and quiet theatrical pointillism, but it lacked the element of bowed strings and metallophones (unless one counts the celesta). Finally, it is worth noting that all of the world music ensembles mentioned above used their instruments in a theatrical context; that was also the context for Fauré's *Voile du bonheur*. So often it is the theater that gives a composer the inspiration to do something new.

The instrumentation of *Le voile du bonheur* betrays the significance of the World's Fairs and Fauré's willingness to displace his style Eastward. His seemingly hodge-podge septet of musicians creates a very deliberate soundscape, allowing the group to function as a sort of imaginary Asian ensemble for Western theater (see Example 9.3). Fauré calls for a percussion player who alternates between two instruments, which Fauré designates in his own spellings as *gong* and *tubophone*. This is the only score in which Fauré used either instrument. It is unclear exactly what instrument would have been used for a *tubophone* part in Paris in 1901. The instrument now known as the tubaphone, once also called a tubus-campanophone, had indeed been recently invented but was rare outside of English bands and vaudeville theaters. It consists of hollow steel tubes arranged in graduated lengths and played like a xylophone.[57] As for the gong, it seems that Fauré (like Messager and Saint-Saëns) knew the difference between a *gong* and a *tam-tam* and wanted an instrument with a central boss or nipple. In *Pénélope* (1907–13) Fauré calls for tam-tam and notates it on the lowest line of a bass clef staff, whereas in *Le voile* he notates the gong part on a clefless staff on the middle

[57] A United States patent by John C. Deagan and Joseph Carroll was registered on August 6, 1889 for a "pipelaphone," fundamentally the same instrument as a tubaphone (US patent No. 408,655). The term *tubophone* is unusual in French and the instrument does not appear (in any spelling) in the *Encyclopédie de musique et Dictionnarie du Conservatoire* (Paris: Delagrave, 1913–30). The modern-day performers from the Orchestre de Paris played the *tubophone* part on tubular bells, but the designation of that instrument as *cloches* (more rarely *tubes-cloches*) in French was well established by Fauré's time, and so it seems likely Fauré would have written "cloches" if he intended them. The effect of the part on tubular bells is nonetheless beautiful. A tubaphone would produce fundamental tones in a higher octave and, in fact, sound more like the highest range of Javanese gamelan instruments (e.g., *saron panerus*, *saron sanga*).

Example 9.3 *Le voile du bonheur*, Scene 3, No. 2, mm. 62–71

line.[58] Of all the timbral aspects of *Le voile*, these two metallophones are the most obvious evidence of Fauré's debt to Asian sonorities at the World's Fairs, but we would also draw attention – as another aspect of that influence – to the way he often allows the solo flute and clarinet to float without harmonic support. Indeed, a surprising proportion of the score altogether abandons Fauré's usual habit of a functional bass line. Fauré also sometimes deploys the harp as a sonorous bell, a surrogate metallophone (see Example 9.2). The articulation marks for these isolated notes on the harp (dot over dash, or staccato over marcato) is telling: it is the same articulation Fauré notated when he wished to evoke bells in his

[58] Perhaps Fauré had been told that gongs of some sort were available at the Théâtre de la Renaissance and trusted Vuillermoz to choose the gong with the best pitch. Messager's opera *Madame Chrysanthème* (1893) premiered at the same theater and calls for a "gong ou cloche (sur le théâtre)," notated on F and G in the upper half of the bass clef.

piano writing. Examples of this notation occur in the third section of his Seventh Nocturne and in the piano part of his song "Prison," both composed in the late 1890s. In these pieces, as in *Le voile du bonheur*, Fauré evokes the sound of a bell by the articulation and textural isolation of a repeated tone or octave.

Le voile's pentatonic pitch content was likely influenced not only by the Asian music at the World's Fairs but also by transcriptions of Chinese music from this same period. Transcriptions in Western notation are what we must reckon with, even though we know they are but faint impressions of Chinese music. The two most frequently printed examples – the "Air chinois" that Fétis included in his *Histoire générale* (1869), and "Madame Wang," first given by van Aalst (1884) and offered again by Tiersot in the series of articles he wrote during the 1900 World's Fair – are very distinct from one another in melodic quality, but have two marked commonalities.[59] First, both are completely pentatonic melodies based on the same collection (D E G A B), with E or G as cofinals; second, both are notated in 2/4. This latter fact would not seem worth stating but for the strange metrical uniformity of Fauré's *Le voile du bonheur*. Every page of the score is in 2/4, a meter that Fauré seldom used, but the one in which most examples of Chinese music were printed in nineteenth-century Western transcriptions. The association of modes focused on E with Chinese melodies also seems marked, for the starting point of Fauré's score is a melody in E pentatonic. The closing music likewise begins on E but wends its way, thanks to the pitch identity of the E Phrygian and C major scales, to an ending on a serene C-major triad with E in the treble.[60]

All of the themes in Fauré's score use a pentatonic system. However, Fauré's use of modality and pentatonicism was not exclusive to his evocations of the Orient. Instead of adding modal inflections to a traditional tonal language, Fauré readily created modal and pentatonic melodies. His

---

[59] F.-J. Fétis, *Histoire générale de la musique*, Vol. 1 (Paris: Firmin Didot, 1869), 60; J. A. van Aalst, *Chinese Music* (Shanghai: The Statistical Department of the Inspectorate General of Customs, 1884), 38.

[60] Two other prominent *chinoiseries* by Fauré's younger contemporaries are also written in 2/4: Manuel de Falla's "Chinoiserie" from *Trois mélodies* (1909), which also takes E as the tonic, and Ravel's "Laideronnette, impératrice des pagodes," from *Ma mère l'Oye* (1910). Saint-Saëns' overture to his opera *La princesse jaune* (1872) is a much earlier example, again cast in 2/4. While it is a *japonerie* rather than a *chinoiserie*, none other than Fauré himself made arrangements of this overture for piano duet (four hands) and two pianos (eight hands). This one-act comedy by Saint-Saëns (libretto by Louis Gallet) is probably the earliest operatic response to *japonisme* as practiced by the Goncourt brothers and is full of irony and jest. As a parody of a cultural craze, it is a senior cousin of Gilbert and Sullivan's *Patience* (1881).

Example 9.4 Fauré, Pie Jesu, Requiem, Op. 48, mm. 35–38

Example 9.5 *Le voile du bonheur*, Scene 15, mm. 305–312

early training in plainchant and Renaissance polyphony gave him fluency in styles that might be extended toward modern diatonic modality or retracted to pentatonicism. We refer readers to the pentatonic, half-stepless endings of the Sanctus, Pie Jesu (see Example 9.4), and In Paradisum of Fauré's Requiem to see how close any of these examples is to the music associated with Tchang-I's blessing, "Le ciel est bon" (see Example 9.5). An expression of divine grace, this music appears twice in the play, when Tchang-I takes up his lute to sing (Scene 10 and Scene 15). Example 9.5 shows the very end of this music, and though the dissonances are freer than in Example 9.4, we recognize the hand that wrote the Pie Jesu.

Alongside these peaceful, oscillating endings, the prominent pentatonic motive heard at the beginning of *La bonne chanson* (1892–4) is another close relation to the themes Fauré invented for *Le voile du bonheur*. "Une Sainte en son auréole" (see Example 9.6) uses a pentatonic melody to evoke the "rare charms" of a medieval "saint in her halo" and "noble ladies of yore." The medieval allusions that suffuse "Une Sainte en son auréole," a song ending with the unusual word "carlovingien" (Carolingian) in the

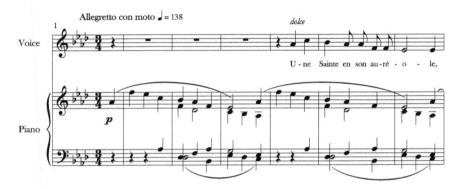

Example 9.6 Fauré, "Une Sainte en son auréole," *La bonne chanson*, mm. 1–6

rhyming position, have a significant, not coincidental, relationship to the pentatonic melodic material in *Le voile du bonheur*. As long ago as 1950, Raymond Schwab pointed out that the French Romantics, and notably Victor Hugo, saw the civilizations of the East *and* of medieval Europe as twin alternatives to Western classicism.[61] Writers like Hugo turned medievalism and orientalism into allies in the larger project of "rewiring" nineteenth-century European art. Hence, the common pitch vocabulary of Fauré's evocations of the Middle Ages and the Orient hearkens back to an old Herderian tradition of something like "world exoticism." In any event, archaic modal melodies, pentatonic or diatonic, were already familiar musical country for Fauré by the time he came to compose *Le voile du bonheur*.[62]

Clemenceau's play is rich in possibilities for layered meanings, which Fauré thoughtfully articulated. His placement of musical material creates his own commentary on the action: he only writes music for scenes where Tchang-I, the main character, enjoys his "veil of happiness." When Tchang-I experiences his world as beautiful, Fauré creates music reflective of this veil. When Tchang-I experiences sight, the nightmare of what he sees is accompanied by silence; the music disappears. At the end of Scene 14, Tchang-I wishes for his "veil of happiness" to be restored. He is able to

---

[61] Raymond Schwab, *The Oriental Renaissance: Europe's Rediscovery of India and the East, 1680–1880*, trans. Gene Patterson-Black and Victor Reinking (New York: Columbia University Press, 1984), 12–13.

[62] Although *Le voile du bonheur* is pentatonic for longer stretches than any other work by Fauré, he does not hesitate to introduce diatonic and chromatic scalar relationships, however sparingly. A typical instance may be observed in Example 9.2: after many measures of tonic pedal (E) and pure pentatonicism, the introduction of F and B♭ in measure 29 shifts the mode to E-Locrian.

Scène XI. *Tou-Fou et Si-Tchun se regardent amouresement et s'enlacent.*

Tou-Fou. Le Youen et le Yang à la robe dorée, [les deux oiseaux de l'amour, c'est nous!]

Example 9.7 *Le voile du bonheur*, Scene 11, mm. 202–215

return to his former state and takes up his lute again in the short final scene (at "Le ciel est bon," whose music ends with Example 9.5). Fauré reinstates lyric plenitude and grants listeners their own musical veil of happiness. Fauré's scoring describes a dichotomy between reality (silence) and dream (musical fabric), signaling to the listener that what may be beautiful may not be reality. For, as Tchang-I peacefully rhapsodizes on his lute again, as he did in Scene 10, a new stage direction sows a jarring element of mockery in the midst of the blind man's joy: his wife and his best friend betray him ("Si-Tchun and Tou-Fou embrace, gazing in each other's eyes").[63]

Fauré lets the noble, melting quality of his closing music arouse our sympathy for Tchang-I and gives no musical quarter to the farce of infidelity that the audience sees (and Tchang-I does not). But the composer acted quite differently in Scene 11. Here Fauré invented a musical analogue for the comedy in Clemenceau's text (see Example 9.7). The strict inversional symmetry between the flute and clarinet may strike the listener as a bit contrived for Fauré, but with a closer attention to the text, we see that he has wittily illustrated the reference to yin and yang in Clemenceau's play. In this scene, we learn that the main character's wife (Si-Tchun) and friend

---

[63] Clemenceau, *Le voile du bonheur* (script) in *La petite illustration* 461 (January 4, 1930), 14.

(Tou-Fou) are having an affair. Clemenceau has Tou-Fou paraphrase Tchang-I's preceding speech in praise of marriage. Now instead of the sacred marriage Tchang-I evoked, Tou-Fou appropriates the image of two lovebirds for his illicit liaison with Tchang-I's wife: "The Yin and the Yang on the golden dress, the two lovebirds; that's us!" These words from the play appear in Fauré's hand on his score as a cue. The flute and clarinet represent the two characters, and the inversional symmetry between them represent the yin and the yang – a bit of Daoist humor that Fauré translated from Clemenceau's conflation of Eastern wisdom and French bedroom farce. (Fauré's music plays as Si-Tchun and Tou-Fou sneak away excitedly to "la chambre nuptiale.")

Le voile du bonheur opens a window on Fauré's contemplation of the perceived stillness of Eastern music, which expanded an existing space of serenity in his own style. And like any good music for the stage, Fauré's score took up the themes and atmosphere of Clemenceau's play. Despite Nectoux's hesitation, the survival of a working copy of the autograph manuscript in full score shows that *Le voile* is securely Fauré's. We have pointed to the character and details of the autograph source as sufficient proof, but to understand the deeper place of the score in Fauré's œuvre, its demonstrable connection to the content of other works of the 1890s is more important. Although *Le voile du bonheur* is strange, it becomes more similar to Fauré's other works the more one studies it. We have only scratched the surface of such connections with our earlier comparisons to the Requiem and *La bonne chanson*. The rhythms, syncopations, and melodic shapes in the duet for flute and clarinet in the second part of Scene 3 (mm. 83–103), for instance, which depict Tchang-I's performance on lute, recall Fauré's song "Mandoline" (lute and mandolin, the instruments of serenade and lyric gratitude, inspired similar music in him). Or again, the measured tremolo passage for strings in Scene 11 recalls the similar "textural music" in the Finale of *Shylock*. While the endings of the Sanctus, Pie Jesu, and In Paradisum, like the later Prelude to *Pelléas et Mélisande* (mm. 1–8), show that Fauré was sometimes willing to reduce his increasingly complex musical style to bare essentials, *Le voile du bonheur* now reveals what we would not otherwise have guessed. There was a further step beyond the serenity of those earlier works: Fauré stripped his music down to a point where it startles us, for *Le voile* brushes close to the edge of silence, a denuded musical *minimum*. Nonetheless, Fauré does something in *Le voile* that he was already master of: he marries dichotomies between West and East, reality and dream, and levels of consciousness.

Encounters with the East: Orientalism in Question

In an article entitled "On the Role and Influence of Arts of the Far East and Japan" (1891), the French art critic Roger Marx hailed "a real encounter, rich and fruitful, of two civilizations."[64] More than a century later, we might not fully appreciate the language of mutuality in this statement, which is so different from the language of domination. That China and Japan were even recognized at all by the French as "civilizations" is significant, as is the fact that they retained their political autonomy in the face of colonial enterprise. This autonomy put them on a different footing *vis-à-vis* European powers than those whose lands suffered colonial domination. We are reminded that not all of the cultures Westerners subjected to exotic inquiry and curiosity were or could be conquered by them. Some, like China and Japan, remaining uncolonized and themselves undertaking their own projects of conquest and colonization, aroused even deeper curiosity. Despite Western inroads into the policies of closure and autonomy exercised by these two empires, they remained somewhat impermeable to Western pressure and guarded their treasures cagily. Thus the orientalism of Clemenceau and Fauré, while not immune to the accusation of appropriation, does not, at least, rearticulate a territorial domination.

Clemenceau's play is a fantasy, and so Fauré had no reason to borrow tunes or seek ethnographic sources for his music. He simply conjured up what were for him acceptable Chinese sounds in a context where European audiences would recognize them as consonant with the atmosphere of the play. The score is a delicate fantasy of elsewhere. As Nasser Al-Taee writes, "European composers throughout history did not indulge in producing 'authentic' Oriental tunes to back up their appropriation of the Orient, because the question of authenticity was not relevant to these projects."[65] The production of authentic Chinese court music was not Fauré's concern; rather, he sought to transport his audience to the imaginary space created by Clemenceau's bittersweet comedy. He had already done the same thing in his music for the imaginary kingdom of Allemonde in his music for Maeterlinck's *Pelléas et Mélisande* two years earlier. It would not be too

[64] "Sur le rôle et l'influence des arts de l'Extrême-Orient et du Japon," *Le Japon artistique* 36 (April 1891); quoted by Patrick Vauday, *La décolonisation du tableau: Art et politique au XIXe siècle, Delacroix, Gauguin, Monet* (Paris: Seuil, 2006), 141.
[65] Nasser Al-Taee, *Representations of the Orient in Western Music: Violence and Sensuality* (Farnham, England and Burlington, VT: Ashgate, 2010), 237.

bold to say that the China of *Le voile du bonheur* is no more real than the completely imaginary Allemonde of Maeterlinck.

Now we must come to terms with the place of *Le voile du bonheur* in the wider world of orientalism. Clemenceau's little play is the best place to start, because it is different from more familiar orientalist fantasies like *Lakmé, Madama Butterfly,* and even Disney's *Aladdin.* How so? First, the human situations in the play are mundane and do not place the characters in a mythic, inaccessible East full of magic and villains, as so many similar works do. Second, all of the characters in the play are Chinese; there are no Westerners like Pinkerton (*Madama Butterfly*) or Gérald (*Lakmé*) to enact betrayal or provide invidious comparisons. Third, although Clemenceau draws on stereotypes of Chinese culture, they are mirrors he turns back on French society in an act of cultural critique. The shortcomings of Tchang-I's well-to-do household are oblique transpositions, digs at social behavior at home in France. More than one character displays gullibility, but none more than Tchang-I, whose unflinching confidence in the completeness and accuracy of government reporting in the *Gazette officielle* (clearly a surrogate for France's *Journal officiel*) provides most of the dialogue in Scene 1. As a journalist, Clemenceau had more than one reason to mock a man who relies on only one source of information! Other problems Tchang-I's household faces were familiar to French social mores at the turn of the century: the ruses of monogamy, outright infidelity, and the lack of parental control over nearly adult children. Tchang-I also experiences the theft of intellectual property (hardly a major Chinese concern in 1901): he discovers that his counselor and fellow mandarin Li-Kiang has taken advantage of his blindness by inserting himself as a co-author in a book of poetry Tchang-I submitted to the Emperor. All in all, Clemenceau's mode of critique here belongs to a less familiar strain of orientalist practice that has its roots in the Enlightenment. Ziauddin Sardar refers to it as "using the Orient to reprove Europe, a coded means of satirizing and pointing out its failures."[66] Clemenceau, a latter-day Voltaire or Montesquieu, felt at home in this intellectual tradition, and indeed, his play has a distinct flavor of Enlightenment skepticism.

Here we return to our earlier assertion that *Le voile du bonheur* is not really a play about China; it is a play about France.[67] Writing in the

---

[66] Sardar, *Orientalism,* 37.

[67] This despite the fact that it was once performed at the Théâtre Antoine in 1919 *in Chinese* with Chinese actors! See Robert de Beauplan's little reception history in *La petite illustration* 461 (January 4, 1930), 16.

immediate wake of the Dreyfus Affair, Clemenceau embedded his play's satirical critique in that particularly charged historical moment.[68] Let us remember that Clemenceau was the owner and editor of *L'Aurore*, the newspaper that published Zola's famous open letter (it was Clemenceau himself who came up with the headline, "J'accuse …!"). Yet it does not take long for satirical fiction to lose its context and edge, and readers today may sympathize with an American reviewer who missed the point of *Le voile du bonheur* seventeen years after its French premiere. The first time the play was performed in the United States in 1918, the New York *Times* described it in the Amusements section:

> *Le Voile du Bonheur*, presented for the first time in America, is a jewel, rare and exquisite, for it holds within it that unique and magnificent blend of eternal truth and perfect beauty. Tchang-I, the blind mandarin, is the symbol of all real truthseekers, who return to their blindness after they have seen life in its true colors. Blind, he takes the flatteries of his friends and wife and servants as true. Seeing, he finds that his wife is unfaithful to him, that his friends sell him, whose benefactor he is robs him. The choice is before him – he returns to blindness. He forgives everything and returns to the lie that is truth, to the darkness that is light.[69]

Here is a complete misconstrual of Clemenceau's intentions. The American reviewer understandably lacked the French political context of 1901 but also chose to overlook even the domestic level of satire in the text. Tchang-I is a fool, not a sage, and certainly not a "truthseeker." His return to blindness, his faith in the infallibility of vested powers and institutions, has to be seen in the light of Clemenceau's unwavering commitment to the Dreyfusard cause, which was the cause of truth and justice at all costs (including ugly stains on the army, government, and church). The quietistic surface of *Le voile du bonheur* should not distract us from its underlying allegory: a fool prefers to remain in a fool's paradise. Clemenceau spent most of his public life slashing at the cushions of falsehood, and Tchang-I's return to the "comfort" of blindness does not show the playwright in a moment of tenderness but rather conveys his ironic pessimism about craven miscarriages of justice in French society.[70]

---

[68] Alfred Dreyfus was freed and given amnesty in 1900 but only restored to full military rank in 1906, twelve years after the Affair began. Many of Dreyfus' supporters were deeply unsatisfied that the amnesty of 1900 hinged on a procedural admission of guilt.

[69] "Clemenceau Fantasy at French Theatre," *The New York Times*, November 12, 1918.

[70] On Clemenceau's despair over the judicial process in this period, see Gregor Dallas, *At the Heart of a Tiger: Clemenceau and His World, 1841–1929* (New York: Carroll & Graf, 1993), 366. The persistence of memory of the Dreyfus Affair in France (in contrast to New York in 1918) is

There is no irony whatsoever in the fact that, in 1922, it would be Clemenceau who doggedly convinced his long-time friend Claude Monet, blind in one eye and losing vision in the other, to get the cataract operation that would give him back his sight and allow him to return to painting in his final years.[71] Likewise, let us re-examine, more closely, Clemenceau's admiration for the Chinese pilgrims Faxian and Xuan-Zang, cited above. He did not praise them for their specific religious devotion or Buddhism but for their devotion to discovering the truth. In direct contrast to the fictional Tchang-I, Faxian and Xuan-Zang *were* truthseekers in Clemenceau's eyes.

In closing, we return to Fauré's score in light of a cultural context in which the history of French painting and design after 1850, and its interaction with Japanese visual art, may be heuristic. In a preface from 1884, Edmond de Goncourt recalled that he and his brother Jules were already involved in the admiration and propagation of Japanese art in Paris in 1851, when only Chinese and Dutch ships were permitted to trade with Japan, and Japanese artifacts were exceedingly rare. In light of the subsequent Japanese influence on French art in the 1870s and 1880s, Edmond de Goncourt was understandably proud of his early connoisseurship of the arts of Japan – "this art," as he declared, "which beyond all doubt is revolutionizing the way we in the West see the world."[72] He adds that "the three great literary and artistic movements of the second half of the nineteenth century" are "the search for truth, the resurrection of eighteenth-century art, and the triumph of *japonisme*."[73] He might have reminded his readers that as recently as 1874, before they were called "Impressionists," Monet and his colleagues were known as "Les japonais."[74]

---

shown by a telling image – a mirror covered with a veil – that was printed to decorate the end of the script of *Le voile du bonheur* in *La petite illustration*, even as late as 1930 (p. 14). The central iconography for Truth among Dreyfusards was a naked woman holding a mirror up to the world. See, among many other sources, Anya Suschitzky, "*Ariane et Barbe-Bleue:* Dukas, the Light, and the Well," *Cambridge Opera Journal* 9, No. 2 (1997), 133–161.

[71] See Jean Martet, *M. Clemenceau peint par lui-même* (Paris: Albin Michel, 1929), 67–69.

[72] Edmond de Goncourt, Preface to Chérie (Paris: Charpentier, 1910), xv: "cet art en train ... de révolutionner l'optique des peuples occidentaux."

[73] Ibid., xv–xvi.

[74] David Bromfield, "Japanese Art, Monet, and the Formation of Impressionism: Cultural Exchange and Appropriation in Later Nineteenth-Century European Art," in *Recovering the Orient: Artists, Scholars, Appropriations*, ed. Andrew Gerstle and Anthony Milner (Chur, Switzerland: Harwood Academic Publishers, 1994), 8, 10.

What Goncourt considered settled stylistic history, however, was still not widely accepted in the public sphere. His comments aroused negative critical reactions, which Goncourt privately bemoaned in his personal journal:

Misguided souls! They have not noticed that right now all of *impressionism* – the banishing of bitumen, etc. – was accomplished through the contemplation and imitation of Japan's *clear impressions*.[75] Nor have they noticed that the brain of a Western artist, in the ornamentation of a plate or whatnot, only conceives and creates a design in the middle of the object, a single decoration, or a decoration composed of two, three, four, or five ornamental details always functioning as pairings or counterweights, and that in modern ceramics the imitation of the ornament thrown to the side of the object, of asymmetrical decoration, was a break from the religion of Greek art, at least in the sphere of ornamentation.

Finally, I have an iron button, a button such as a Japanese man would use to attach his tobacco pouch to his belt, and on this button, under the leg of an unseen crane – a crane flying beyond the nielloed medallion – we see the crane's reflection in the waters of a moonlit stream. Don't you think that people among whom a craftsman has such powers of imagination is not a people apt to be a teacher to other peoples?

And when I said that *japonisme* was revolutionizing the way we in the West see the world, I was affirming that *japonisme* was bringing the West a new *coloration*, a new *system of ornamentation*, finally, if you will, a *poetic fantasy* in the creation of the art object that never existed in the most perfect decorative objects of the Middle Ages and Renaissance.[76]

This spirited passage is worth quoting at length because it shows a French critic thinking of a foreign art in terms of its independent integrity and forms, an attitude which we will call "second-degree" orientalism, in contrast to a more superficial "first-degree" orientalism. Where a first-degree orientalist depicts Oriental themes within a Western frame and technique, forcing them into an alien order or context, a second-degree orientalist allows the observation of an Eastern form to decenter Western techniques and hence achieve a work whose structure and appearance has been radically changed from Western craft norms, regardless of its content. Second-degree orientalism does not borrow in order to leer but in order to learn.

---

[75] "Impressions claires": *claire* could also mean light in color or transparent (unmodulated pigment) in this phrase.
[76] Edmond et Jules de Goncourt, *Journal: Mémoires de la vie littéraire, 1866–1886*, ed. Robert Ricatte (Paris: Fasquelle and Flammarion, 1956; reprinted by Robert Laffont, 2004), 1065 (entry of April 19, 1884).

The Impressionists were by no means consistent in their approach to oriental materials. Monet's portrait of his wife Camille, dressed in an elaborate kimono and surrounded by a meaningless display of Japanese fans (*La japonaise*, 1876), seems to us an example of first-degree orientalism. The canvas unfurls foreign objects on and around a Western woman for leering consumption. Patrick Vauday suggests that Monet may not have taken the painting very seriously from the start, since he gave it an almost redundant generic subtitle: *Japonerie.*[77] In 1918, Monet left no room for doubt, referring to the painting as a *saleté* ("a piece of filth"). David Bromfield remarks, "Monet was not simply referring to the technical quality of the work but to its close relation to the genre of erotic geisha painting that had been a speciality of artists like Tissot and that represented the appropriation of Japanese culture into the most banal of Western cultural forms."[78] In contrast, *La rue Montorgueil à Paris (Fête de 30 juin 1878)*, with its aggressive primary colors, aerial point of perspective, tiny human figures, and vibrant animation shows "second-degree" influence from Japanese painting, despite its wholly French subject and endlessly patriotic tricolor flags. A musical parallel to Monet's portrait of his wife in Japanese clothing is bound to be inexact, but two songs mentioned earlier, Bizet's "Adieux de l'hôtesse arabe" and Delibes' "Filles de Cadix," approximate the same effect: they throw stereotyped Arabic or Andalusian fabrics onto a pre-existent formal scheme. If Fauré's "Roses d'Ispahan" might fall into the same category, what makes *Le voile du bonheur* different?

In *La décolonisation du tableau*, Patrick Vauday describes two different ways of responding to a non-Western influence: by the reproduction of cultural differences (*par différence*), or by a kind of collaboration with them (*par ressemblance et connivence*). The latter method usually hinges on discovering in the art of another culture something one already has in common with it, something which answers a creative need and sparks, in Vauday's words, a surprising "transformation of the other into oneself, and of oneself into the other."[79] Vauday's two paths correspond, more or less, to our first-degree and second-degree orientalisms. But Vauday adds a key insight: the idea of discovery, in the other, of a form that corresponds to an expressive habit or need. "In these circumstances, the other is not reduced

---

[77] Vauday, *La décolonisation du tableau*, 134.

[78] See Bromfield, "Japanese Art," 40, where he discusses the sale in 1918 that occasioned Monet's comment. The translation of "saleté" and the quoted passage are from Bromfield.

[79] Vauday, *La décolonisation du tableau*, 141.

to an object of curiosity but instead recognized as a subject with a voice of his or her own, open to questioning and sharing."[80] Obviously, it was not by dressing Western figures in kimonos that the optics of French painting were radically changed by Japanese art. Rather, the transformation occurred through new techniques of asymmetry, line, color, perspective, and so forth, which the Impressionist painters seized upon in Japanese art as sympathetic to aesthetic aims and instincts of their own. Indeed, several of the formal pictorial elements Vauday goes on to list may be transposed to the domain of music: fragmentariness, asymmetry, simplification, pure colors . . . These – consistent traits of *Le voile du bonheur* – may now appear in a different light, as Fauré's deliberate "self-othering" of style through contact with Eastern musical arts. Yet, as with Monet and Pissarro, Fauré absorbed these enticing affordances as a way of extending latent tendencies in his own style. That, at least, is what we hoped to show with a few of the examples in the previous section.

Vauday summarizes the affordances that Japanese art gave the Impressionists as a "translation," not merely an "importation": the "joyful experience of translating oneself through another."[81] One could say French musicians who worked in parallel to Monet around 1900, including Fauré and Debussy, also experienced this expansion in the possibilities of "translation" – of both artistic self and imaginary place. In the music of the Far East, each composer found something that confirmed his own musical predilections. And in pursuing that "something" they redirected their existing musical strategies toward new sounds that made their music just a bit more like the art of the other. The pentatonic collection, though almost banal in its familiarity, was a crucial "pitch-way" that allowed composers to tune into something foreign and then find new expressive liberation in it. One could even call the pentatonic scale the universal solvent of music East and West. It allowed a shift into a space where something new might happen. The displacement was still part of the fantasy of orientalism, but it was a step toward the unknown, rather than an acquisition from a fixed position. Such an attitude might also be described in terms of the difference between receptivity and domination, or between learning and knowing. Clemenceau proved his Asian *bona fides* through his actions and writings. Fauré is in a weaker position because he was such a private figure. We can only guess at his thought about the East through the nearly isolated compositional dare that is *Le voile du bonheur*.

---

[80] Ibid., 135.   [81] Ibid., 141–142.

STEVEN RINGS

Scholars of French music have long known the name Vladimir Jankélévitch, but it is only in recent years that he has captured the attention of musicologists more generally. This is due almost entirely to the efforts of Carolyn Abbate, whose much-debated 2004 essay "Music – Drastic or Gnostic?" gives Jankélévitch pride of place.[1] A year before that essay, Abbate had published a translation of Jankélévitch's 1961 book *Music and the Ineffable*, which was the focus of a special session at the 2010 annual meeting of the American Musicological Society and a subsequent colloquy in the *Journal of the American Musicological Society*.[2] As a result of Abbate's provocative work, Jankélévitch has emerged as a figurehead for a certain style of thought about music: one that valorizes the ineffable immediacies of real-time musical experience (the drastic) and expresses profound skepticism toward talk about music (the gnostic).[3]

If Theodor Adorno acted for a generation of new musicologists as a philosophical authority for assertions of music's worldly and social legibility, then Jankélévitch has acted as a patron saint for a new generation's claims for music's *illegibility*, as a phenomenon that always exceeds the discursive. That Jankélévitch has taken on this significance is perhaps symptomatic of a post–New Musicological swerve in the discipline, one characterized in part by a weariness or dissatisfaction with highly textualized approaches to musical meaning and desirous of a return to a less mediated engagement with music's sonic and somatic effects.[4]

---

[1] This fact obscures an interesting wrinkle in Jankélévitch's North American reception history: William Austin had been teaching the French thinker's writings for decades at Cornell prior to Abbate's published interventions in the early 2000s. (I thank Byron Adams for sharing this information.)

[2] Carolyn Abbate, "Music – Drastic or Gnostic?" *Critical Inquiry* 30 (2004), 505–536; Vladimir Jankélévitch, *Music and the Ineffable*, trans. Carolyn Abbate (Princeton: Princeton University Press, 2003); Michael Gallope and Brian Kane (eds.), "Vladimir Jankélévitch's Philosophy of Music," *Journal of the American Musicological Society* 65 (2012), 215–256.

[3] For a valuable counterpoint to Abbate's engagement with Jankélévitch – with an emphasis on Henri Bergson, Charles Sanders Peirce, and Fauré's *mélodies* – see Stephen Rumph, "Fauré and the Effable: Theatricality, Reflection, and Semiosis in the *mélodies*," *Journal of the American Musicological Society* 68 (2015), 497–558.

[4] For a range of views on this disciplinary turn – some critical and ambivalent – see the essays in Gallope and Kane, "Jankélévitch's Philosophy."

But the resulting polemics, with their tendency toward Manichean dualisms – drastic *or* gnostic, performance *or* work, interpretation *or* silence – have not done justice to the full, perplexing range of Jankélévitch's thought. His writings on music are far more capacious, nimble, and inconsistent than the recent musicological literature suggests.[5] To see this rhetorical diversity in practice, we need look no further than his writings on Fauré, a composer who was in many ways the touchstone of his musical thought, and who animated that thought in all of its contradictory multiplicity. The philosopher knew Fauré's children personally and wrote about their father with a hagiographic devotion unmatched in his writings on any other musician. Fauré pops up with great frequency in Jankélévitch's general writings on music and indeed in many of his philosophical essays, rubbing shoulders with Plotinus, Schelling, and Bergson – often in the same sentence.

Music as Sounding Philosophy

As some readers may not be familiar with Jankélévitch, it is worth pausing for a brief introduction to his career and work. He was primarily a moral philosopher, holding the chair in that subject at the Sorbonne from 1951 until 1979.[6] While he never enjoyed the celebrity of a Derrida, Foucault, or Lacan – and indeed felt increasingly out of step with the star culture of French philosophy in the post-war years – he became a charismatic mentor in Parisian intellectual circles and was much beloved by his students, among them Levinas and Catherine Clément. A student of Henri Bergson, he remained a devout Bergsonian for his entire career, amplifying and extending his teacher's uncompromising arguments about the unrepresentability of temporal experience. Jankélévitch published prolifically, nearly a book a year, alternating between weighty philosophical tomes and

---

[5] The most philosophically ambitious demonstration of this point in the anglophone literature is Michael Gallope, *Deep Refrains: Music, Philosophy, and the Ineffable* (Chicago: University of Chicago Press, 2017), 165–203. Gallope avoids facile binaries and emphasizes the inconsistent plenitude of Jankélévitch's thought, going so far as to dub his chapter "Jankélévitch's Inconsistency."

[6] For concise English-language overviews of Jankélévitch's life and thought, see Andrew Kelley's introduction to Vladimir Jankélévitch, *Forgiveness*, trans. Andrew Kelley (Chicago: University of Chicago Press, 2005), vii–xix, and the brief essays by Arnold Davidson and Carolyn Abbate in the front matter of *Music and the Ineffable*, vii–xx. Readers of French interested in a more in-depth monographic treatment may consult Isabelle de Montmollin, *La philosophie de Vladimir Jankélévitch* (Paris: Presses universitaires de France, 2000).

volumes on music. As a child he hoped to be a concert pianist, but ultimately decided that he did not have the temperament for it – too nervous, he said. He nevertheless played piano throughout his life – even playing four-hand music with Roland Barthes – and lectured extensively on music. Indeed, music evidently played a profound role in *shaping* his philosophical thought; he stated in an interview toward the end of his life that his philosophical ideas took shape as much at the piano as at a writing desk. Arnold Davidson has argued that one of the most remarkable things about Jankélévitch's writing is the way in which he treats music as an equal to philosophy, even a kind of implicit philosophy. As Davidson puts it: "Nobody else would have had the intellectual audacity and assurance to describe Satie and Debussy in the same breath as Plato, endowing each with their own philosophical force."[7]

Music as sounding philosophy: if any composer fulfilled that promise for Jankélévitch, it was Fauré. The former's first book on music was about Fauré's songs (*Gabriel Fauré et ses mélodies*: Paris: Plon, 1938); he republished it thirty-six years later in greatly expanded form. This latter volume, *Fauré et l'inexprimable* (Paris: Plon, 1974; hereafter, *FI*), ranges widely in style, content, and method, the prose tacking between close attention to musical detail – often winding around notated examples – and philosophical meditations on affect, meaning, and ethics.[8] Alongside brilliant musings on Fauré's famed reticence and elusiveness – and what we might call the music's "sounding ethics" – we find discussions of notes, chords, themes, and forms, as well as some surprisingly traditional hermeneutic readings. Yet Jankélévitch's thought and his prose remain always in motion, never coming to rest at any single location for long, at one moment cool and aloof, the next swooping in close to a musical detail, only then to swerve back out to broader philosophical and moral considerations. The motion of his thought is in fact itself rather Fauréan: constantly in flux, often hovering elusively just out of reach, and hesitant to touch down for long, until the inevitable final measure.[9]

---

[7] From Davidson's introduction to Vladimir Jankélévitch, "Pelléas and Pénélope," trans. Arnold I. Davidson and Nancy R. Knezevic, *Critical Inquiry* 26 (2000), 585.

[8] The first part of *FI* reprints *Gabriel Fauré et ses mélodies*, the second is a discussion of the piano and chamber music, and the third ("Ambiguity, Tranquility of Soul, and Charm in Fauré's Works") addresses more general philosophical and aesthetic concerns, some of which I address below.

[9] For discussion of these and other characteristics of Fauré's aesthetic, see Carlo Caballero, *Fauré and French Musical Aesthetics* (Cambridge: Cambridge University Press, 2001) and James Sobaskie, "Allusion in the Music of Gabriel Fauré," in *Regarding Fauré*, ed. Tom Gordon (Amsterdam: Gordon and Breach, 1999), 163–205.

In short, Jankélévitch's writings on Fauré are more beguilingly plentiful than Abbate's polemics of drasticity – with their tendency toward an ethics of scarcity, proscription, and discursive silence – would have us believe.[10] Now, one may well wish to depart from Jankélévitch in this regard and advocate for the sort of asceticism that an Abbatean retreat from the gnostic entails. But I think we have more to learn from Jankélévitch, and – perhaps more relevant to the readers of this volume – more to learn about Fauré, via Jankélévitch. He felt that Fauré had as much to teach as any philosopher and found in his music – in addition to a fathomless reservoir of aesthetic pleasures – profound ethical and philosophical implications, grasped through the ears and fingers.

In what follows, I will listen alongside Jankélévitch to one of his favorite pieces: Fauré's Thirteenth Nocturne, Op. 119.[11] In so doing, I will perform a continuity of discourses – analytical, interpretive, philosophical – taking a stance deliberately athwart the Manichean dualisms of anglophone musicology's recent ineffable turn. My argument will be ostensive rather than propositional, an act of showing rather than telling. Specifically, I will strategically braid Jankélévitch's thoughts on the Nocturne with my own analytical observations, in an effort to suture discourses that have been overly dichotomized in the recent Jankélévitch revival. In so doing, I will demonstrate that Fauré's extraordinary final piano work, while exceeding any discourse aimed at it, does not recede in the face of analytical or interpretive attention. To the contrary, as Jankélévitch's own decades-long fascination with the composer attests, this music becomes *more* elusive, not less, the closer we listen. The example of his own engagement with Fauré opens the door to richer, more abundant interpretive practice, one that does not proscribe certain modes of expression – be they analytical or hermeneutic – but that also steadfastly resists *reducing* the sounding music to any such representations. To theorize this aporia, I will draw at the end of the chapter on Michael Gallope's recent discussion of two Jankélévitchian terms of art: quiddity and quoddity. An attention to quiddity and quoddity – carefully theorized and attentively held in mind – points the

---

[10] I am speaking here primarily of the polemic that drives Abbate's "Music – Drastic or Gnostic?"

[11] The present chapter picks up and expands upon my thinking about this Nocturne and Jankélévitch's engagement with it as begun in "Talking and Listening with Jankélévitch," my contribution to Gallope and Kane, "Jankélévitch's Philosophy," 218–223. That essay, in its turn, had picked up the thread from my earlier article on Jankélévitch and French music, "*Mystères limpides*: Time and Transformation in Debussy's *Des pas sur la neige*," 19th-Century Music 32 (2008), 178–208. See also my "Lourenço, Transfigured Night, and Musical Writing," Revista portuguesa de musicologia 3 (2016), 107–130, which explores a related set of issues.

way toward an interpretive ethics of abundance and plenitude, rather than one of prohibition and lack, while still remaining mindful of Jankélévitch's ethics – and Fauré's aesthetics – of reticence and modesty.

Jankélévitch and the Thirteenth Nocturne

Let us begin with Jankélévitch's own words on the Thirteenth Nocturne, which appear in Part 2 of *FI*. As we will refer back to this excerpt at various points in the discussion that follows, I present it here in full (the translation is mine, as are all translations in the chapter):

The Nocturne in B Minor (1922), almost contemporary with the trio, *L'horizon chimérique*, and the Second Cello Sonata, is the austere work of old age. Three main ideas share in the development of the Thirteenth Nocturne. First a chant, modestly draped over a few scale degrees of the middle register, gropes amid insidious rustling in the arid search for a *je-ne-sais-quoi*. Is it the anguish of sickness that forces the notes to huddle like this, one against the other? Throughout Fauré's last works – "Danseuse" [*Mirages*], for example – the proximity of the two hands, the abundance of seconds and thirds, creates nodules and harsh frictions. – The second idea, much broader, forcefully affirms an insistent, fateful, obstinately hammered motive, which later develops into canonical imitations. The left and right hands trade these seven notes back and forth. – And then follows the great lyrical explosion. The andante suddenly gives way to an allegro in G♯ minor. The Thirteenth Nocturne, reaching the end of its fumbling search, launches itself with a fire and impetuosity that are wholly vernal. Finally, the irresistible *élan* falls away bit by bit. The last page of the Nocturne – after such storms, hopes, and tumults – picks up the thread of the initial, profound meditation. The First, Sixth, and Seventh Nocturnes return like this, ending at their beginning. The left hand murmurs the protesting affirmation of the second theme *mezzo voce*: the second scale degree, lowered a semitone, irresistibly tilts the fateful theme toward the tonic, toward rest, toward night. One might be tempted when considering a second degree of the Phrygian scale to ask whether Fauré himself, speaking to his son about the *air de danse* from *Caligula* and its apparently Hypolydian scale, had not indirectly put us on guard against retrospective interpretations of his language. For no one is less of a grammarian than Gabriel Fauré! Let's turn to Philippe Fauré-Fremiet, who expresses in incomparable terms the sense of his father's last nocturne in his "Notes on the Interpretation of the Works": ". . . it exalts and shines in zenithal splendor; it becomes an affirmation of joy and glory, while the second theme, tormented, in response drags in its train the hammered bass notes of an unappeasable human desire . . . The distress becomes light, desire anguish. Without doubt we are returning to earth: the beautiful theme descends back into the middle register, slowly resuming the melancholy plaint of the opening. But one last return of the second theme – appeased – carries us, over a B-minor chord, to a conclusion of beneficent serenity."[12]

The Thirteenth Nocturne sums up – not at all biographically (for Fauré never related such a thing) but ideally and retrospectively – the general sense of a human life: the Nocturne, in contrast to the life of Fauré himself, begins with anxious searching on paths where one stumbles: "I went along dangerous paths, painfully uncertain ..."[13] Just so, Liszt's marvelous fugue in the variations on *Weinen, Klagen* gropes ahead [*tâtonne*]. And then there is the future, the takeoff of hope, the ardent youthfulness of a confidence left intact. "The sea is infinite and my dreams are wild."[14] Winter has ended,[15] and with winter the agoraphobia, the fear of great open spaces and the vast plains of the world. All of the air and all of the sea![16] And to finish: uncertainty pulled out of itself, lifted free [*hors de ses gonds*] by the wind of wild hope and transfigured into serene resignation. To have known by turns fear, hope and despair, infinite weariness, and, at the trials' end, acquiescence and wisdom, – is this not the destiny of man? (*FI*, 248–250)

There is so much to notice in this excerpt, and we will have occasion to dwell on several of its most striking passages. Note first that this is an interpretation of a work, not of a performance (*pace* Abbate). Despite his commitment to the ephemeral moment of music-as-performed, Jankélévitch did not overturn the work concept; he remained committed to pieces and made scores the objects for philosophical contemplation – indeed, notated musical examples abound in his writings on music.[17] Also, observe the fluid, unfussy motion between interpretive language (the Nocturne is a work of old age and sickness, pitches huddle and rustle, the formal trajectory resembles a human life, etc.) and matter-of-fact analytical observations. Among the latter, Jankélévitch identifies three principal themes, traces the movement's ternary form, and even comments on a Phrygian inflection when the second theme is played in the bass. Only on this last point does he waver somewhat, wondering whether it is permissible to use such technical language in discussing the music of this supposed anti-grammarian. But the worry dissolves as quickly as it came, giving way to a quotation from Philippe Fauré-Fremiet: Jankélévitch allows the composer's son to rhapsodize for him. Having regained his voice, he

[12] Philippe Fauré-Fremiet, *Gabriel Fauré*, second edition (Paris: A. Michel, 1957), 164.
[13] Jankélévitch quotes the fourth song of Fauré's *La bonne chanson*, Op. 61, "J'allais par des chemins perfides."
[14] Quoting the first song of *L'horizon chimérique*, Op. 118, "La mer est infinie."
[15] Quoting the ninth song of *La bonne chanson*, "L'hiver a cessé."
[16] Not from a Fauré song, but from Maeterlinck's play *Pelléas et Mélisande*.
[17] As Gallope observes in *Deep Refrains*, Chapter 3, passim.

Example 10.1 Fauré, Thirteenth Nocturne in B Minor, Op. 119, mm. 1–4

then launches his second paragraph, which zooms out to consider the work's large-scale form and its resemblance to a human life. It is a characteristically idiosyncratic paragraph – the ecstatic quotations from Fauré songs and Debussy's opera are quintessential Jankélévitch – but one is also struck by something else: here the supposed enemy of hermeneutics veers suspiciously close to a hermeneutic reading.

We will return to the question of hermeneutics below. First, though, I will weave Jankélévitch's more local observations with some of my own. Let us begin by attending to the themes he identifies. Example 10.1 shows the work's opening theme, which Jankélévitch calls a "chant, modestly draped over a few scale degrees of the middle register." The French word *chant* might also be translated as "song," but the archaizing English cognate (chant) seems particularly apt here, for this is music in a self-consciously antique style, with four real voices; some have dubbed it Fauré's motet style.[18] In it we sense his deep familiarity with Renaissance polyphony, which he studied as a boy at the École Niedermeyer. Note the prevalence of stepwise motion, which gives the texture a Palestrinian, held-back quality, and also a sort of expressive blankness. Each voice contains exactly one leap in this opening phrase; all else is stepwise motion. The reader can find these leaps easily by singing, playing, or visually tracing each line. (I have enclosed the upper voices at the end of measure 4 in parentheses as they form an upbeat to the second phrase.)

The leap in the top voice comes right at the opening: a descending third. As Example 10.2 shows, Fauré recoups this third with stepwise motion in the opposite direction, in classic gap-fill fashion – another subtle Palestrinian gesture. This configuration – leap down followed by stepwise ascent – becomes a kind of flexible motto for the movement.

---

[18] See, for example, Graham Johnson, *Gabriel Fauré: The Songs and Their Poets*, with translations of the song texts by Richard Stokes (Farnham, Surrey: Ashgate, 2009), 229.

Example 10.2 Gap-fill motto in the upper voice of Op. 119, mm. 1–2

This motto recurs throughout the piece, sometimes literally, but more often transformed; it underlies all three themes that Jankélévitch discusses, along with several more subsidiary ones. As Example 10.3a shows, Fauré sometimes changes the size of the opening leap: here it is a descending octave. Note that both the leaping gesture and scalar ascent are repeated. At other times, Fauré iterates just the descending third, illuminated by exquisite shifts in harmonic lighting, as shown in Example 10.3b. The motto is also the basis for the secondary themes in the movement. As Example 10.3c shows, it underlies the assertive theme that sounds first in measure 22, an impassioned variant of the opening chant. It is also evident in the insistent whole-tone gesture that Jankélévitch calls the "thème fatidique" – the fateful (or ominous) theme. This theme recurs throughout the work, often "obstinately hammered," as Jankélévitch says, and frequently sounding in canonic imitation. Example 10.3d shows both the descending third embedded in the theme and the incipient scalar ascent that follows. The ardent theme that begins the B section (m. 55) – Jankélévitch's third theme – is also related to the motto. As Example 10.3e illustrates, the initial descending interval is now a second, and the stepwise ascent is longer, but the gestural parallels are clear. (The resemblance is reinforced by the rhythm, to which we will return below.)

This exercise is useful, but it risks making Fauré's music seem clearer than it is. These related themes inhabit a dense and perplexing world of harmonic evasion and contrapuntal severity, the whole shot through with that characteristically Fauréan mix of nonchalance and rigor. In the B-section theme shown in Example 10.3e, for example, harmonic swerves, metric play, and ambiguities in phrase structure defamiliarize the motto – we may sense the thematic similarity, but only obliquely, hearing it out of the corner of our ears, as it were, so preoccupied are we by the otherwise bewildering surroundings.

The famous elusiveness of Fauré's music – a common topic in the literature on the composer, which Carlo Caballero explores in penetrating detail in his monograph – is everywhere in evidence in this late work.[19]

---

[19] Caballero, *Fauré and French Musical Aesthetics.*

Example 10.3 Transformations of the motto of Op. 119 in subsequent themes

It may be interesting to note that the composer himself worried about this aspect of his music, especially as regards first hearings; he said that he wished all listeners could begin with a *third* hearing rather than a first, so that the piece would make a more precise

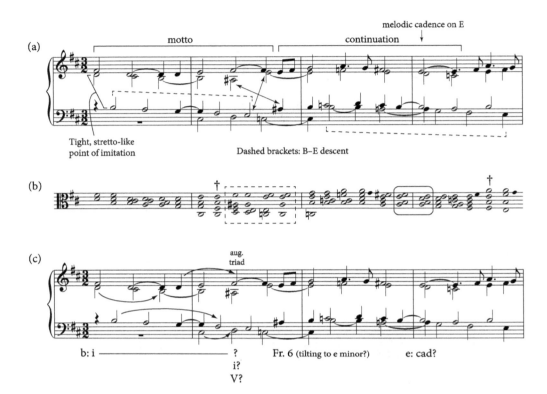

Example 10.4 Contrapuntal and harmonic density in Op. 119, mm. 1–4
(a) Imitative and interlaced contrapuntal activity in lower three voices, beneath the motto and its continuation
(b) Spacing in the verticalities arising from the counterpoint
(c) Tonal trajectories and uncertainties

impression.[20] But even on better acquaintance, something in the Nocturne often seems to hover just out of reach. This is classic Jankélévitchian territory: he is compelled by exactly such moments, when Fauré's music seems to withdraw or recede, an almost-grasped clarity giving way to cool puzzlement.

The sheer textural density of Fauré's motet style contributes to this puzzlement: there is too much to hear, and none of it is given the space to sound unobstructed (indeed, the phrase presents the pianist with

---

[20] "Quel dommage qu'on ne puisse pas toujours commencer par la troisième audition!" Letter to Marie Clerc, September 17, 1877, in Gabriel Fauré, *Correspondance suivie de Lettres à Madame H.*, ed. Jean Michel-Nectoux (Paris: Fayard, 2015), 65. The composer refers to the Romance for Violin and Piano, Op. 28.

considerable challenges of voicing). Example 10.4a returns us to the opening phrase. The example analyzes the phrase structure of the upper voice more explicitly: the opening motto is followed by a continuation that leads to a melodic cadence on E. But beneath this elegant trajectory there is a welter of contrapuntal activity, a dense weave. The tenor follows the alto in a tight point of imitation; their stepwise descents end in tritone leaps,[21] which sound in disorienting voice exchange (marked by the crossing arrows).[22] As the dashed brackets show, the tenor and bass also interact in loose imitation: the descending B-to-E fifth that begins the tenor recurs later in the very same register, but now technically in the bass voice.

The harmony further blurs these linear relationships: aurally arresting verticalities continually smudge the contrapuntal strata. I experience the result as a peculiar warping of my attention: when I attend to lines, perplexing harmonies obtrude, but when I then attend to the verticalities, my ear is drawn back to the integrity of the lines. I tend to sense line or harmony only obliquely, as I put it above, as objects in my peripheral hearing.

Fauré's harmonic spacing adds to the effect. As Jankélévitch notes, the pitches seem to "huddle together" here, occupying a very small compass in the middle of the keyboard. The single-staff representation of Example 10.4b shows that huddling. Note especially the preponderance of vertical seconds, made visible by their angled alignment. Jankélévitch observes that "the proximity of the two hands – the abundance of seconds and thirds – creates nodules and harsh frictions." The harshest such nodule surrounds the bar line of measure 4 – a rounded box in the example encloses the chords in question. The two harmonies on either side of this bar line contain two vertical seconds each, clouding the very moment of the melody's cadential arrival on E in a haze of seconds. Even at those moments

---

[21] While the upper voice more or less observes Palestrinian decorum in its diatonic leap-and-fill, the lower voices do not. Their intervals are very *un*-Palestrinian – tritones in alto and tenor, a major seventh in the bass – and the two middle voices follow their leaps by a step in the *same* direction, before the reversal. Yet none of this strikes the ear with any particular force or precision, given the sheer number of details competing for attention, the narrow registral compass, and the muted *mezzo piano* dynamic.

[22] Diana Deutsch has observed that in some contexts listeners have difficulty telling whether a melodic tritone is ascending or descending (she calls this the "tritone paradox"). Fauré's placement of the two voice-exchanging tritones in such close proximity – they share the same two pitch classes, and indeed the same middle *pitch* – invites just such mishearing and confusion. See Diana Deutsch, "A Musical Paradox," *Music Perception* 3 (1986), 275–280, and her webpage on the phenomenon: http://deutsch.ucsd.edu/psychology/pages.php?i=206, accessed April 14, 2018.

when the chords are widely spaced, they remain perplexing. For example, the two most evenly spaced verticalities in the passage, marked with daggers (†) above the staff, are both stacks of perfect fourths. These are in fact members of the very set-class of the two chords that surround the bar line of measure 4: all are versions of tetrachord [0257] – a relatively euphonious harmony nevertheless far from tertian clarity. The other passage of widely spaced harmonies, in measure 2, projects pitches from a single whole-tone collection. Thus, while the cadence in measure 4 is occluded in a haze of seconds and fourths, the motto's conclusion is shrouded in whole-tone mist.

More traditional modes of tonal analysis also illuminate this process of occlusion. The arrows in Example 10.4c show how each line arrives on a member of the tonic triad at the end of its first linear gesture. At the moment when soprano, tenor, and bass arrive at their tonic pitches, however, the alto slips to an A♯, creating an augmented triad that throws the harmonic situation into doubt. Rather than clarifying the situation in favor of either a tonic or dominant hearing, the augmented triad shades into a French sixth chord on the third beat. The native key of this chord – at least in common-practice tonal harmony – is E minor, though a French sixth on the lowered second degree in B minor would be a close second. Whatever its key, the chord does not resolve properly: the bass, rather than moving down by step, holds on for one beat too long, and then leaps up to resolve in the wrong octave, leaving the C♮ orphaned in the lower register. The cadence that follows seems in part to deliver on the promise of E, but it projects neither an explicit dominant nor tonic harmony in that key. The functional harmonies are conspicuous in their sonic absence, seemingly hovering just out of earshot.

The elusive nature of the phrase was not lost on Jankélévitch. The music here, he says, "gropes amid insidious rustling in the arid search for a *je-ne-sais-quoi*." This last – *je-ne-sais-quoi*, or "I don't know what" – is of course a familiar locution in French. But it has great importance for Jankélévitch, as a central term of art in his philosophy. One of his most ambitious philosophical treatises, published in three volumes in 1957, is entitled *Le Je-ne-sais-quoi et le Presque-rien* (The I-Don't-Know-What and the Almost-Nothing). Here is the opening of Volume 1:

There is something that is, so to speak, the bad conscience of the rationalist's good conscience, and the ultimate scruple of strong minds; something that protests and "murmurs" within us against the success of reductionist enterprises. This something is comparable ... to the malaise of a conscience unsatisfied before an incomplete truth [i.e., science]. There is something obscure and indemonstrable ... whose invisible presence fills us, yet whose inexplicable absence leaves us curiously disquieted, something that does not exist and is yet the most important thing among all important things, the only thing that is worth saying and yet precisely *the one thing that cannot be said!* ... The nostalgia for *something else*, the feeling *that there is something else* – this pathos of incompleteness animates a type of negative philosophy that has always been on the margins, though sometimes at the center, of esoteric philosophy. Plato – who knows, when he says unsayable things, to abandon dialectical discourse for mystical narrative – Plato speaks in the *Symposium* of "something else" ... that cannot be expressed, and that can only be suggested in riddles.[23]

We might find Jankélévitch's frank mysticism unnerving, but this line of thought, in one form or another, is not so foreign to French philosophy. It is firmly in the tradition that Gary Gutting calls "spiritualism," which rests on "an assertion of the metaphysical and ethical primacy of the individual mind [*l'esprit*], against the claims of materialism, empiricism, and certain forms of idealism."[24] The tradition originates with figures like Maine de Biran in the early nineteenth century and continues on up through Bergson and Jankélévitch in the twentieth. In all of these thinkers we encounter a skepticism toward the claims of natural science, amid arguments that crucial realms of knowledge and experience resist its totalizing grasp. We can detect distant echoes of this tradition in more familiar French thinkers of the twentieth century, who posited various terms of art for that which resists rationalist thought (or, in some cases, is *produced* by rationalist thought, as its necessary supplement): Lacan's real, Deleuze's virtual, Derrida's *différance*, Levinas' unknowable Other. To be sure, there are crucial differences between these thinkers and Jankélévitch. Yet the comparison does make clear that, in positing a *certain something* that eludes all attempts at rational capture, he is in good company.

Fauré is for Jankélévitch the quintessential composer of the *je-ne-sais-quoi*. The elusive aspects of Fauré's music that we explored above are the very details that Jankélévitch valorizes. He describes Fauré as a composer exquisitely attuned to the *je-ne-sais-quoi*, his music always gesturing toward an absence. It is music in which the "nostalgia for something else" is made sonically palpable. At one point, he poetically analogizes this to Penelope waiting for Odysseus: "Fauré's music is like Penelope, ... who

---

[23] Vladimir Jankélévitch, *Le Je-ne-sais-quoi et le Presque-rien* (Paris: Presses universitaire de France, 1957; reprinted and expanded edition, Vol. 1 [Paris: Éditions du Seuil, 1980]), 1–2.

[24] Gary Gutting, *French Philosophy in the Twentieth Century* (Cambridge: Cambridge University Press, 2001), 9–14, quote at 10. A related critical tradition (or -ism) informing Jankélévitch's thought was *vitalism*; see Kelley's introduction to Jankélévitch, *Forgiveness*, xv, and Gallope, *Deep Refrains*, Chapter 3.

dreams, her eyes elsewhere, and thinks of her absent lover" (*FI*, 351–352). In theorizing this Fauréan *je-ne-sais-quoi*, Jankélévitch mobilizes a field of paradoxes that he senses in the music. We have already encountered some of these, most notably a mixing of nonchalance and severity that I mentioned in passing; Jankélévitch dubs this quality "evasive rigor" and "negligent precision." He senses other paradoxes in Fauré's music as well, among them "contained force," "unpredictable predictability," and "mobile immobility."[25]

The most common example of the latter is a progression that veers wildly away from its tonic only to find it again at the last instant: the phrase as a whole goes nowhere but it covers vast harmonic ground. Jankélévitch discusses the phenomenon at several points in his writings on Fauré; as above, Odysseus and the other characters that populate Fauré's opera *Pénélope* are typically at hand to add metaphorical heft:

Just as the nurse Euryclea recognizes Odysseus under the rags of the beggar, just so the auditory memory recognizes the tonic pitch [*le ton fundamental*] that has been unrecognized [*méconnu*] over the course of the harmonic transmutations; and just as Odysseus himself, at the end of his long trek, rediscovers the Ithaca of his nostalgia, Fauréan discourse, after many more or less remote circuits and excursions rediscovers the Ithaca of the initial tonality. That which we call "circular modulation," which is in fact a *simulated* modulation, brings us back in the same way to our homeland [*nous ramène ainsi dans notre patrie*]; "circular modulation," is – like Odysseus's journey – a return. (*FI*, 275)

Jankélévitch here illuminates a central aspect of Fauréan kinetics and motion: his music seems animated by a restless, inner harmonic propulsion, but by phrase's end it so often finds anchor again at its tonal starting point. Such phrases enact Odysseus' fidelity to Penelope: no matter how far the hero is pulled off course, he always returns faithfully to Ithaca. This is Jankélévitch's "circular modulation." Genuine change of key through traditional modulation is less common in Fauré's music than wide-ranging motion *within* or *around* keys, with the tonal Ithaca assured at journey's beginning and end. When it comes to true changes of key – as in the

---

[25] Such paradoxical locutions pepper Jankélévitch's writings on music, not just in the Fauré books. See, for example, part two of *Music and the Ineffable*, titled "The Inexpressive 'Espressivo.'" Michael Gallope offers a lucid survey of this opposition as well as several other related antinomies in Jankélévitch's musical thought, in *Deep Refrains*, 184–191, arguing that they float in an "unwoven dialectic" in the philosopher's thought. As Gallope's section heading – "Charme" – indicates, these unstable pairings can be understood as various articulations of Jankélévitch's organizing concept of musical "charm," which Arnold Davidson discusses in his introductory essay to *Music and the Ineffable*, vii–xii.

transition to the B section of the Thirteenth Nocturne – the modulation can be brittle and abrupt, far removed from the supple if wayward kinetics of the local harmonic peripatetics at the phrase level.

Examples of Jankélévitch's "circular modulations" are legion; one very clear instance is the theme that begins the present nocturne's B section. Example 10.5b shows the score of measures 55–58. As the annotations beneath the staff indicate, the theme begins clearly in G♯ minor before swerving precipitously away in measures 56 and 57 (the label, G♯ minor *méconnu*, adopts Jankélévitch's term from the block quotation above), only to return just as unexpectedly to the tonic in measure 58 (G♯ minor!). The phrase bows out harmonically in its middle – as though pulled by some external force – only to snap back at the last instant.

The phrase also seems to be bent by temporal forces, yielding the kind of metric elusiveness that Caballero explores. As Example 10.5a – at the top of the example – shows, the phrase harbors residues of the 3/2 meter from the opening, despite the shift to a notated 2/2. The annotations also make clear that the end of the phrase sounds at first like a new beginning, as the motto rhythm seems to repeat: the phrase seems to wrap back metrically around to its beginning. The result is a strangely circular sort of musical time, in which the music at once progresses and makes no progress; the relationship to the discussion of "circular modulation" above should be clear. Moreover, the specific sense of 3/2 is further supported by the harmony. As Example 10.5c indicates, the middle 3/2 measure contains the perplexing harmonic swerve in E minor, while the outer measures project G♯ minor. The notation in Example 10.5c shows that the bass line outlines the tonic (G♯-minor) triad in descent, but that the arpeggiation is blown off course in the middle 3/2 measure; the change to up-stems in that measure makes the harmonic departure from the straight course visibly clear. Example 10.5d fleshes out the complete harmonic texture, providing a Roman numeral analysis; the boxed area shows that the pivot between G♯ minor and E minor occurs via an augmented triad. This triad plays a very similar syntactical role to the one in Example 10.4c: it clouds the arrival on a putative tonic and initiates a zone of peripatetic tonal uncertainty. The double-headed arrow in Example 10.5d is meant to show that Fauré could have avoided this tonal detour by reversing two semitonally adjacent pitches in the interior voice leading; had he done so, the tonally unambiguous progression in Example 10.5e would have resulted. As the phrase is actually composed, though, the augmented triad deflects the phrase's G♯-minor course, creating an unexpected opening – it is the portal through which the harmonic swerve occurs.

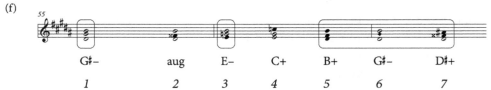

Example 10.5 Aspects of the theme that begins the B section of Op. 119, mm. 55–58

(a) The theme hints at the motto rhythm (and meter) from the A section

(b) The theme departs from and returns to G♯ minor, though it swerves wildly away in mm. 56–57

(c) Functional bass line reading, showing alignment of the middle "3/2 measure" with the zone of tonal uncertainty

(d) Fuller harmonic representation of the passage

(e) The first "3/2 measure" recomposed to show a normative tonic prolongation

(f) The triads passed through in the theme

It will not surprise students of recent harmonic theory to learn that there is much efficient voice leading afoot here.[26] Example 10.5f shows the triads that structure the phrase. The chords are numbered *1–7* for future reference. From chord *2* on, open noteheads indicate common tones from the previous harmony; solid note heads indicate a pitch that has moved only one semitone from the previous chord; and diamond noteheads indicate a pitch that has moved a whole tone from the previous chord. One immediately notes the preponderance of open note heads, and the fact that only one voice moves by whole tone in the whole phrase; all other motion is by semitones. As it turns out, the five consonant triads in rounded boxes in the example are all only one semitone away from the "portal" augmented triad. The sole remaining triad, C major, is a semitone away from E minor. This suggests a voice-leading space that Richard Cohn calls a "Weitzmann region," in honor of the nineteenth-century champion of the augmented triad, Carl Friedrich Weitzmann.[27] Example 10.6 shows the relevant Weitzmann region, plus the C-major addendum, which is enclosed in brackets to make clear that it is adjacent to the region but not formally *part* of it. Chords not sounded in the Fauré passage are grayed out. The italicized numbers from Example 10.5f now label stages on the phrase's wayward swing through this space, away from and back to the G♯-minor node (which is followed in chord *7* by its dominant, D♯ major). Fauré's progression begins at the G♯-minor chord (*1*), and seems to be moving toward its dominant, D♯ major, but it steps heedlessly on the augmented triad (*2*) and is pulled through the looking glass to E minor (*3*). After a side trip to C major (*4*), it passes through B major (*5*) on the way back to G♯ minor (*6*) and its dominant (*7*). Note how the progression swings around the augmented triad as though it is a center of gravity; I don't want to push Jankélévitch's Homeric metaphor too hard, but the augmented triad sure

[26] I am thinking both of neo-Riemannian theory (as in the work of Richard Cohn) and of geometrical music theory (as in the work of Dmitri Tymoczko). For representative monographs, see Richard Cohn, *Audacious Euphony: Chromaticism and the Triad's Second Nature* (New York: Oxford University Press, 2012) and Dmitri Tymoczko, *A Geometry of Music* (New York: Oxford University Press, 2011). My own work in transformational theory – Steven Rings, *Tonality and Transformation* (New York: Oxford University Press, 2011) – provides an alternative perspective, focusing on tonal character and quality rather than on efficient voice-leading. Example 10.6 is indebted principally to Tymoczko's work.

[27] See Richard Cohn, "Weitzmann's Regions, My Cycles, and Douthett's Dancing Cubes," *Music Theory Spectrum* 22 (2000), 89–103; Cohn, *Audacious Euphony*, Chapter 4; and Steven Rings, "Neo-Riemannian Values, Paleo- and Neo-," in *The Oxford Handbook of Neo-Riemannian Music Theories*, ed. Edward Gollin and Alexander Rehding (New York: Oxford University Press, 2011), 487–511.

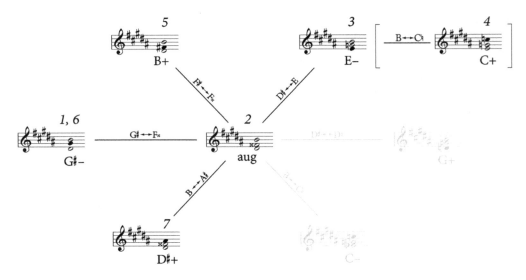

Example 10.6 Weitzmann region (plus C+ adjacency)
Italicized numerals indicate the triadic stages of Example 10.5f.
Grayed-out nodes represent chords that do not sound in the passage.

looks like Charybdis in this image. The metaphor is only partially apt, for the augmented triad is the force that both abets the phrase's harmonic torsion and reins in the resulting motion, bringing us safely back to port at our point of origin. As in so many phrases in Fauré, the augmented triad is one agent of the music's mobile immobility.

Conclusion: Quiddities and Quoddities

To return to issues I sketched at the paper's outset, I am fully aware that the juxtaposition of such "technological" music theory with Jankélévitchian ideas may seem incongruous, given recent interdisciplinary fissures. And Jankélévitch, to be sure, was often critical of analysis; this aspect of his thought has been amplified in the Abbate-led revival to a wholesale indictment. But a close reading of Jankélévitch's writings reveals a slightly more complex picture. While he was personally disinclined to analyze, he was not immune to the pleasures and insights that analysis could provide. In his Fauré volume, for example, he praises three highly technical analytical monographs on Fauré – one of them by a German author![28] At one

---

[28] See *FI*, 12. The authors are Françoise Gervais, Amy Dommel-Diény, and Max Favre.

Figure 10.1 Analytical image from Amy Dommel-Diény's study of Fauré's *Theme and Variations*

point, for example, we read: "The remarkable analysis of Madame Dommel-Diény makes us feel the 'absolute calm' that reigns in these shimmering passages" (*FI*, 241).

Lest the reader think that the book in question is theoretically "lightweight," lacking anything that we would recognize as technical analysis, Figure 10.1 shows one representative image from her monograph, in which Dommel-Diény is trying to disentangle the thorny enharmonicism of the very passage in the *Theme and Variations* that Jankélévitch is discussing.[29] This is hardly the most detailed such example (her figures can occasionally resemble Schenkerian sketches in size and amount of detail).

The crucial point is that Jankélévitch did not judge all analytical talk illegitimate. Rather, in some circumstances, he was alive to its potential to open, direct, and focus our ears, aiming them toward the music's extra-linguistic surplus. Note what he says: Dommel-Diény's "remarkable analysis ... makes us feel" [*nous fait sentir*] the "absolute calm" of the passage. He is concerned not with the propositional content of the analysis, but the experience that it begets. And it is here that we can most productively understand the relationship between the drastic and the gnostic in his thought. The two are not in a mutually exclusive agon, the one always crowding out the other; rather, gnostic reflection – at its most successful – can act as a quickening agent to drastic experience. We need to be mindful, however, not to confuse the propositional content of some gnostic statement with the drastic experience it may engender. This is true whether the statement is a technical analysis, or a hermeneutic gloss, as in

[29] Amy Dommel-Diény, *L'Harmonie vivante.* Vol. 5, fasc. 12: *L'Analyse harmonique en examples de J.-S. Bach à Debussy* (Alençon, France: Éditions A. Dommel-Diény, 1974), 40, example 28.

Jankélévitch's analogizing of the entire Nocturne to the course of a human life in the large quotation near the beginning of this chapter.

In *Deep Refrains*, Michael Gallope has theorized the relationship between irreducible temporal experience and mediation of that experience – among other things, thought and talk about it – with unusual sensitivity, drawing on Jankélévitch's own concepts of quiddity and quoddity, which Gallope calls a "dualism" that animates the philosopher's thought:

In his *Philosophie première* (1954), Jankélévitch develops this dualism as one between quiddity (a conceptual and intellectual order) and what he calls "quoddity." Quoddity is the "thatness" of something, its indescribable and contingent existence as a specific fact.[30]

Figure 10.2a reproduces Gallope's Figure 3.1, which he describes thus:

On the left, quiddity organizes this force of absolute creativity into an Apollonian grid of symbols, definitions, and concepts mediated by the intellect. On the right, I have represented quoddity with a star of irregularly radiating lines that reflect the qualitative multiplicity of *durée* at work in the concrete facticity of every instant.[31]

For our present purposes, think of quoddity as Fauré's (or, really, anyone's) music experienced in time, in all of its extradiscursive and ephemeral presence. Quiddity is then any set of words, concepts, intellectual frameworks, interpretations, analyses that we bring to bear on that experience. As Gallope notes, a crucial initial step for Jankélévitch is to distinguish quiddity clearly from quoddity, in Bergsonian fashion. But Jankélévitch then departs from Bergson in

showing that quoddity or *durée* cannot be presented to experience without interventions from quidditive, symbolic filters. These orders are permanently and paradoxically enmeshed within one another.[32]

Gallope presents two more pictures to illustrate the ways in which quoddity and quiddity interact in Jankélévitch's thought, reproduced here as Figures 10.2b and c. The former shows a quidditive *fidelity* to quodditive experience:

The curve of quoddity [Gallope's curved line] is the facticity of an irreversible musical experience [think: Fauré's music experienced in real time, hitting the ears and produced by physical bodies and instruments]. It stretches from left to right. A receding grid in the center of the figure that points upward to the right represents one's quidditive and linguistic fidelity to the quoddity of music's

[30] Gallope, *Deep Refrains*, 173.   [31] Ibid., 174.   [32] Ibid.

(a)

(b)

(c)

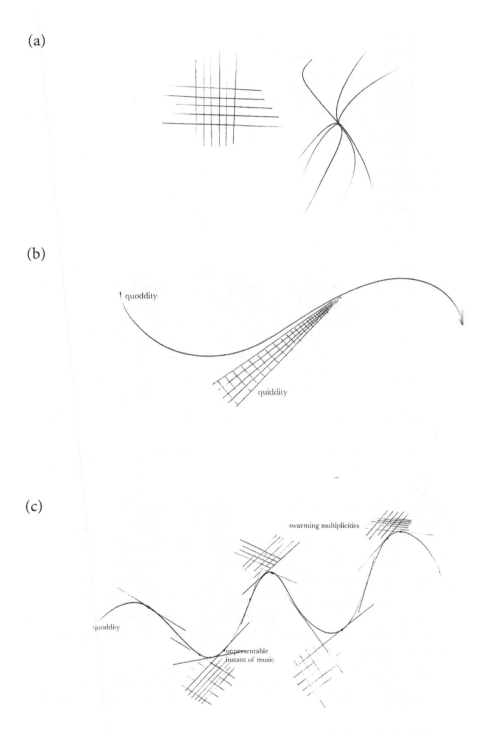

quoddity

quiddity

swarming multiplicities

quoddity

unpresentable
instant of music

Figure 10.2 (a) Quiddity (left) and quoddity (right) (174, Figure 3.1); (b) Quiddity's fidelity to quoddity (178, Figure 3.3); (c) Music's speculative multiplicities (191, Figure 3.4) From *Deep Refrains: Music, Philosophy, and the Ineffable* by Michael Gallope. © 2017 by The University of Chicago. Reproduced by permission. The captions are Gallope's.

temporal inconsistency [think: Jankélévitch's loquacious response to the music, and perhaps ours]. It approaches in the manner of an asymptote. (177–178)

Finally, Figure 10.2c shows how music's quodditive presence gives rise to speculative multiplicities, swarms of quodditive discourses that cluster around the music's fleeting quodditive swerves. It is not hard to see how this image provides an attractive framework for thinking about our work above: Jankélévitch's reading of the Nocturne as a life lived, his Homeric metaphors, my analyses of smudged counterpoint and circular modulations – these are so many quodditive grids that arise in proximity to music's sounding presence, its quodditive irreducibility.

But Gallope, following Jankélévitch, takes a proscriptive turn here, which I do not wish to follow:

But this dialectic is one of asymptotes and asides rather than particulars and totalities – its loquacity traffics in oblique descriptions and quixotic changes in direction, rather than in focused interpretations of details, fragments, or hidden depths. It is incommensurable rather than contradictory; for Jankélévitch music and language are subject to a strict gap or hiatus. His unwoven dialectics are based in a hyperactive fidelity actualized through an ethics of impersonality and inexpression. (191)

In other words, only some kinds of talk – fractured, skittish, Gallic, cool, mercurial – can express fidelity to music's ephemeral thatness. Gallope is indeed right to characterize Jankélévitch's thought in this way: the philosopher's writings show considerable animus toward certain modes of quodditive being and proliferation in music's presence – hostility is not too strong a word. Jankélévitch's intolerance for cognitive diversity and his spasms of unseemly *ad hominem* attack aimed at thinkers who differ from him – "Maniac antihedonism [read: music analysis] is the mark of the technician and is akin in its frivolity to a love for Viennese waltzes"[33] – strike a jarring note in a thinker otherwise so exquisitely attuned to human difference.

Yet Jankélévitch's inconsistency saves him. As soon as his focus is back on his own interpretations – the fruits of his own quodditive actions – and not the words or interpretive deeds of others, his gaze and rhetoric soften again. Consider this surprisingly pragmatist position, which we might take as a defense of his interpretation of the Thirteenth Nocturne quoted near the beginning of this chapter:

A sonata *is like* a précis of the human adventure that is bordered by death and birth – but is not *itself* this adventure . . . Everything hangs upon the meaning of

---

[33] Jankélévitch, *Music and the Ineffable*, 102.

the verb *to be* and the adverb *like* . . . *Only* an awareness that a way of speaking is, simply, a way of speaking can keep us honest.[34]

In other words, don't confuse quiddity with quoddity. Remember that our ways of speaking about music are indeed just that, and that our musical experiences will always outrun them – or better, swerve from our grid-like mediations. Also implicit in Jankélévitch's quote: don't apologize for quiddity. It is inseparable from our many modes of being in music's presence; we are quidditive beings. This strikes me as an eminently reasonable antidote to the Manichean either/or dualisms of the recent Jankélévitch revival, not to mention a corrective to the philosopher's own intellectual intolerance.

I will add in closing that the swerving, asymptotic gestures of Gallope's figures shown in Figure 10.1b and c strike me as quintessentially Fauréan. His music can indeed often feel like an ungraspable curve, never precisely measurable, but generative of thought, reflection, and affect in abundance. These quidditive residues linger long after the music's sine wave has faded into silence. Perhaps more than anything else, this is Fauré's *parfum impérissable* – the thought that lingers on, reanimating a fugitive music just past.

---

[34] Ibid., 14, italics original.

Index

Printed in the USA
CPSIA information can be obtained
at www.ICGtesting.com
JSHW061544131223
53753JS00010B/95